Cambridge IGCSE™

Core Mathematics

EXAM PREPARATION AND PRACTICE

Martin Noon, Katherine Pate & Dicky Susanto

with Digital access

Shaftesbury Road, Cambridge CB2 8EA, United Kingdom

One Liberty Plaza, 20th Floor, New York, NY 10006, USA

477 Williamstown Road, Port Melbourne, VIC 3207, Australia

314–321, 3rd Floor, Plot 3, Splendor Forum, Jasola District Centre, New Delhi – 110025, India

Cambridge University Press & Assessment is a department of the University of Cambridge.

We share the University's mission to contribute to society through the pursuit of education, learning and research at the highest international levels of excellence.

www.cambridge.org

Information on this title: www.cambridge.org/9781009829465

© Cambridge University Press & Assessment 2026

First published 2026

Exam Preparation and Practice to support Third edition 2023

20 19 18 17 16 15 14 13 12 11 10 9 8 7 6 5 4 3 2 1

Printed in Malaysia by Vivar Printing

A catalogue record for this publication is available from the British Library

ISBN   978-1-009-82946-5   Exam Preparation and Practice with Digital Access (2 Years)

ISBN   978-1-009-82943-4   Digital Exam Preparation and Practice (2 Years)

ISBN   978-1-009-82945-8   Exam Preparation and Practice - eBook

Additional resources for this publication at www.cambridge.org/9781009829465

Cover image neokan/Getty Images

....

....

2025 Cambridge Dedicated Teacher Awards

Our **Cambridge Dedicated Teacher Awards** are an opportunity to show appreciation for the incredible work teachers do every day.

Thank you to everyone who nominated this year; we have been inspired and moved by all of your stories. Well done to all of our nominees for your dedication to learning and for inspiring the next generation of thinkers, leaders and innovators.

Congratulations to our winners!

Global Winner

Sub-Saharan Africa

Portia Dzilah

Pakro-Adjinase St. James Anglican Basic School, Ghana

East Asia

Yun Xie

Yew Wah International Education School of Shanghai Lingang, China

Europe

Oleksandr Zhuk

Zaporizhzhia Special Comprehensive Boarding Xchool, Dzherelo, Ukraine

Latin America

Eduardo Pérez

Instituto Técnico Guaimaral, Colombia

North America

Isabel de Feria

Marjory Stoneman Douglas Elementary, USA

Middle East and North Africa

Farrukh Saleem

Pakistan International School Jeddah English Section, Saudi Arabia

Pakistan

Adnan Ahmed Usmani

Bahria Town School and College, Pakistan

South Asia

Sakina Bharmal

The Galaxy School - Wadi, India

Southeast Asia & Pacific

Polly Neville

Denla British School Bangkok, Thailand

For more information about our dedicated teachers and their stories, go to **dedicatedteacher.cambridge.org**

Contents

Past Paper Practice Questions Resource Sheets

There are extra digital questions for this title found online at Cambridge GO.

For more information on how to access and use your digital resource, please see inside the front cover.

> How to use this series

This suite of resources supports learners and teachers following the Cambridge IGCSE™ and IGCSE (9–1) Mathematics syllabuses (0580/0980). Up-to-date metacognition techniques have been incorporated throughout the resources to meet the changes in the syllabuses content and develop a complete understanding of mathematics for learners. All of the components in the series are designed to work together.

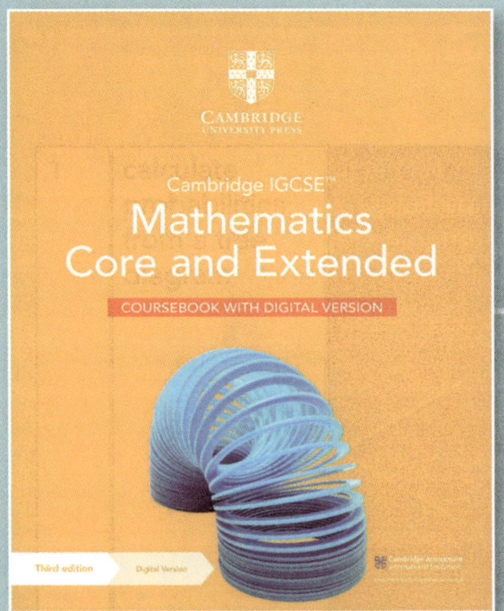

The coursebook contains 23 chapters that together offer complete coverage of the syllabus. We have worked with NRICH to provide a variety of project activities, designed to engage learners and strengthen their problem solving skills. Each chapter contains opportunities for formative assessment, differentiation and peer and self-assessment offering learners the support needed to make progress. Cambridge Online Mathematics is available through the digital/ print bundle option or on its own without the print coursebook. Learners can review content digitally, explore worked examples and test their knowledge with quiz questions and answers. Teachers benefit from the ability to set tests and tasks with the added auto-marking functionality and a reporting dashboard to help track learner progress quickly and easily.

The digital teacher's resource provides extensive guidance on how to teach the course, including suggestions for differentiation, formative assessment and language support, teaching ideas and PowerPoints. The Teaching Skills Focus shows teachers how to incorporate a variety of key pedagogical techniques into teaching, including differentiation, assessment for learning, and metacognition. Answers for all components are accessible to teachers for free on the Cambridge GO platform.

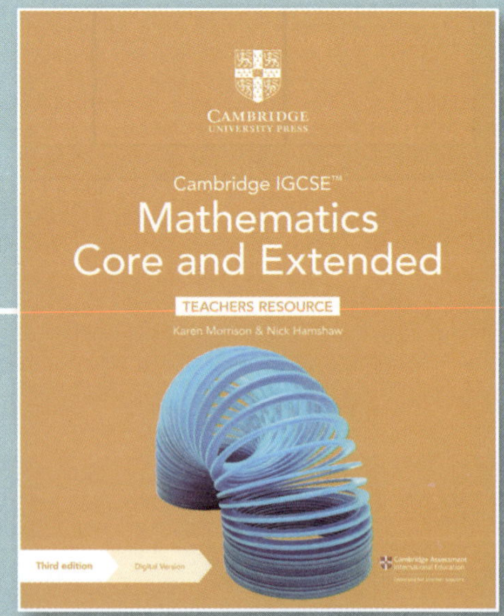

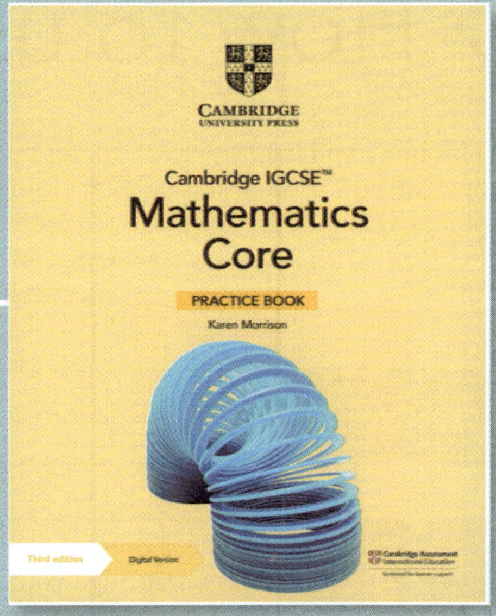

A Practice Book is available for learners that wish to have extra questions to work through. This resource which can be used in class or assigned as homework, provides a wide variety of extra maths activities and questions to help learners consolidate their learning and prepare for assessment. Tips are also regularly featured to give learners extra advice and guidance on the different areas of maths they encounter. Access to the digital versions of the practice books is included, and answers can be found either here or in the back of the books.

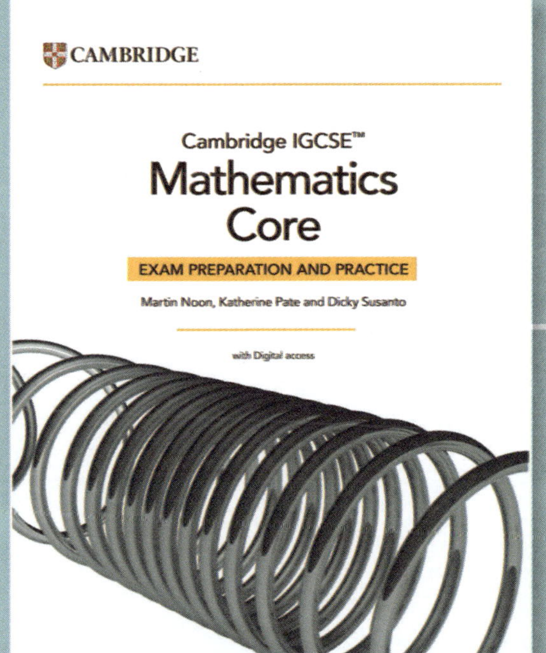

The Exam Preparation and Practice resource provides dedicated support for learners in preparing for their final assessments. Hundreds of questions in the book and accompanying digital resource will help learners to check that they understand, and can recall, syllabus concepts. To help learners to show what they know in an exam context, a checklist of exam skills with corresponding questions, and past paper question practice, is also included. Self-assessment and reflection features support learners to identify any areas that need further practice. This resource should be used alongside the coursebook, throughout the course of study, so learners can most effectively increase their confidence and readiness for their exams.

> How to use this book

This book will help you to check that you **know** the content of the syllabus and practise how to **show** this understanding in an exam. It will also help you be cognitively prepared and in the **flow**, ready for your exam. Research has shown that it is important that you do all three of these things, so we have designed the Know, Show, Flow approach to help you prepare effectively for exams.

| Know | You will need to consolidate and then recall a lot of syllabus content. |

| Show | You should demonstrate your knowledge in the context of a Cambridge exam. |

| Flow | You should be cognitively engaged and ready to learn. This means reducing test anxiety. |

Exam skills checklist

Category	Exam skill
Understanding the question	Recognise different question types
	Understand command words
	Mark scheme awareness
Providing an appropriate response	Understand connections between concepts
	Keep to time
	Know what a good answer looks like
Developing supportive behaviours	Reflect on progress
	Manage test anxiety

This **Exam skills checklist** helps you to develop the awareness, behaviours and habits that will support you when revising and preparing for your exams. For more exam skills advice, including understanding command words and managing your time effectively, please go to the **Exam skills chapter**.

Know

The full syllabus content of your IGCSE Core Mathematics course is covered in your Cambridge coursebook. This book will provide you with different types of questions to support you as you prepare for your exams. You will answer **Knowledge recall questions** that are designed to make sure you understand a topic, and **Recall and connect questions** to help you recall past learning and connect different concepts.

KNOWLEDGE FOCUS

Knowledge focus boxes summarise the topics that you will answer questions on in each chapter of this book. You can refer back to your Cambridge coursebook to remind yourself of the full detail of the syllabus content.

You will find **Knowledge recall questions** to make sure you understand a topic, and **Recall and connect questions** to help you recall past learning and connect different concepts. It is recommended that you answer the Knowledge recall questions just after you have covered the relevant topic in class, and then return to them at a later point to check you have properly understood the content.

Knowledge recall question

Testing yourself is a good way to check that your understanding is secure. These questions will help you to recall the core knowledge you have acquired during your course, and highlight any areas where you may need more practice. They are indicated with a blue bar with a gap, at the side of the page. We recommend that you answer the Knowledge recall questions just after you have covered the relevant topic in class, and then return to them at a later point to check you have properly understood the content.

≪ RECALL AND CONNECT 1 ≪

To consolidate your learning, you need to test your memory frequently. These questions will test that you remember what you learned in previous chapters, in addition to what you are practising in the current chapter.

UNDERSTAND THIS TERM

These list the important vocabulary that you should understand for each chapter. Definitions are provided in the glossary of your Cambridge coursebook.

 This icon shows you where you should complete an exercise without using your calculator.

Show

Exam questions test specific knowledge, skills and understanding. You need to be prepared so that you have the best opportunity to show what you know in the time you have during the exam. In addition to practising recall of the syllabus content, it is important to build your exam skills throughout the year.

EXAM SKILLS FOCUS

This feature outlines the exam skills you will practise in each chapter, alongside the Knowledge focus. They are drawn from the core set of eight exam skills, listed in the exam skills checklist. You will practise specific exam skills, such as understanding command words, within each chapter. More general exam skills, such as managing text anxiety, are covered in the Exam skills chapter.

Exam skills question

These questions will help you to develop your exam skills and demonstrate your understanding. To help you become familiar with exam-style questioning, these questions follow the style and use the language of real exam questions, and have allocated marks. They are indicated with a solid red bar at the side of the page.

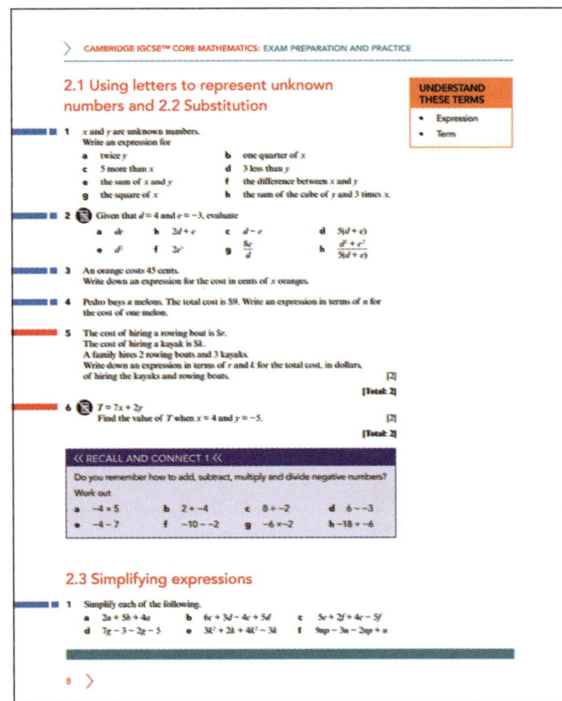

Looking at sample answers to past paper questions helps you to understand what to aim for.

The **Exam practice** sections in this resource contain example student responses and examiner-style commentary showing how the answer could be improved (both written by the authors).

Flow

Preparing for exams can be stressful. One of the approaches recommended by educational psychologists to help with this stress is to improve behaviours around exam preparation. This involves testing yourself in manageable chunks, accompanied by self-evaluation. You should avoid cramming, and build in more preparation time. This book is structured to help you do this.

Increasing your ability to recognise the signs of exam-related stress and working through some techniques for how to cope with it will help to make your exam preparation manageable.

REFLECTION

This feature asks you to think about the approach that you take to your exam preparation, and how you might improve this in the future. Reflecting on how you plan, monitor and evaluate your revision and preparation will help you to do your best in your exams.

SELF-ASSESSMENT CHECKLIST

These checklists return to the Learning intentions from your coursebook, as well as the Exam skills focus boxes from each chapter. The statements that relate to Exam skills are indicated with a solid red bar at the side of the page. Checking in on how confident you feel in each of these areas will help you to focus your exam preparation. The 'Show it' prompts will allow you to test your rating. You should revisit any areas that you rate 'Needs more work' or 'Almost there'.

Now I can	Show it	Needs more work	Almost there	Confident to move on

Increasing your ability to recognise the signs of exam-related stress and working through some techniques for how to cope with it will help to make your exam preparation manageable. The **Exam skills chapter** will support you with this.

Syllabus assessment objectives for IGCSE Core Mathematics

You should be familiar with the Assessment Objectives from the syllabus, as you will need to show evidence of these requirements in your responses.

The assessment objectives for this syllabus are:

Assessment objective	IGCSE weighting
AO1: Knowledge and understanding of mathematical techniques	60–70%
AO2: Analyse, interpret and communicate mathematically	30–40%

If a question asks you to complete a diagram/table/graph, you can find a printable copy of this in the Past Paper Practice Questions Resource Sheets, which are available to download from Cambridge GO.

Digital questions

Extra digital questions, in the form of **Multiple choice** and **Flip cards**, for all chapters can be found online at Cambridge GO. For more information on how to access and use your digital resource, please see inside the front cover.

- Provides lots of additional practice to reinforce knowledge and understanding

- Gives instant feedback to support autonomy over your own learning

- Encourages self-assessment to understand your strengths and weaknesses

- User-friendly design to help with easy navigation

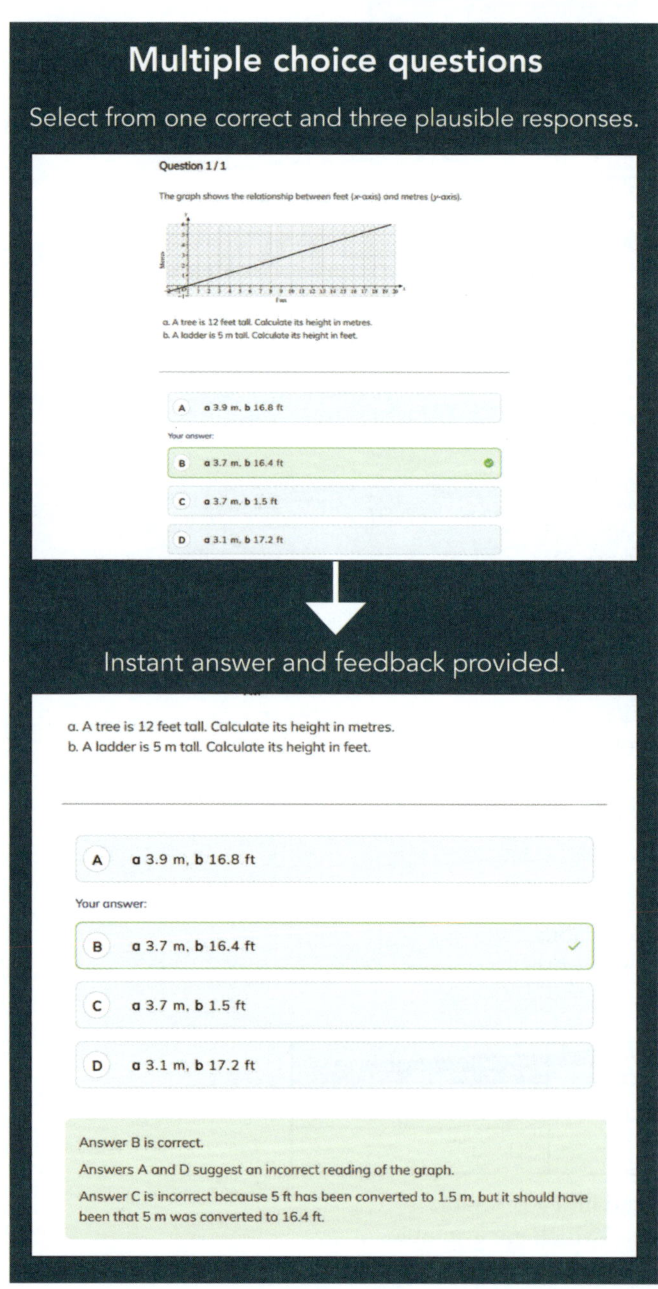

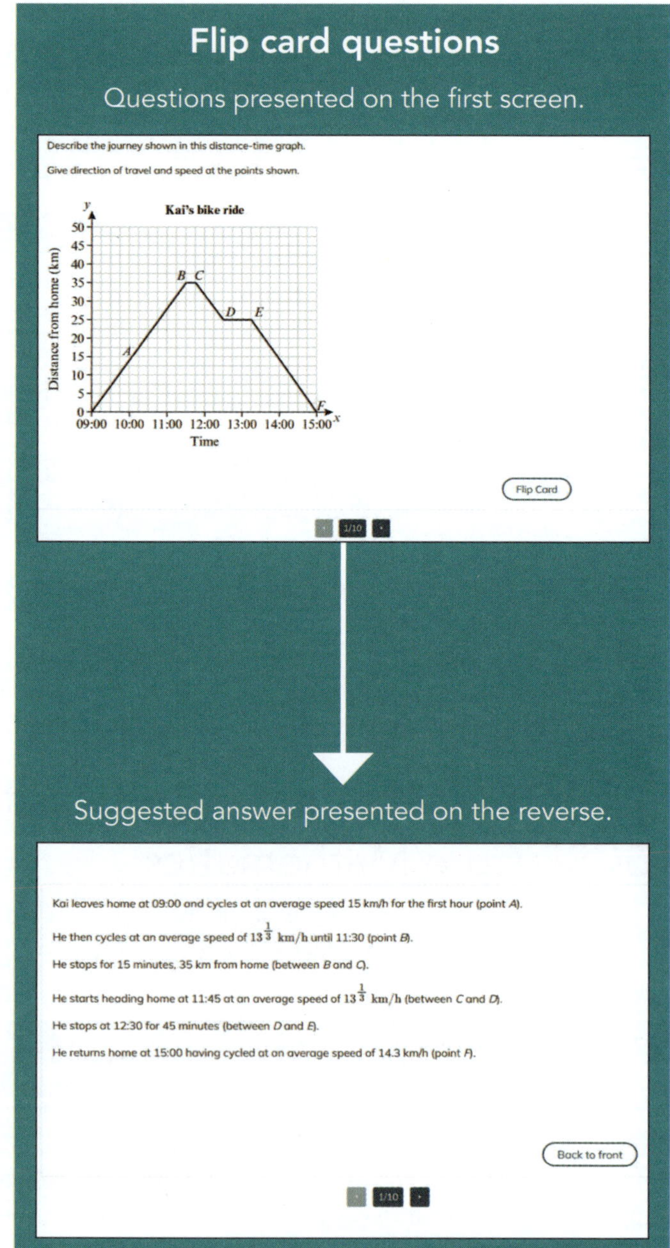

Exam skills

by Lucy Parsons

What's the point of this book?

Most students make one really basic mistake when they're preparing for exams. What is it? It's focusing far too much on learning 'stuff' – that's facts, figures, ideas, information – and not nearly enough time practising exam skills.

The students who work really, really hard but are disappointed with their results are nearly always students who focus on memorising stuff. They think to themselves, 'I'll do practice papers once I've revised everything.' The trouble is, they start doing practice papers too late to really develop and improve how they communicate what they know.

What could they do differently?

When your final exam script is assessed, it should contain specific language, information and thinking skills in your answers. If you read a question in an exam and you have no idea what you need to do to give a good answer, the likelihood is that your answer won't be as brilliant as it could be. That means your grade won't reflect the hard work you've put into revising for the exam.

There are different types of questions used in exams to assess different skills. You need to know how to recognise these question types and understand what you need to show in your answers.

So, how do you understand what to do in each question type?

That's what this book is all about. But first a little background.

Meet Benjamin Bloom

The psychologist Benjamin Bloom developed a way of classifying and valuing different skills we use when we learn, such as analysis and recalling information. We call these thinking skills. It's known as Bloom's Taxonomy and it's what most exam questions are based around.

If you understand Bloom's Taxonomy, you can understand what any type of question requires you to do. So, what does it look like?

Bloom's Taxonomy of thinking skills

Increasing difficulty →

Evaluation — **Passing judgement** on something

Synthesis — **Putting together knowledge,** understanding, application and analysis **to create something new**

Analysis — **Taking apart** information or data in order to **discover relationships**, motives, causes, patterns and connections

Application — **Using knowledge** and understanding in **new and different circumstances**

Understanding — **Distinguishing between two similar ideas** or things by using knowledge to **recognise the difference**

Knowledge — **Recalling, memorising and knowing**

The key things to take away from this diagram are:

- Knowledge and understanding are known as lower-level thinking skills. They are less difficult than the other thinking skills. Exam questions that just test you on what you know are usually worth the lowest number of marks.

- All the other thinking skills are worth higher numbers of marks in exam questions. These questions need you to have some foundational knowledge and understanding but are far more about how you think than what you know. They involve:

  - Taking what you know and using it in unfamiliar situations (application).

  - Going deeper into information to discover relationships, motives, causes, patterns and connections (analysis).

  - Using what you know and think to create something new – whether that's an essay, long-answer exam question a solution to a maths problem, or a piece of art (synthesis).

  - Assessing the value of something, e.g. the reliability of the results of a scientific experiment (evaluation).

In this introductory chapter, you'll be shown how to develop the skills that enable you to communicate what you know and how you think. This will help you achieve to the best of your abilities. In the rest of the book, you'll have a chance to practise these exam skills by understanding how questions work and understanding what you need to show in your answers.

Every time you pick up this book and do a few questions, you're getting closer to achieving your dream results. So, let's get started!

Exam preparation and revision skills

What is revision?

If you think about it, the word 'revision' has two parts to it:

- re – which means 'again'

- vision – which is about seeing.

So, revision is literally about 'seeing again'. This means you're looking at something that you've already learned.

Typically, a teacher will teach you something in class. You may then do some questions on it, write about it in some way, or even do a presentation. You might then have an end-of-topic test sometime later. To prepare for this test, you need to 'look again' or revise what you were originally taught.

Step 1: Making knowledge stick

Every time you come back to something you've learned or revised you're improving your understanding and memory of that particular piece of knowledge. This is called **spaced retrieval**. This is how human memory works. If you don't use a piece of knowledge by recalling it, you lose it.

Everything we learn has to be physically stored in our brains by creating neural connections – joining brain cells together. The more often we 'retrieve' or recall a particular piece of knowledge, the stronger the neural connection gets. It's like lifting weights – the more often you lift, the stronger you get.

However, if you don't use a piece of knowledge for a long time, your brain wants to recycle the brain cells and use them for another purpose. The neural connections get weaker until they finally break, and the memory has gone. This is why it's really important to return often to things that you've learned in the past.

Great ways of doing this in your revision include:

- Testing yourself using flip cards – use the ones available in the digital resources for this book.

- Testing yourself (or getting someone else to test you) using questions you've created about the topic.

- Checking your recall of previous topics by answering the Recall and connect questions in this book.

- Blurting – writing everything you can remember about a topic on a piece of paper in one colour. Then, checking what you missed out and filling it in with another colour. You can do this over and over again until you feel confident that you remember everything.

- Answering practice questions – use the ones in this book.

- Getting a good night's sleep to help consolidate your learning.

> **The importance of sleep and creating long-term memory**
>
> When you go to sleep at night, your brain goes through an important process of taking information from your short-term memory and storing it in your long-term memory.
>
> This means that getting a good night's sleep is a very important part of revision. If you don't get enough good quality sleep, you'll actually be making your revision much, much harder.

Step 2: Developing your exam skills

We've already talked about the importance of exam skills, and how many students neglect them because they're worried about covering all the knowledge.

What actually works best is developing your exam skills at the same time as learning the knowledge.

What does this look like in your studies?

- Learning something at school and your teacher setting you questions from this book or from past papers. This tests your recall as well as developing your exam skills.

- Choosing a topic to revise, learning the content and then choosing some questions from this book to test yourself at the same time as developing your exam skills.

The reason why practising your exam skills is so important is that it helps you to get good at communicating what you know and what you think. The more often you do that, the more fluent you'll become in showing what you know in your answers.

Step 3: Getting feedback

The final step is to get feedback on your work.

If you're testing yourself, the feedback is what you got wrong or what you forgot. This means you then need to go back to those things to remind yourself or improve your understanding. Then, you can test yourself again and get more feedback. You can also congratulate yourself for the things you got right – it's important to celebrate any success, big or small.

If you're doing past paper questions or the practice questions in this book, you will need to mark your work. Marking your work is one of the most important things you can do to improve. It's possible to make significant improvements in your marks in a very short space of time when you start marking your work.

Why is marking your own work so powerful? It's because it teaches you to identify the strengths and weaknesses of your own work. When you look at the mark scheme and see how it's structured, you will understand what is needed in your answers to get the results you want.

This doesn't just apply to the knowledge you demonstrate in your answers. It also applies to the language you use and whether it's appropriately subject-specific, the structure of your answer, how you present it on the page and many other factors. Understanding, practising and improving on these things are transformative for your results.

The most important thing about revision

The most important way to make your revision successful is to make it active.

Sometimes, students say they're revising when they sit staring at their textbook or notes for hours at a time. However, this is a really ineffective way to revise because it's passive. In order to make knowledge and skills stick, you need to be doing something like the suggestions in the following diagram. That's why testing yourself and pushing yourself to answer questions that test higher-level thinking skills are so effective. At times, you might actually be able to feel the physical changes happening in your brain as you develop this new knowledge and these new skills. That doesn't come about without effort.

The important thing to remember is that while active revision feels much more like hard work than passive revision, you don't actually need to do nearly as much of it. That's because you remember knowledge and skills when you use active revision. When you use passive revision, it is much, much harder for the knowledge and skills to stick in your memory.

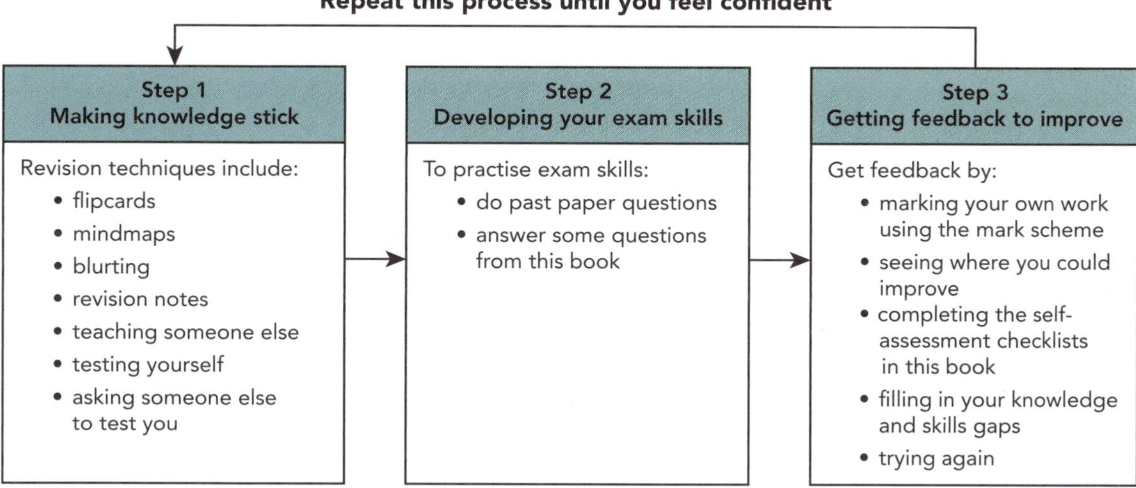

How to improve your exam skills

This book helps you to improve in eight different areas of exam skills, which are divided across three categories. These skills are highlighted in this book in the Exam skills focus at the start of each chapter and developed throughout the book using targeted questions, advice and reflections.

1   **Understand the questions: what are you being asked to do?**

   •   Know your question types.

   •   Understand command words.

   •   Work with mark scheme awareness.

2   **How to answer questions brilliantly**

   •   Understand connections between concepts.

   •   Keep to time.

   •   Know what a good answer looks like.

3   **Give yourself the best chance of success**

   •   Reflection on progress.

   •   How to manage test anxiety.

Understand the questions: what are you being asked to do?

Know your question types

In any exam, there will be a range of different question types. These different question types will test different types of thinking skills from Bloom's Taxonomy.

It is very important that you learn to recognise different questions types. If you do lots of past papers, over time you will begin to recognise the structure of the paper for each of your subjects. You will know which types of questions may come first and which ones are more likely to come at the end of the paper. You can also complete past paper questions in the Exam practice sections in this book for additional practice.

You will also recognise the differences between questions worth a lower number of marks and questions worth more marks. The key differences are:

- how much you will need to write in your answer

- how sophisticated your answer needs to be in terms of the detail you give and the depth of thinking you show.

Types of questions

1 Multiple-choice questions

Multiple-choice questions are generally worth smaller numbers of marks. You will be given several possible answers to the question, and you will have to work out which one is correct using your knowledge and skills.

There is a chance of you getting the right answer with multiple-choice questions even if you don't know the answer. This is why you must **always give an answer for multiple-choice questions** as it means there is a chance you will earn the mark.

Multiple-choice questions are often harder than they appear. The possible answers can be very similar to each other. This means you must be confident in how you work out answers or have a high level of understanding to tell the difference between the possible answers.

Being confident in your subject knowledge and doing lots of practice multiple-choice questions will set you up for success. Use the resources in this book and the accompanying online resources to build your confidence.

This example of a multiple-choice question is worth one mark. You can see that all the answers have one part in common with at least one other answer. For example, palisade cells is included in three of the possible answers. That's why you have to really know the detail of your content knowledge to do well with multiple-choice questions.

Which two types of cells are found in plant leaves?

A   Palisade mesophyll and stomata

B   Palisade mesophyll and root hair

C   Stomata and chloroplast

D   Chloroplast and palisade mesophyll

2 Questions requiring longer-form answers

Questions requiring longer-form answers need you to write out your answer yourself.

With these questions, take careful note of how many marks are available and how much space you've been given for your answer. These two things will give you a good idea about how much you should say and how much time you should spend on the question.

A rough rule to follow is to write one sentence, or make one point, for each mark that is available. You will get better and better at these longer form questions the more you practise them.

In this example of a history question, you can see it is worth four marks. It is not asking for an explanation, just for you to list Lloyd George's aims. Therefore, you need to make four correct points in order to get full marks.

What were Lloyd George's aims during negotiations leading to the
Treaty of Versailles?   [4]

3 Essay questions

Essay questions are the longest questions you will be asked to answer in an exam. They examine the higher-order thinking skills from Bloom's Taxonomy such as analysis, synthesis and evaluation.

To do well in essay questions, you need to talk about what you know, giving your opinion, comparing one concept or example to another, and evaluating your own ideas or the ones you're discussing in your answer.

You also need to have a strong structure and logical argument that guides the reader through your thought process. This usually means having an introduction, some main body paragraphs that discuss one point at a time, and a conclusion.

Essay questions are usually level-marked. This means that you don't get one mark per point you make. Instead, you're given marks for the quality of the ideas you're sharing as well as how well you present those ideas through the subject-specific language you use and the structure of your essay.

Practising essays and becoming familiar with the mark scheme is the only way to get really good at them.

Understand command words

What are command words?

Command words are the most important words in every exam question. This is because command words tell you what you need to do in your answer. Do you remember Bloom's Taxonomy? Command words tell you which thinking skill you need to demonstrate in the answer to each question.

Two very common command words are **describe** and **explain**.

When you see the command word describe in a question, you're being asked to show lower-order thinking skills like knowledge and understanding. The question will either be worth fewer marks, or you will need to make more points if it is worth more marks.

The command word explain is asking you to show higher-order thinking skills. When you see the command word explain, you need to be able to say how or why something happens.

You need to understand all of the relevant command words for the subjects you are taking. Ask your teacher where to find them if you are not sure. It's best not to try to memorise the list of command words, but to become familiar with what command words are asking for by doing lots of practice questions and marking your own work.

How to work with command words

When you first see an exam question, read it through once. Then, read it through again and identify the command word(s). Underline the command word(s) to make it clear to yourself which they are every time you refer back to the question.

You may also want to identify the **content** words in the question and underline them with a different colour. Content words tell you which area of knowledge you need to draw on to answer the question.

In this example, command words are shown in red and underlined with content words in **blue and bold**:

1 a Explain **four** reasons why **governments** might **support business start-ups**.   [8]

*Adapted from Cambridge IGCSE Business Studies (0450)
Q1a Paper 21 June 2022*

Marking your own work using the mark scheme will help you get even better at understanding command words and knowing how to give good answers for each.

Work with mark scheme awareness

The most transformative thing that any student can do to improve their marks is to work with mark schemes. This means using mark schemes to mark your own work at every opportunity.

Many students are very nervous about marking their own work as they do not feel experienced or qualified enough. However, being brave enough to try to mark your own work and taking the time to get good at it will improve your marks hugely.

Why marking your own work makes such a big difference

Marking your own work can help you to improve your answers in the following ways:

1 Answering the question

Having a deep and detailed understanding of what is required by the question enables you to answer the question more clearly and more accurately.

It can also help you to give the required information using fewer words and in less time, as you can avoid including unrelated points or topics in your answer.

2 Using subject-specific vocabulary

Every subject has subject-specific vocabulary. This includes technical terms for objects or concepts in a subject, such as mitosis and meiosis in biology. It also includes how you talk about the subject, using appropriate vocabulary that may differ from everyday language. For example, in any science subject you might be asked to describe the trend on a graph.

Your answer could say it 'goes up fast' or your answer could say it 'increases rapidly'. You would not get marks for saying 'it goes up fast', but you would for saying it 'increases rapidly'. This is the difference between everyday language and formal, scientific language.

When you answer lots of practice questions, you become fluent in the language specific to your subject.

3   Knowing how much to write

It's very common for students to either write too much or too little to answer questions. Becoming familiar with the mark schemes for many different questions will help you to gain a better understanding of how much you need to write in order to get a good mark.

4   Structuring your answer

There are often clues in questions about how to structure your answer. However, mark schemes give you an even stronger idea of the structure you hould use in your answers.

For example, if a question says:

'Describe and explain two reasons why…'

You can give a clear answer by:

- Describing reason 1
- Explaining reason 1
- Describing reason 2
- Explaining reason 2

Having a very clear structure will also make it easier to identify where you have earned marks. This means that you're more likely to be awarded the number of marks you deserve.

5   Keeping to time

Answering the question, using subject-specific vocabulary, knowing how much to write and giving a clear structure to your answer will all help you to keep to time in an exam. You will not waste time by writing too much for any answer. Therefore, you will have sufficient time to give a good answer to every question.

How to answer exam questions brilliantly

Understand connections between concepts

One of the higher-level thinking skills in Bloom's Taxonomy is **synthesis**. Synthesis means making connections between different areas of knowledge. You may have heard about synoptic links. Making synoptic links is the same as showing the thinking skill of synthesis.

Exam questions that ask you to show your synthesis skills are usually worth the highest number of marks on an exam paper. To write good answers to these questions, you need to spend time thinking about the links between the topics you've studied before you arrive in your exam. A great way of doing this is using mind maps.

How to create a mind map

To create a mind map:

1   Use a large piece of paper and several different coloured pens.

2 Write the name of your subject in the middle. Then, write the key topic areas evenly spaced around the edge, each with a different colour.

3 Then, around each topic area, start to write the detail of what you can remember. If you find something that is connected with something you studied in another topic, you can draw a line linking the two things together.

This is a good way of practising your retrieval of information as well as linking topics together.

Answering synoptic exam questions

You will recognise questions that require you to make links between concepts because they have a higher number of marks. You will have practised them using this book and the accompanying resources.

To answer a synoptic exam question:

1 **Identify the command and content words**. You are more likely to find command words like **discuss** and **explain** in these questions. They might also have phrases like 'the connection between'.

2 **Make a plan for your answer**. It is worth taking a short amount of time to think about what you're going to write in your answer. Think carefully about what information you're going to put in, the links between the different pieces of information and how you're going to structure your answer to make your ideas clear.

3 **Use linking words and phrases in your answer**. For example, 'therefore', 'because', 'due to', 'since' or 'this means that'.

Here is an example of an English Literature exam question that requires you to make synoptic links in your answer.

1 Discuss **Carol Ann Duffy's exploration of childhood** in her poetry.

Refer to **two** poems in your answer. [25]

Content words are shown in blue; command words are shown in red.

This question is asking you to explore the theme of childhood in Duffy's poetry. You need to choose two of her poems to refer to in your answer. This means you need a good knowledge of her poetry, and to be familiar with her exploration of childhood, so that you can easily select two poems that will give you plenty to say in your answer.

Keep to time

Managing your time in exams is really important. Some students do not achieve to the best of their abilities because they run out of time to answer all the questions. However, if you manage your time well, you will be able to attempt every question on the exam paper.

Why is it important to attempt all the questions on an exam paper?

If you attempt every question on a paper, you have the best chance of achieving the highest mark you are capable of.

Students who manage their time poorly in exams will often spend far too long on some questions and not even attempt others. Most students are unlikely to get full marks on many questions, but you will get zero marks for the questions you don't answer. You can maximise your marks by giving an answer to every question.

Minutes per mark

The most important way to keep to time is knowing how many minutes you can spend on each mark.

For example, if your exam paper has 90 marks available and you have 90 minutes, you know there is 1 mark per minute.

Therefore, if you have a 5 mark question, you should spend five minutes on it.

Sometimes, you can give a good answer in less time than you have budgeted using the minutes per mark technique. If this happens, you will have more time to spend on questions that use higher-order thinking skills, or more time on checking your work.

How to get faster at answering exam questions

The best way to get faster at answering exam questions is to do lots of practice. You should practise each question type that will be in your exam, marking your own work, so that you know precisely how that question works and what is required by the question. Use the questions in this book to get better and better at answering each question type.

Use the 'Slow, Slow, Quick' technique to get faster.

Take your time answering questions when you first start practising them. You may answer them with the support of the textbook, your notes or the mark scheme. These things will support you with your content knowledge, the language you use in your answer and the structure of your answer.

Every time you practise this question type, you will get more confident and faster. You will become experienced with this question type, so that it is easy for you to recall the subject knowledge and write it down using the correct language and a good structure.

Calculating marks per minute

Use this calculation to work out how long you have for each mark:

Total time in the exam / Number of marks available = Minutes per mark

Calculate how long you have for a question worth more than one mark like this:

Minutes per mark × Marks available for this question
= Number of minutes for this question

What about time to check your work?

It is a very good idea to check your work at the end of an exam. You need to work out if this is feasible with the minutes per mark available to you. If you're always rushing to finish the questions, you shouldn't budget checking time. However, if you usually have time to spare, then you can budget checking time.

To include checking time in your minutes per mark calculation:

(Total time in the exam – Checking time) / Number of marks available
= Minutes per mark

Know what a good answer looks like

It is much easier to give a good answer if you know what a good answer looks like.

Use these methods to know what a good answer looks like.

1 **Sample answers** – you can find sample answers in these places:

   - from your teacher

   - written by your friends or other members of your class

   - in this book.

2 **Look at mark schemes** – mark schemes are full of information about what you should include in your answers. Get familiar with mark schemes to gain a better understanding of the type of things a good answer would contain.

3 **Feedback from your teacher** – if you are finding it difficult to improve your exam skills for a particular type of question, ask your teacher for detailed feedback. You should also look at their comments on your work in detail.

Give yourself the best chance of success

Reflection on progress

As you prepare for your exam, it's important to reflect on your progress. Taking time to think about what you're doing well and what could be improved brings more focus to your revision. Reflecting on progress also helps you to continuously improve your knowledge and exam skills.

How do you reflect on progress?

Use the 'reflection' feature in this book to help you reflect on your progress during your exam preparation. Then, at the end of each revision session, take a few minutes to think about the following:

	What went well? What would you do the same next time?	What didn't go well? What would you do differently next time?
Your subject knowledge		
How you revised your subject knowledge – did you use active retrieval techniques?		
Your use of subject-specific and academic language		
Understanding the question by identifying command words and content words		
Giving a clear structure to your answer		
Keeping to time		
Marking your own work		

Remember to check for silly mistakes – things like missing the units out after you carefully calculated your answer.

Use the mark scheme to mark your own work. Every time you mark your own work, you will be recognising the good and bad aspects of your work, so that you can progressively give better answers over time.

When do you need to come back to this topic or skill?

Earlier in this section of the book, we talked about revision skills and the importance of spaced retrieval. When you reflect on your progress, you need to think about how soon you need to return to the topic or skill you've just been focusing on.

For example, if you were really disappointed with your subject knowledge, it would be a good idea to do some more active retrieval and practice questions on this topic tomorrow. However, if you did really well you can feel confident you know this topic and come back to it again in three weeks' or a month's time.

The same goes for exam skills. If you were disappointed with how you answered the question, you should look at some sample answers and try this type of question again soon. However, if you did well, you can move on to other types of exam questions.

Improving your memory of subject knowledge

Sometimes students slip back into using passive revision techniques, such as only reading the coursebook or their notes, rather than also using active revision techniques, like testing themselves using flip cards or blurting.

You can avoid this mistake by observing how well your learning is working as you revise. You should be thinking to yourself, 'Am I remembering this? Am I understanding this? Is this revision working?'

If the answer to any of those questions is 'no', then you need to change what you're doing to revise this particular topic. For example, if you don't understand, you could look up your topic in a different textbook in the school library to see if a different explanation helps. Or you could see if you can find a video online that brings the idea to life.

You are in control

When you're studying for exams it's easy to think that your teachers are in charge. However, you have to remember that you are studying for your exams and the results you get will be yours and no one else's.

That means you have to take responsibility for all your exam preparation. You have the power to change how you're preparing if what you're doing isn't working. You also have control over what you revise and when: you can make sure you focus on your weaker topics and skills to improve your achievement in the subject.

This isn't always easy to do. Sometimes you have to find an inner ability that you have not used before. But, if you are determined enough to do well, you can find what it takes to focus, improve and keep going.

What is test anxiety?

Do you get worried or anxious about exams? Does your worry or anxiety impact how well you do in tests and exams?

Test anxiety is part of your natural stress response.

The stress response evolved in animals and humans many thousands of years ago to help keep them alive. Let's look at an example.

The stress response in the wild

Imagine an impala grazing in the grasslands of east Africa. It's happily and calmly eating grass in its herd in what we would call the parasympathetic state of rest and repair.

Then the impala sees a lion. The impala suddenly panics because its life is in danger. This state of panic is also known as the stressed or sympathetic state. The sympathetic state presents itself in three forms: flight, fight and freeze.

The impala starts to run away from the lion. Running away is known as the flight stress response.

The impala might not be fast enough to run away from the lion. The lion catches it but has a loose grip. The impala struggles to try to get away. This struggle is the fight stress response.

However, the lion gets an even stronger grip on the impala. Now the only chance of the impala surviving is playing dead. The impala goes limp, its heart rate and breathing slows. This is called the freeze stress response. The lion believes that it has killed the impala so it drops the impala to the ground. Now the impala can switch back into the flight response and run away.

The impala is now safe – the different stages of the stress response have saved its life.

What has the impala got to do with your exams?

When you feel test anxiety, you have the same physiological stress responses as an impala being hunted by a lion. Unfortunately, the human nervous system cannot tell the difference between a life-threatening situation, such as being chased by a lion, and the stress of taking an exam.

If you understand how the stress response works in the human nervous system, you will be able to learn techniques to reduce test anxiety.

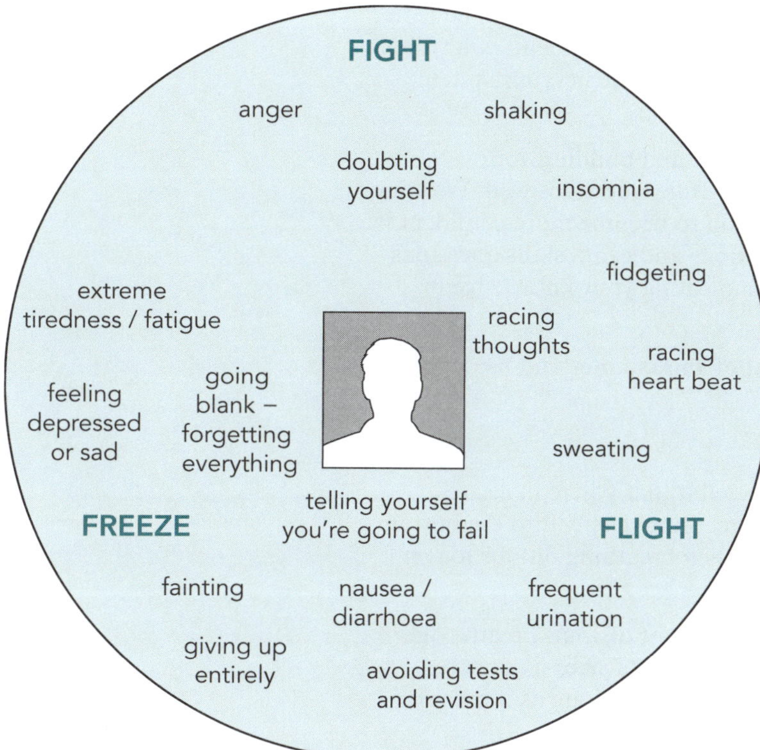

The role of the vagus nerve in test anxiety

The vagus nerve is the part of your nervous system that determines your stress response. Vagus means 'wandering' in Latin, so the vagus nerve is also known as the 'wandering nerve'. The vagus nerve wanders from your brain, down each side of your body, to nearly all your organs, including your lungs, heart, kidneys, liver, digestive system and bladder.

If you are in a stressful situation, like an exam, your vagus nerve sends a message to all these different organs to activate their stress response. Here are some common examples:

- **Heart** beats faster.
- **Kidneys** produce more adrenaline so that you can run, making you fidgety and distracted.
- **Digestive system** and **bladder** want to eliminate all waste products so that energy can be used for fight or flight.

If you want to feel calmer about your revision and exams, you need to do two things to help you move into the parasympathetic, or rest and repair, state:

1   Work with your vagus nerve to send messages of safety through your body.
2   Change your perception of the test so that you see it as safe and not dangerous.

How to cope with test anxiety

1   Be well prepared

Good preparation is the most important part of managing test anxiety. The better your preparation, the more confident you will be. If you are confident, you will not perceive the test or exam as dangerous, so the sympathetic nervous system responses of fight, flight and freeze are less likely to happen.

This book is all about helping you to be well prepared and building your confidence in your knowledge and ability to answer exam questions well. Working through the knowledge recall questions will help you to become more confident in your knowledge of the subject. The practice questions and exam skills questions will help you to become more confident in communicating your knowledge in an exam.

To be well prepared, look at the advice in the rest of this chapter and use it as you work through the questions in this book.

2   Work with your vagus nerve

The easiest way to work with your vagus nerve to tell it that you're in a safe situation is through your breathing. This means breathing deeply into the bottom of your lungs, so that your stomach expands, and then breathing out for longer than you breathed in. You can do this with counting.

Breathe in deeply, expanding your abdomen, for the count of four; breathe out drawing your navel back towards your spine for the count of five, six or seven. Repeat this at least three times. However, you can do it for as long as it takes for you to feel calm.

The important thing is that you breathe out for longer than you breathe in. This is because when you breathe in, your heart rate increases slightly, and when you breathe out, your heart rate decreases slightly. If you're spending more time breathing out overall, you will be decreasing your heart rate over time.

3   Feel it

Anxiety is an uncomfortable, difficult thing to feel. That means that many people try to run away from anxious feelings. However, this means the stress just gets stored in your body for you to feel later.

When you feel anxious, follow these four steps:

1   Pause.
2   Place one hand on your heart and one hand on your stomach.
3   Notice what you're feeling.
4   Stay with your feelings.

What you will find is that if you are willing to experience what you feel for a minute or two, the feeling of anxiety will usually pass very quickly.

4 Write or talk it out

If your thoughts are moving very quickly, it is often better to get them out of your mind and on to paper.

You could take a few minutes to write down everything that comes through your mind, then rip up your paper and throw it away. If you don't like writing, you can speak aloud alone or to someone you trust.

Other ways to break the stress cycle

Exercise and movement	Being friendly	Laughter
• Run or walk. • Dance. • Lift weights. • Yoga. Anything that involves moving your body is helpful.	• Chat to someone in your study break. • Talk to the cashier when you buy your lunch.	• Watch or listen to a funny show on TV or online. • Talk with someone who makes you laugh. • Look at photos of fun times.
Have a hug	**Releasing emotions**	**Creativity**
• Hug a friend or relative. • Cuddle a pet e.g. a cat. Hug for 20 seconds or until you feel calm and relaxed.	It is healthy to release negative or sad emotions. Crying is often a quick way to get rid of these difficult feelings so if you feel like you need to cry, allow it.	• Paint, draw or sketch. • Sew, knit or crochet. • Cook, build something.

If you have long-term symptoms of anxiety, it is important to tell someone you trust and ask for help.

Your perfect revision session

1 Intention

What do you want to achieve in this revision session?
- Choose an area of knowledge or an exam skill that you want to focus on.
- Choose some questions from this book that focus on this knowledge area or skill.
- Gather any other resources you will need e.g. pen, paper, flashcards, coursebook.

2 Focus

Set your focus for the session
- Remove distractions from your study area e.g. leave your phone in another room.
- Write down on a piece of paper or sticky note the knowledge area or skill you're intending to focus on.
- Close your eyes and take three deep breaths, with the exhale longer than the inhale.

3 Revision

Revise your knowledge and understanding
- To improve your knowledge and understanding of the topic, use your coursebook, notes or flashcards, including active learning techniques.
- To improve your exam skills, look at previous answers, teacher feedback, mark schemes, sample answers or examiners' reports.

4 Practice

Answer practice questions
- Use the questions in this book, or in the additional online resources, to practise your exam skills.
- If the exam is soon, do this in timed conditions without the support of the coursebook or your notes.
- If the exam is a long time away, you can use your notes and resources to help you.

5 Feedback

Mark your answers
- Use mark schemes to mark your work.
- Reflect on what you've done well and what you could do to improve next time.

6 Next steps

What have you learned about your progress from this revision session?
What do you need to do next?
- What did you do well? Feel good about these things, and know it's safe to set these things aside for a while.
- What do you need to work on? How are you going to improve? Make a plan to get better at the things you didn't do well or didn't know.

7 Rest

Take a break
- Do something completely different to rest: get up, move or do something creative or practical.
- Remember that rest is an important part of studying, as it gives your brain a chance to integrate your learning.

1 Review of number concepts

When you read an examination question, look carefully at the command word used. It is important to understand what each command word means and what it is asking you to do. In this chapter, look out for the questions containing the command words 'write' and 'write down'.

Write	give an answer in a specific form.
Write down	give an answer without significant working.

When an examination question uses the command words 'write down', it is asking for a brief, direct answer that you can find without doing much or any working. In some 'write down' questions, you may be able to copy some of the information given in the question.

If a question uses the command word 'write', it is asking you to write an answer in a particular form, for example as a decimal, as a fraction or as a power.

You will take two mathematics examinations. Paper 1 is a non-calculator paper so you will need to be able to answer some questions without a calculator. In this chapter, some questions are labelled 🔢. You should try to answer these without using a calculator.

1.1 Different types of number, 1.2 Multiples and factors and 1.3 Prime numbers

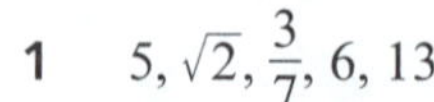

1 $5, \sqrt{2}, \frac{3}{7}, 6, 13$

From this list of numbers, write down

a   an even number   b   an integer

c   the rational numbers   d   an irrational number

e   a prime number.

2 a   List all the factors of 12.

b   Write down the prime factors of 12.

3 List the first four multiples of 12.

4 Find the lowest common multiple (LCM) of 8 and 6.

5 Find the highest common factor (HCF) of 24 and 42.

6 Write 54 as the product of its prime factors.

7 $60 = 2 \times 2 \times 3 \times 5, 105 = 3 \times 5 \times 7$

a   Find the HCF of 60 and 105.

b   Find the LCM of 60 and 105.

8 51, 52, 53, 54, 55, 56, 57, 58, 59
From this list of numbers, write down

a   a multiple of 18   [1]

b   a factor of 168   [1]

c   the prime numbers.   [2]

[Total: 4]

9 a   Write 240 as a product of its prime factors.   [2]

b   Find the lowest common multiple (LCM) of 240 and 140.   [2]

[Total: 4]

≪ RECALL AND CONNECT 1 ≪

Each digit in a number has a place value.

a   What is the value of the 7 in 47 206?

b   What is the value of the 7 in 25 731?

How can you use place value to help you write a number in words?
For example, how do you write 25 731 in words?

> **UNDERSTAND THESE TERMS**
> - Integer
> - Rational number
> - Irrational number
> - Prime number
> - Factor
> - Multiple
> - Product

1.4 Working with directed numbers

1 Copy and complete the statements with the correct sign type, < or >.

  a $-5 \ldots\ldots 4$ **b** $-3 \ldots\ldots -12$ **c** $-2 \ldots\ldots -27$ **d** $-5 \ldots\ldots -2$

2 Find the answers to these calculations.

  a $-3 + 7$ **b** $4 - 10$ **c** $-2 - 5$ **d** $7 + -2$

  e $8 - -5$ **f** $-4 - -3$ **g** 3×-5 **h** -4×-2

  i -6×2 **j** $12 \div -2$ **k** $-18 \div -3$ **l** $-9 \div 3$

3 Use a calculator to work out

  a the difference between -40 and 175

  b the sum of 130 and -84

  c the product of 15 and -23.

4 Find two integers that give -21 when added, and give 38 when multiplied.   [2]

                                                                    [Total: 2]

5 Find the temperature that is $6\,°C$ warmer than $-2\,°C$.   [1]

                                                                    [Total: 1]

6 One day the temperature in Seoul is $2\,°C$ and the temperature in Helsinki is $-7\,°C$.
   Work out the difference in temperature between these two cities.   [1]

                                                                    [Total: 1]

《 RECALL AND CONNECT 2 《

Write a calculation to find the difference between 5 and 8.

Now write calculations to find

a the difference between -10 and 13

b the difference between -10 and -14.

Does knowing how to find the difference between two positive numbers help you to find the difference between two numbers where one or both are negative?

UNDERSTAND THESE TERMS

- Index
- Index notation
- Reciprocal
- Cube number
- Cube root
- Square number
- Square root
- Power

1.5 Powers, roots and laws of indices

1 Work out

  a 3^2 **b** 5^3 **c** 7^2

2 Find the value of

  a $\sqrt{144}$ **b** 6^0 **c** 4^3 **d** $\sqrt[3]{8}$

3 Use a calculator to find the value of

  a $\sqrt{1296}$ **b** 19^2 **c** 2^4 **d** $\sqrt[5]{3125}$

4  Evaluate

   a 7^{-1} **b** $\left(\dfrac{1}{3}\right)^{-1}$ **c** $\left(\dfrac{4}{9}\right)^{-1}$

5 Write 45 as the product of its prime factors. Give your answer in index form.

6 Simplify each expression. Give your answer in index form.

   a $5^3 \times 5^4$ **b** $7^6 \div 7^2$ **c** $3^2 \times 3^{-4}$ **d** $(2^2)^3$

7  Write down the reciprocal of $\dfrac{1}{8}$.   [1]

                                                     [Total: 1]

8  24, 25, 26, 27, 28

   From this list of numbers, write down

   a a cube number   [1]

   b a square number.   [1]

                                                        [Total: 2]

9  **a** Write $\dfrac{5^3 \times 5^4}{5^7}$ as a single power of 5.   [1]

   b Write the value of 5^{-2} as a decimal.   [1]

                                                        [Total: 2]

≪ RECALL AND CONNECT 3 ≪

What is 11^2?

What is the cube root of 125?

Learning the square numbers from 1^2 to 12^2 and the cube numbers from 1^3 to 5^3 and 10^3 will help you find squares, cubes and roots without a calculator.

1.6 Order of operations

1 Write down what each letter stands for in 'BODMAS'.

2  Work out

   a $2 \times 3 + 4$ **b** $6 + 3 \times 4$ **c** $3 \times 7 - 2 \times 4$

3 Work out

   a $2 \times (3 + 4)$ **b** $(6 - 3) \times 4$ **c** $(3 + 9) \div (8 - 2)$

4 Evaluate

   a $4^2 + 5$ **b** $(4 + 5)^2$ **c** $4^2 + 5^2$

5 Add a pair of brackets to make this calculation correct.
$5 \times 9 + 12 \div 3 = 35$ [1]

                                                     [Total: 1]

6 Find the value of $4^6 \div 2^5$.   [2]

                                                        [Total: 2]

7  **a**   Work out $-5 \times -6 \div -2$.   [1]

  b   Work out
  i $13 + 6 \times 4 - 1$ [1]
  ii $13 + 6 \times (4 - 1)$ [1]

[Total: 3]

1.7 Rounding and estimating

1   Round each number correct to 2 decimal places.

  a   36.548   **b**   0.732   **c**   0.295   **d**   0.999

2   Round each number correct to
  i   the nearest 100
  ii   the nearest 1000.

  a   23 406   **b**   15 870   **c**   9650   **d**   428 766

3   Round each number correct to
  i   1 significant figure
  ii   3 significant figures.

  a   2457   **b**   11.32   **c**   36 519   **d**   0.048 75

4    By writing each number in the calculation correct to 1 significant figure, work out an estimate for the value of

$$\frac{7.96 \times 3.4}{1.25 + 4.9}.$$

You must show all your working.   [2]

[Total: 2]

5  **a**   Write 32 485 correct to
  i   the nearest thousand   [1]
  ii   the nearest ten.   [1]

  b   By writing each number in the calculation correct to 1 significant figure, work out an estimate for the value of

$$\frac{4.6^2 + 98}{8.3 - 2.7}.$$

You must show all your working.   [2]

[Total: 4]

REFLECTION

Look at all the non-calculator questions you answered in this chapter.

Write a list of the number skills, facts and rules you used in these questions. How confident are you that you can remember all of these? Are there any that you need to practise to help you answer non-calculator questions?

Highlight any you need to learn. When you think you have learned them, ask someone to use your list to test you on them.

SELF-ASSESSMENT CHECKLIST

Let's revisit the Knowledge and Exam skills focus for this chapter.
Decide how confident you are with each statement.

	Now I can	Show it	Needs more work	Almost there	Confident to move on
1	identify different types of number	Write the definitions of factor, integer, irrational number, multiple, rational number, prime number and product.			
2	write numbers in prime factor form	Write 30 as the product of prime factors. Write 98 as the product of prime factors, in index form.			
3	calculate with negative numbers	Work out **a** $-5 - 4$ **b** $-5 - -4$ **c** -5×-4 **d** $20 \div -5$			
4	recall and use the laws of indices	Write as a single power **a** $3^4 \times 3^5$ **b** $2^8 \div 2^2$ **c** $(5^3)^0$			
5	recall the order of operations	Calculate $9 + 6 \times 7 - 8 \div (6 - 4)$.			
6	round numbers to a given number of decimal places or significant figures	Round 4.6527 **a** to 3 decimal places **b** to 2 significant figures.			
7	estimate the answer to calculations by first rounding all the numbers in the calculation to 1 significant figure	Estimate the value of $\dfrac{5.7^2}{8.75 + 3.1}$.			
8	understand the command words 'write down' and 'write'	What is the difference between 'write down' and 'write'?			
9	work out the answers to non-calculator and calculator questions.	Without using a calculator, work out **a** 9^2 **b** $\sqrt[3]{-27}$ Use a calculator to work out **c** 8^3 **d** $\sqrt{392.04}$			

2 Making sense of algebra

In this chapter you will answer questions on:

- using letters to represent numbers
- writing algebraic expressions to represent mathematical information
- substituting numbers for words and letters in expressions
- adding and subtracting like terms to simplify expressions
- multiplying and dividing to simplify expressions
- expanding and simplifying expressions by removing brackets
- using index notation in algebra
- learning and applying the laws of indices to simplify expressions.

In this chapter you will:

- show that you understand the command words 'write down' and can answer 'write down' questions
- show that you can understand and use the marks available in an examination question to help you write good answers to questions.

When you read an examination question, look carefully at the command word used. It is important to understand what each command word means and what it is asking you to do. In this chapter, look out for the questions containing the command words 'write down'.

| Write down | give an answer without significant working. |

When an examination question uses the command words 'write down', it is asking for a brief, direct answer that you can find without much or any working. To answer a 'write down' question, you use the letters and numbers given in the question.

The number of marks for an examination question can help you understand how much work you need to do. If a question has one mark, then it will usually only require one or two straightforward steps to reach the answer. If a question is worth two or more marks there will usually be either marks for working or for different parts of the answer, for example the different terms of an expression.

2.1 Using letters to represent unknown numbers and 2.2 Substitution

UNDERSTAND THESE TERMS

- Expression
- Term

1 x and y are unknown numbers.
Write an expression for

   a twice y **b** one quarter of x

   c 5 more than x **d** 3 less than y

   e the sum of x and y **f** the difference between x and y

   g the square of x **h** the sum of the cube of y and 3 times x.

2  Given that $d = 4$ and $e = -3$, evaluate

   a de **b** $2d + e$ **c** $d - e$ **d** $5(d + e)$

   e d^2 **f** $2e^3$ **g** $\dfrac{8e}{d}$ **h** $\dfrac{d^2 + e^2}{5(d + e)}$

3 An orange costs 45 cents.
Write down an expression for the cost in cents of x oranges.

4 Pedro buys n melons. The total cost is \$9. Write an expression in terms of n for the cost of one melon.

5 The cost of hiring a rowing boat is \$$r$.
The cost of hiring a kayak is \$$k$.
A family hires 2 rowing boats and 3 kayaks.
Write down an expression in terms of r and k for the total cost, in dollars,
of hiring the kayaks and rowing boats.   [2]

      [Total: 2]

6 $T = 7x + 2y$
Find the value of T when $x = 4$ and $y = -5$.   [2]

      [Total: 2]

≪ RECALL AND CONNECT 1 ≪

Do you remember how to add, subtract, multiply and divide negative numbers?

Work out

   a -4×5 **b** $2 + -4$ **c** $8 \div -2$ **d** $6 - -3$

   e $-4 - 7$ **f** $-10 - -2$ **g** -6×-2 **h** $-18 \div -6$

2.3 Simplifying expressions

1 Simplify each of the following.

   a $2a + 5b + 4a$ **b** $6c + 3d - 4c + 5d$ **c** $5e + 2f + 4e - 5f$

   d $7g - 3 - 2g - 5$ **e** $3k^2 + 2k + 4k^2 - 3k$ **f** $9np - 3n - 2np + n$

2 Write an expression for the perimeter, P, of each of shape. Give your answer in its simplest form.

a

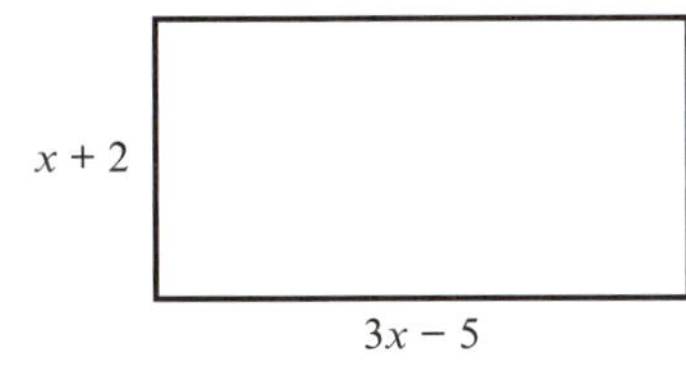

b

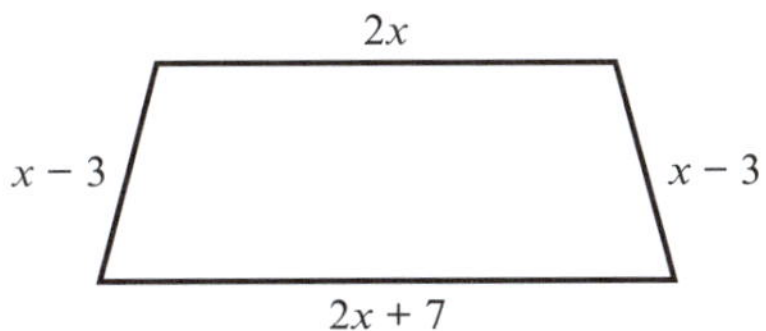

3 Simplify each of the following.

a $3a \times 5$

b $6c \times 3d$

c $-5e \times 4e$

d $2ab \times 4ab$

e $3 \times 5a^2b \times 2a$

f $3g \times 2gh \times 4hk$

4 Simplify each of the following.

a $\dfrac{12x}{4}$

b $\dfrac{8y}{4y}$

c $\dfrac{15y^2}{3y}$

d $\dfrac{20rt}{5t}$

e $\dfrac{3abc}{6ab}$

f $14y^2 \div 2y$

g $9x^2y^3 \div 3xy$

h $\dfrac{12x}{5y} \times \dfrac{10y}{3}$

5 Simplify $2x - 5x + 8x$. [1]

[Total: 1]

6 a Simplify $n + 5n - 2n$. [1]

b Simplify $11t - 3t \times 5$. [1]

c

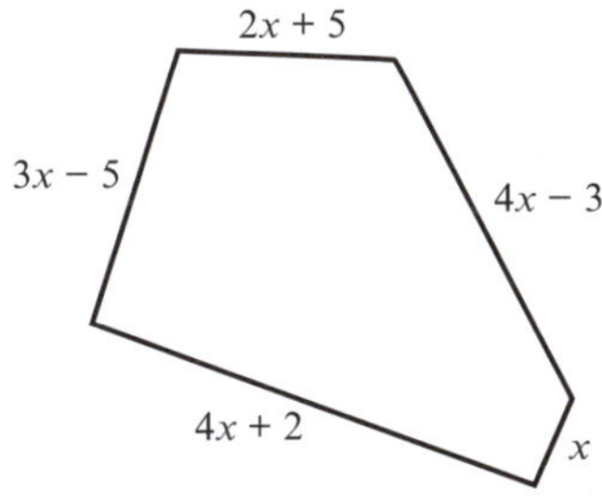

Write down an expression for the perimeter of this shape.
Give your answer in its simplest form. [2]

[Total: 4]

≪ RECALL AND CONNECT 2 ≪

Write the answers to these equations using indices.

a $2^2 \times 2 = 2^\square$ **b** $x^2 \times x = x^\square$ **c** $5^3 \div 5 = 5^\square$ **d** $y^3 \div y = y^\square$

What do you notice about the rules for multiplying and dividing numbers with powers, and for multiplying and dividing letter terms with powers?

2.4 Working with brackets

1 Expand each of the following.

    a $2(a + 7)$ **b** $3(x - 5)$ **c** $b(b - 3)$ **d** $2c(c + 4)$

    e $5(2x + 3)$ **f** $4(5d - 2e)$ **g** $2f^2(3f - 2g)$ **h** $4h^2k(5 - 2k)$

2 Write an expression using brackets for the area, A, of each rectangle.
Then expand the brackets.

    a

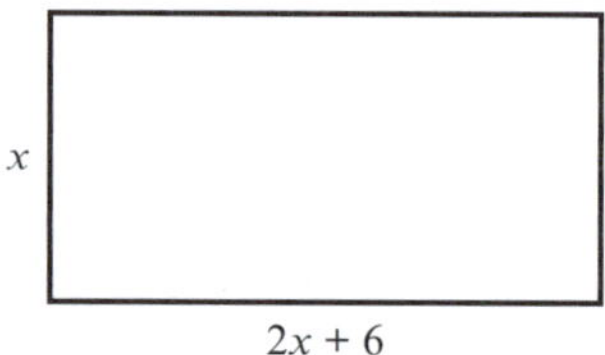

    b

3 Leonie is x years old.
Matt is 3 years older than Leonie.
Jody is twice as old as Matt.
Write down an expression in terms of x for Jody's age.

4 Expand and simplify each of the following.

    a $4(a + 3) + 2a$ **b** $5(2x - 6) + 4$

    c $2(b - 1) - 3b + 5$ **d** $3c(c + 3) + c(c - 2)$

5 Expand each of the following.

    a $-2(d + 5)$ **b** $-3(y - 4)$

    c $-6(2e - 3f)$ **d** $-2g(3g + 8)$

6 Expand and simplify each of the following.

    a $-4(h + 2) + 5h$ **b** $10x - 5(x + 1)$

    c $7(y - 1) - 3(y + 5)$ **d** $3t(t + 3) - (t^2 - 2t)$

7 Expand and simplify $5(2b - 4) + 3(b + 2)$.   [2]

    [Total: 2]

8 Simplify.

    a $5a - 3b + 2a - b$ [2]

    b $4(2x + 5) - 3(x - 1)$ [2]

    [Total: 4]

REFLECTION

When you answered Question 8a, how many terms were in your answer?

How does this relate to the number of marks for this question?

2.5 Indices

1   Write each expression using index notation.

   a $n \times n \times n$

   b $r \times r \times r \times r \times r \times r \times r$

2   Simplify each of the following.

   a $a^2 \times a^3$

   b $4b^2 \times 2b$

   c $-3c^5 \times 4c^2d$

   d $5e^3f \times 3ef^2$

3   Simplify each of the following.

   a $\dfrac{x^8}{x^2}$
   b $\dfrac{10m^4}{2m}$
   c $\dfrac{12n^4q}{3n^3}$
   d $\dfrac{4p^5r^2}{8p^3r}$

4   Simplify each of the following.

   a $(x^2)^3$
   b $(2y^3)^2$
   c $(4x^5y^2)^2$
   d $(6x^5)^0$

5   Simplify each of the following.
Give your answers with positive indices.

   a $x^3 \div x^4$
   b $y^2 \div y^7$
   c $5t^{-2} \times 3t^{-3}$
   d $(2x^5)^{-2}$

6   Simplify $15x^9 \div 5x^3$. [2]

[Total: 2]

7 $5^{12} \div 5^x = 5^3$
Find the value of x. [1]

[Total: 1]

8   Simplify.

   a $(y^6)^3$ [1]

   b $\left(\dfrac{9}{x}\right)^{-2}$ [1]

[Total: 2]

❰❰ RECALL AND CONNECT 3 ❰❰

Simplify each of the following.

a 2^0
   b x^0
   c 5^{-1}

d y^{-1}
   e 5^{-2}
   f y^{-2}

What do you notice about the rules for zero and negative indices for numbers and for letters?

REFLECTION

How can you learn and remember the index laws for numbers and for algebra (letters)?

What strategy did you find useful to learn how to use and apply the index rules for numbers? Can you update this strategy to include examples of the index rules for letters?

How can you apply your methods of learning and remembering these rules to other rules in different topics?

SELF-ASSESSMENT CHECKLIST

Let's revisit the Knowledge and Exam skills focus for this chapter.
Decide how confident you are with each statement.

	Now I can	Show it	Needs more work	Almost there	Confident to move on
1	write algebraic expressions	Pens cost $\$x$ each and rulers cost $\$y$ each. Write down an expression for the total cost of 12 pens and 5 rulers.			
2	substitute values into an expression	Make up some expressions using a, b and c. Evaluate your expressions when $a = 4$, $b = 5$ and $c = -1$.			
3	simplify expressions by collecting like terms	Simplify **a** $5x - 3x + 6x$ **b** $2y - 3 - 6y + 8$ **c** $-3x^2 + 2x + 5x^2 - x$			
4	multiply and divide expressions	Simplify **a** $2a \times c$ **b** $3b \times 4a$ **c** $7bc \times 2bc$ **d** $\dfrac{6def}{3df}$			
5	expand and simplify expressions with brackets	Expand **a** $3(x + 8)$ **b** $5(2y - 3)$ **c** $2x(3x - 4y)$. Expand and simplify **d** $10(x + 4) + 3(x - 2)$ **e** $8(y - 1) - 5(y + 2)$			

CONTINUED

	Now I can	Show it	Needs more work	Almost there	Confident to move on
6	simplify expressions with indices	Simplify **a** $(3x)^0$ **b** t^{-3} **c** $2x^3 \times 5x^4$ **d** $12y^7 \div 3y^3$.			
7	understand the command words 'write down'	This square has side length y. y □ Write down an expression for **a** the perimeter **b** the area. How can you use the information given in the question to help you write your answer?			
8	use the marks given for a question to help write good answers to questions.	This question is worth two marks. What does this tell you? $y = 3x + 4t$ Find the value of y when $x = 5$ and $y = -2$. [2]			

3 Lines, angles and shapes

In this chapter you will answer questions on:

- using the correct terms to talk about points, lines, angles and shapes
- classifying, measuring and constructing angles
- calculating unknown angles using angle relationships
- talking about the properties of triangles, quadrilaterals, circles and polygons
- constructing triangles using a ruler and a pair of compasses.

In this chapter you will:

- show that you understand the 'give' and 'construct' command words and can answer 'give' and 'construct' questions
- show that you can understand and answer different types of questions, for example those that need calculations and those that need written answers.

When you read an examination question, look carefully at the command word used. It is important to understand what each command word means and what it is asking you to do. In this chapter, look out for the questions containing the command words 'construct' and 'give'.

Construct	make an accurate drawing.
Give	produce an answer from a given source or recall/memory.

When an examination question uses the command word 'construct', you are being asked to use mathematical instruments to draw accurately. It is likely the instruments you are expected to use will be set out in the question, so you will always need to make sure you take all the required items to an examination. When constructing with compasses and a straight edge, you will need to make sure all arcs and lines you use to make the construction are clear.

When an examination question uses the command word 'give', it is asking you to write an answer using facts or information you have learned and remembered. In this chapter, questions will ask you to give reasons why an answer is correct. This means you need to write down any geometric facts you have used. For example, when you have calculated a missing angle in a triangle, you can give the reason 'the angles in a triangle sum to 180°'.

3.1 Lines and angles

1   Answer the questions about this shape.

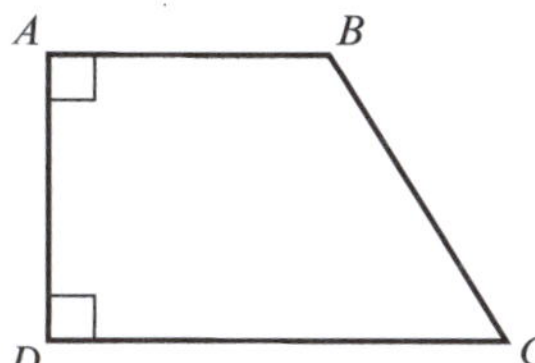

a   Which two sides are parallel?

b   Which two sides are perpendicular?

c   What type of angle is angle ABC?

d   What type of angle is angle BCD?

2   For each diagram, find the missing angle and give a geometric reason for your answer.

a

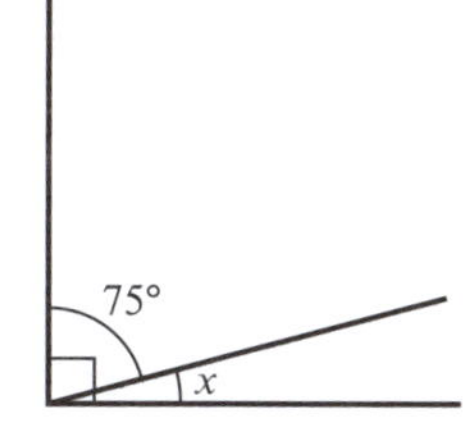

b

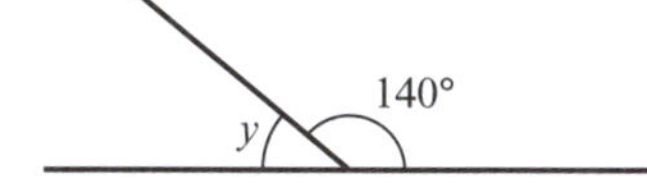

c

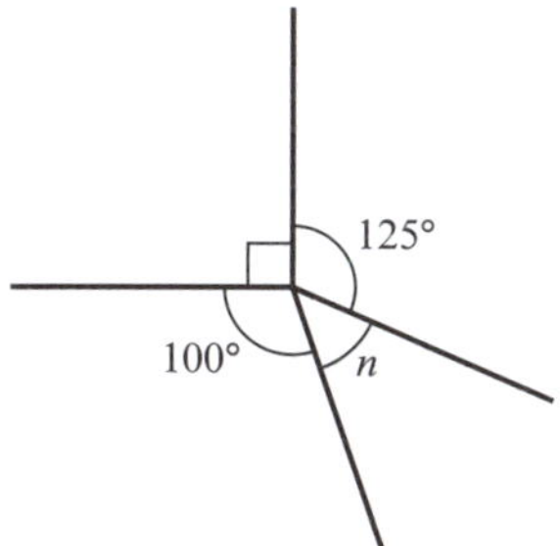

3   The diagram shows two straight lines that cross.

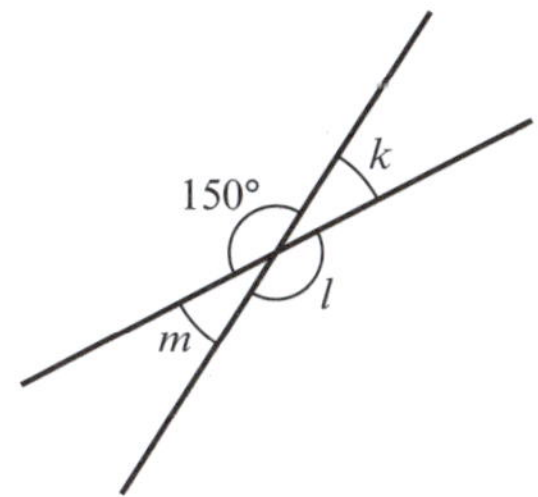

Give a geometric reason for each of these statements.

a   The value of angle l is 150°.   b   The value of angle k is 30°.

4 Write down the letters of

   a two co-interior angles

   b two pairs of corresponding angles

   c two alternate angles

   d two pairs of vertically opposite angles.

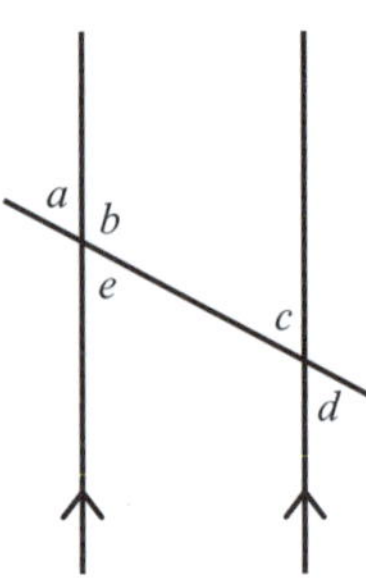

5 Find the value of x.

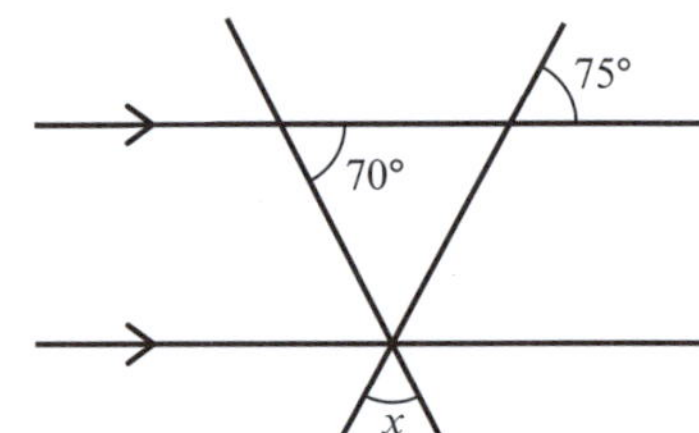

NOT TO SCALE

6

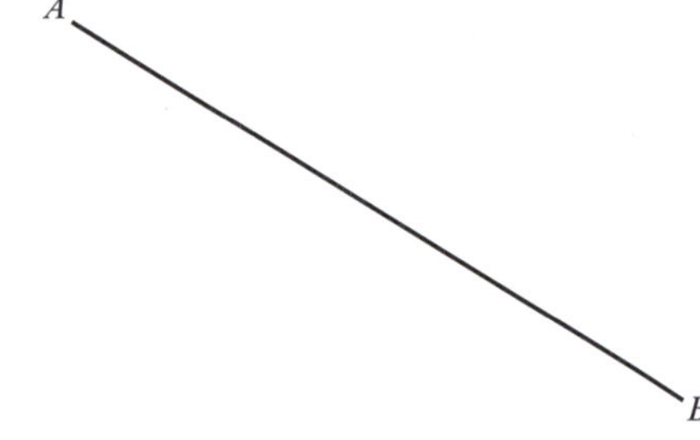

   a Measure the length of the line segment AB in millimetres. [1]

   b Mark the mid-point, M, of AB. [1]

   c Draw a line through M that is perpendicular to AB. [1]

[Total: 3]

7 **a**

     i Measure angle y. [1]

     ii Write down the mathematical name for angle y. [1]

   b

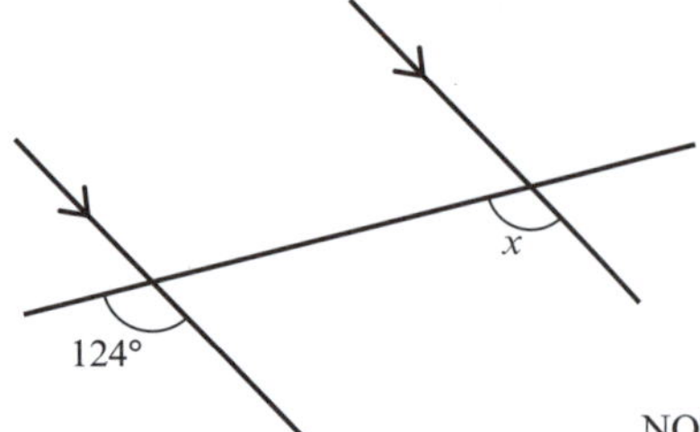

NOT TO SCALE

The diagram shows a pair of parallel lines and a straight line.
Give a geometric reason why the value of x is 124°. [1]

[Total: 3]

3.2 Triangles, 3.3 Quadrilaterals and 3.4 Polygons

1   Write down the name of each triangle.

a 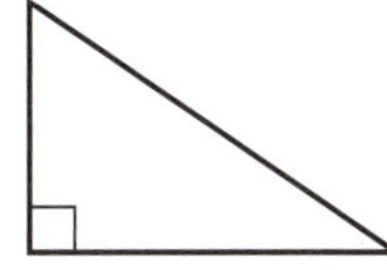

b 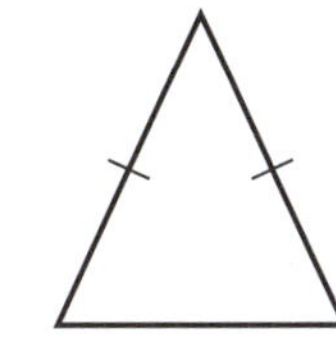

c 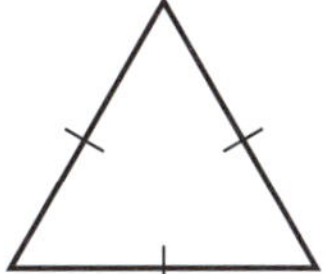

d 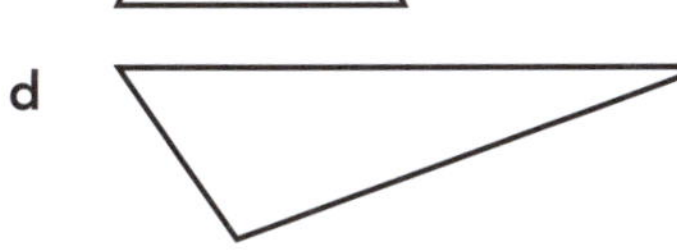

2   Find the angles labelled with letters in each triangle. The diagrams are not to scale.

a 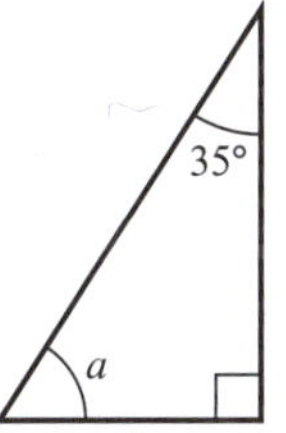

b 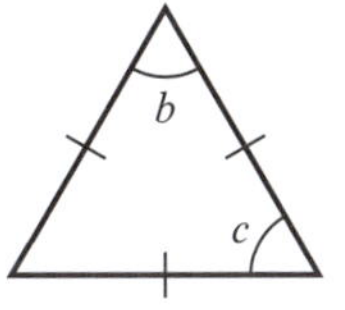

c 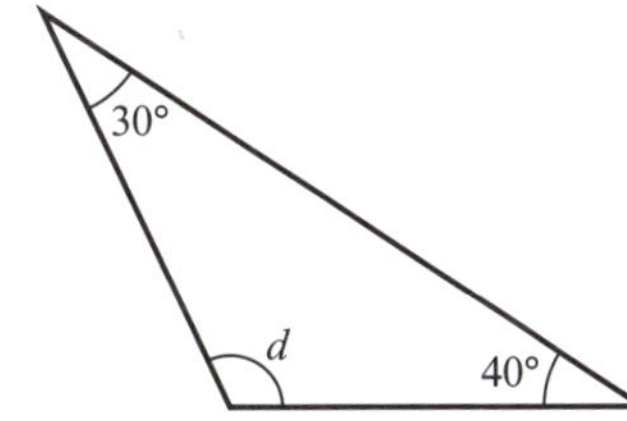

d 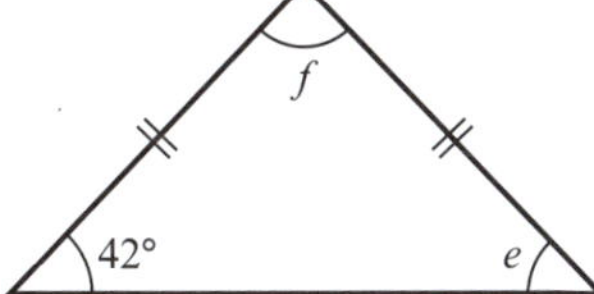

e 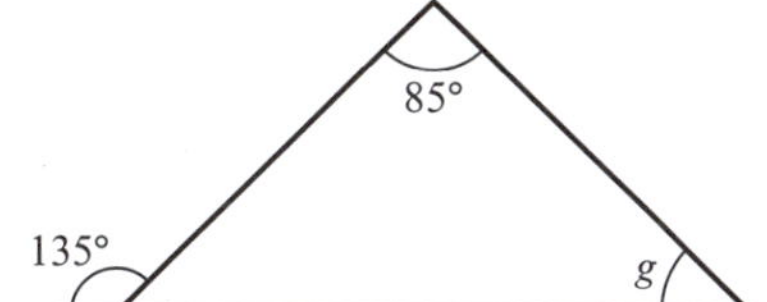

3   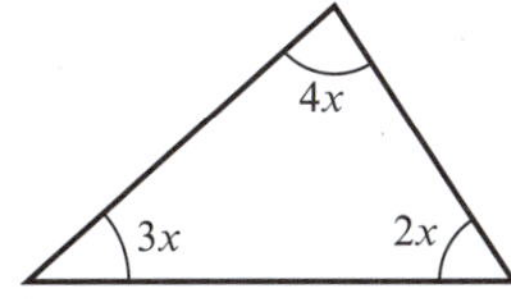

Work out the size of each angle in this triangle.
Give a geometric reason for your answer.

« RECALL AND CONNECT 1 «

Write down an expression to help you solve the problem in Question 3.

4   Sketch each quadrilateral from this list:
rectangle, parallelogram, kite, rhombus, isosceles trapezium
On each sketch, label any

i   parallel sides   ii   equal sides   iii   equal angles.

5 Find the angles labelled with letters in each quadrilateral.
The diagrams are not to scale. (Hint: Think about the rules for co-interior angles in parallel lines.)

a
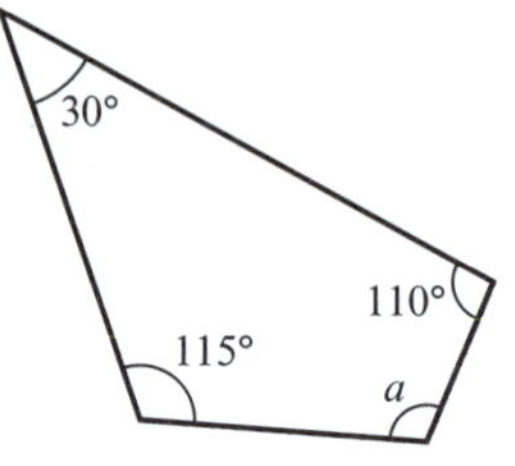

b
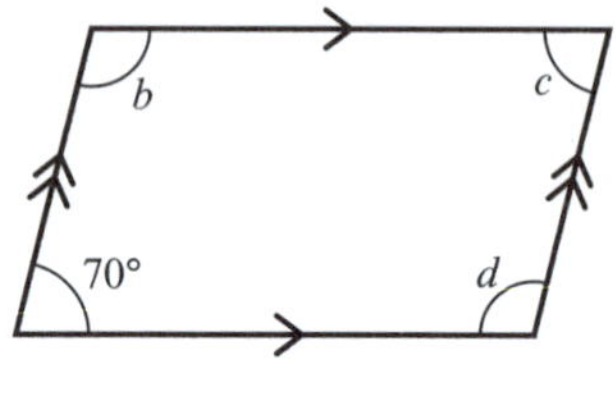

c
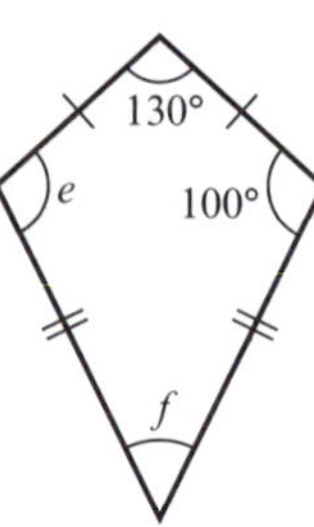

d
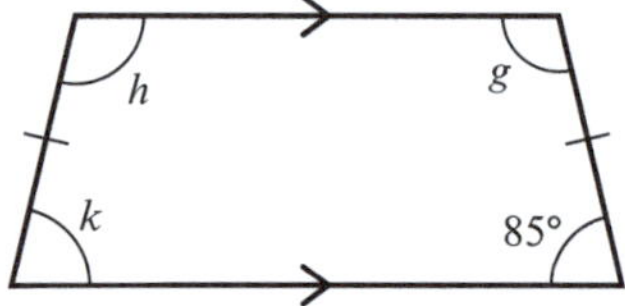

e
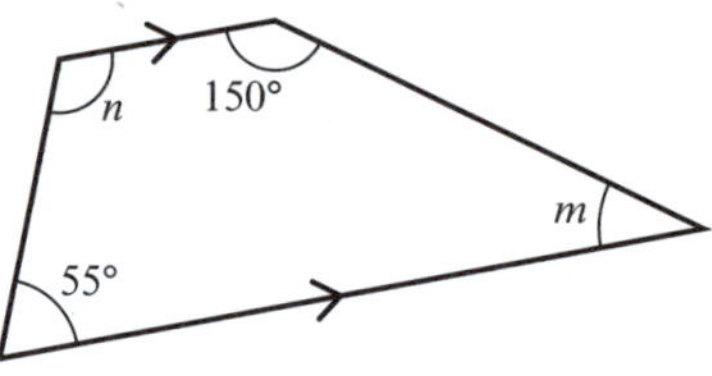

6 **a** How many sides does a decagon have?

   b What is the name of a polygon with five sides?

7 **a** Work out the angle sum of a pentagon.

   b Work out the size of one interior angle of a regular pentagon.

8 Angle x is an exterior angle of a regular octagon.

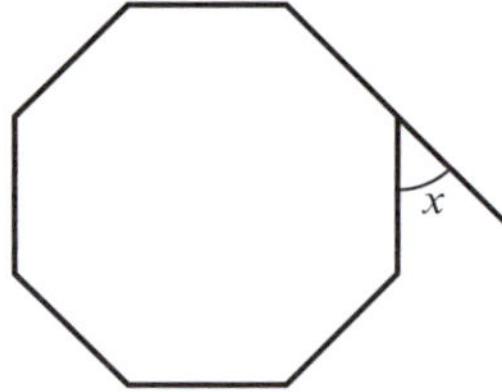

Work out the size of angle x.

9 

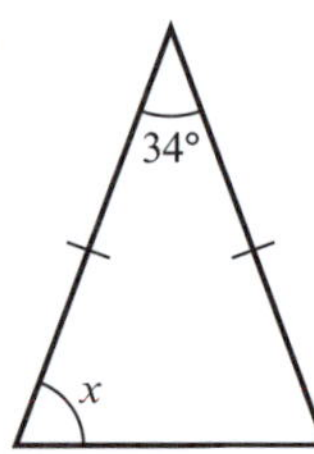

NOT TO SCALE

The diagram shows an isosceles triangle.
Find the value of x.   [2]

[Total: 2]

10 The diagram shows a quadrilateral.

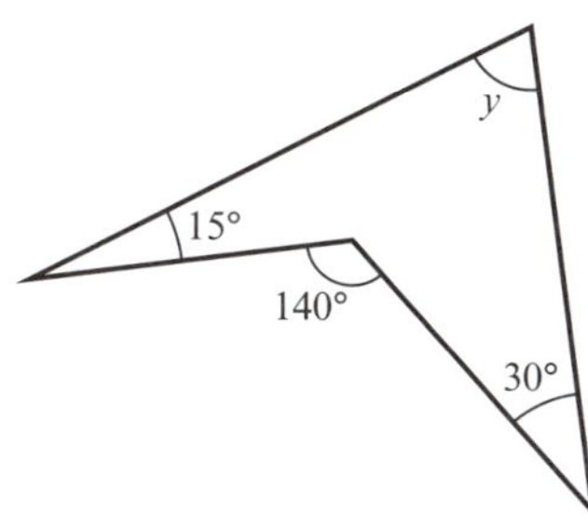

Find the value of y and give a geometric reason for your answer. [3]

[Total: 3]

11 a Show that the interior angle of a regular hexagon is 120°. [1]

b

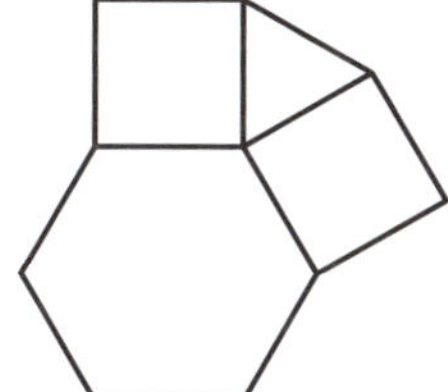

Show that a regular hexagon, two squares and an equilateral triangle meet at a point without any gaps. [1]

[Total: 2]

REFLECTION

Do you find that drawings help you visualise questions better?
What diagrams might you draw to help you solve problems about angles in triangles and quadrilaterals?

What other ways can help you remember angle facts and properties of shapes? What works best for you?

3.5 Circles

1 Write down the names of each part of this circle labelled with a letter.
O is the centre of the circle.

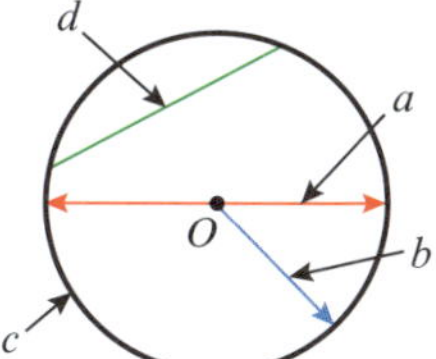

2   Use a pair of compasses to draw a circle.
Draw and label

   a a chord   **b** a major segment   **c** a minor segment.

3   Use a pair of compasses to draw a circle.
Draw and label

   a a minor sector   **b** a major sector

   c a minor arc   **d** a major arc.

4 

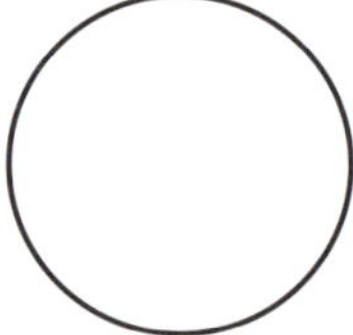

   a Assume the diameter of this circle is 3.4 cm.
Write down the radius of this circle in cm.   [1]

   b On the diagram, draw a tangent.   [1]

                      [Total: 2]

5 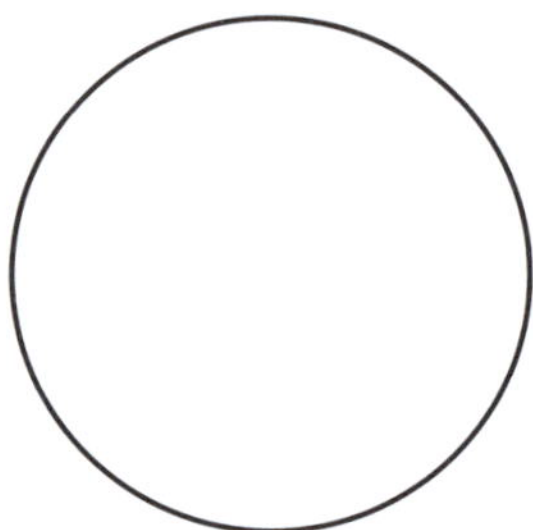

   a The diagram shows a circle. On the circle, draw a chord.   [1]

   b Another circle has radius 27 mm.
Write down the diameter of this circle in cm.   [1]

                      [Total: 2]

REFLECTION

How can you memorise the names for the parts of a circle? You might remember them alphabetically. You might remember diagrams that show them.
You might remember them in groups, for example:

- radius, diameter, tangent

- circumference, arc

- chord, segment

- radius, sector.

How will you memorise these names?

3.6 Construction

1   Using a ruler and a pair of compasses, construct this triangle accurately.
Leave in your construction arcs.

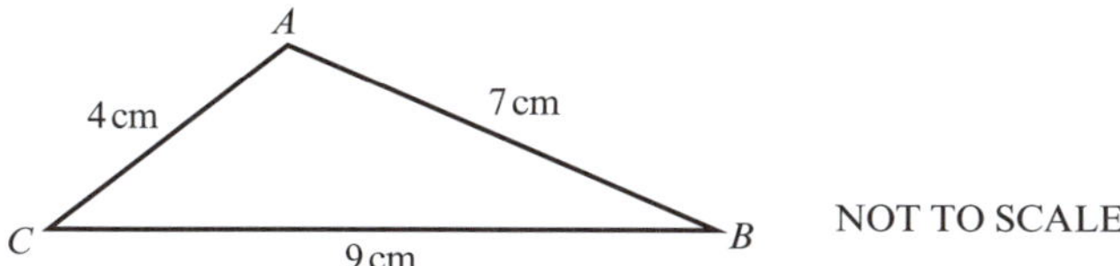

2   Construct an equilateral triangle with side 5 cm. (Hint: Use a ruler and a pair of compasses.)

3   Construct an isosceles triangle with sides 6 cm, 8 cm and 8 cm. (Hint: Use a ruler and a pair of compasses.)

4   Using a ruler and a pair of compasses, construct this diagram accurately.
Leave in your construction arcs.

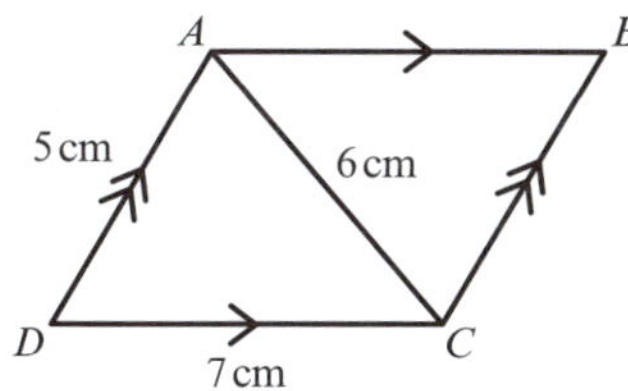

5   In triangle ABC, $AC = 6.5$ cm and $BC = 5$ cm.

a   Using a ruler and a pair of compasses only, construct triangle ABC.
Leave in your construction arcs.
The line AB has been drawn for you.

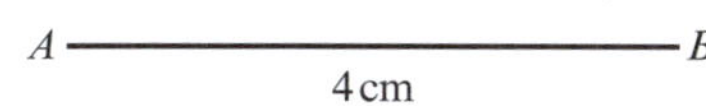

[2]

b   Write down the mathematical name for this type of triangle.   [1]

[Total: 3]

6 In triangle PQR, $PR = 10\,$cm and $QR = 8\,$cm.

  a Using a ruler and a pair of compasses only, construct triangle PQR.
Leave in your construction arcs.
The line PQ has been drawn for you.

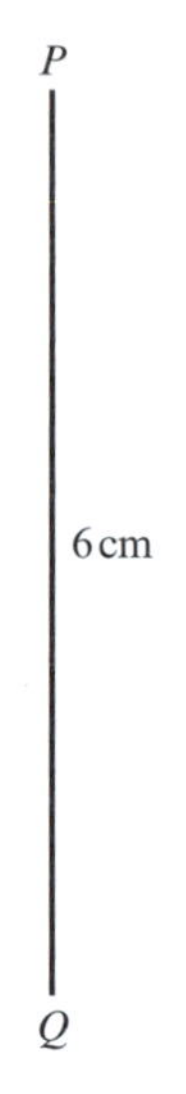

    [2]

  b Write down the mathematical name for this type of triangle. [1]

  c Measure the distance from Q to the midpoint of PR.
Give your answer in millimetres. [1]

[Total: 4]

≪ RECALL AND CONNECT 2 ≪

Convert these measurements

  a 11.7 cm = _____ mm   **b** 300 mm = _____ cm   **c** 0.9 cm = _____ mm.

SELF-ASSESSMENT CHECKLIST

Let's revisit the Knowledge and Exam skills focus for this chapter.
Decide how confident you are with each statement.

	Now I can	Show it	Needs more work	Almost there	Confident to move on
1	draw perpendicular and parallel lines	Use a ruler to draw a straight line segment AB. Draw a line parallel to AB. Label the midpoint, M, of AB. Draw a line through M and perpendicular to AB.			
2	identify types of angles	Sketch • an acute angle • an obtuse angle • a reflex angle.			
3	find angles in parallel lines	Find the angles labelled with letters.			
4	find angles in triangles	Find the angles labelled with letters.			
5	find angles in quadrilaterals	$ABCD$ is a rhombus. Find angle x.			
6	work out the angle sum of a polygon	Work out the angle sum of a 12-sided polygon.			
7	find the exterior angle of a regular polygon	Find the exterior angle of a regular nonagon (a 9-sided polygon).			

CONTINUED

	Now I can	Show it	Needs more work	Almost there	Confident to move on
8	name the parts of a circle	Write down the name of each part of the circle shown.			
9	construct a triangle using ruler and a pair of compasses only	Construct a triangle with sides 5 cm, 7 cm and 10 cm.			
10	understand the command word 'construct'	Using a ruler and a pair of compasses, construct an equilateral triangle with side length 7.5 cm.			
11	understand the command word 'give'	$2x + 50 = 180$ Give a geometric reason why this equation is correct.			
12	understand how to answer different types of questions.	Look at the exam skills questions in this chapter, sort them into those that require a written answer and those that require a construction (drawn) answer. Do any of them fit into both categories?			

4 Collecting, organising and displaying data

When you read an examination question, look carefully at the command word used. It is important to understand what each command word means and what it is asking you to do. In this chapter, look out for the questions containing the command words 'state' and 'explain'.

State	express in clear terms.
Explain	set out purposes or reasons/make the relationships between things clear/say why and/or how and support with relevant evidence.

When an examination question uses the command word 'state', it is asking for a short, clear answer. You do not need to include an explanation.

When an examination question uses the command word 'explain', it means you should include a mathematical reason or justification. Make sure your answer shows the thinking behind your solution. Show your working and make sure your explanation covers all aspects of the question.

When answering examination questions, you should think about what to include to give the best possible answer. In this chapter, you will be asked to draw graphs and charts. To give a good answer to a question asking you to draw graphs or charts, you should make sure that you label any axes or scales and include a key if needed (for example, for a stem-and-leaf diagram). Make sure you draw bars and measure lines as accurately as possible. As you work through the exam skills questions, once you have written each answer, think about how you might be able to improve it.

4.1 Collecting and classifying data

> **UNDERSTAND THESE TERMS**
> - Numerical data
> - Categorical data
> - Discrete data
> - Continuous data
> - Primary data
> - Secondary data

1   Shane goes to three supermarkets to collect data on the prices of bread and milk. Lucy collects data on the prices of bread and milk from the supermarkets' websites.

    a   Who collected primary data?   **b**   Who collected secondary data?

2   Identify each of the following data sets as numerical or categorical.

    a   Colours of rope   **b**   Lengths of rope

    c   Soft drink flavours   **d**   Amount of soft drink in a can

3   Identify each of the following data sets as discrete or continuous.

    a   Number of eggs in a nest   **b**   Masses of newborn kittens

    c   Volume of water in a pond   **d**   Number of matches in a box

4   Mica wants to find out which country won the most medals at the last Olympic Games.

    a   How could Mica collect this data?

    b   Is it primary or secondary data?

    c   Is the data categorical or numerical?

« RECALL AND CONNECT 1 «

Continuous data is usually collected by measuring.

What instruments and units can you use to measure the following quantities?

- Length
- Mass
- Volume
- Temperature

REFLECTION

Have you successfully memorised the definitions of the key terms in the box?

Try testing yourself by saying or writing the definitions without looking at them and then check whether your definitions were correct. If you don't recall them all correctly, test yourself again every few days until you can.

By doing this you can avoid 'cramming' – trying to memorise a lot of information in a short time before the exam – which can cause anxiety and is not a reliable way to prepare.

4.2 Organising data

1   Copy and complete the frequency table.

Colour of T-shirt	Tally	Frequency
Blue	卌 卌	
Green		15
Red	卌 |||	
White		26
Black	卌 卌 卌 ||	
	Total	

UNDERSTAND THESE TERMS

- Two-way table
- Tally mark
- Class interval

2   Here are some students' marks in a maths test.

15	22	41	36	28	9	31	45
38	11	42	29	31	14	27	43
48	26	15	19	37	40	38	26

Organise the data into a grouped frequency table.

3   The back-to-back stem-and-leaf diagram shows the lengths of worms from two different soil samples.

```
      Sample A                    Sample B

                          4  |  8  9
                          5  |  3  7  9
                   7      6  |  0  2
          9  6  6  1      7  |  4  5  5  6  7  9  9
                5  5  3   8  |  3
             7  6  2  0   9  |
                8  3  1  10  |
```

Key: Sample A   7 | 6 represents 6.7 cm

       Sample B   4 | 8 represents 4.8 cm

a   How many worms were measured in sample A?

b   How many worms from sample A were longer than 8 cm?

c   How many worms from sample B were less than 6 cm long?

d   Joe says, 'The longest worm in Sample B is 83 cm long'. Explain why Joe is wrong.

e   What does this stem-and-leaf diagram tell you about the lengths of the worms in the two samples?

4 Copy and complete this two-way table for the worm length data from the stem-and-leaf diagram in Question 3.

	Length of worm		
	4.0–5.9 cm	6.0–7.9 cm	8.0–10.9 cm
Sample A			
Sample B			

5 The numbers of visitors to a library is recorded each day for 14 days.

12	14	25	18	30	21	11
19	22	13	34	12	16	24

a Copy and complete the stem-and-leaf diagram.

1	
2	
3	

Key: 1|2 represents 12 visitors   [2]

b Sasha says that on more than half of the days there were fewer than 20 visitors to the library. Is she correct? Explain your answer. [1]

[Total: 3]

> **REFLECTION**
>
> In which other subjects do you use charts and diagrams? How could what you have learned about these in maths help you with these other subjects?

4.3 Using charts to display data

1 Here are three types of chart. Select the correct chart for each description.

      bar chart   composite bar chart   dual bar chart

a Shows two sets of data in bars side-by-side.
b Displays data in a series of bars plotted against a scale on the axis.
c Shows a whole set of data in one bar, broken down into groups.

2 Sara sells small, medium and large T-shirts.
The table shows the numbers of each size she sells in two weeks.

	Small	Medium	Large
Week 1	25	30	15
Week 2	10	40	20

a Draw a dual bar chart to display this data to show the difference in sales in the two weeks.

b Draw a composite bar chart to show the sales of each size in the two weeks.

> **UNDERSTAND THESE TERMS**
>
> - Composite bar chart
> - Dual bar chart
> - Pie chart
> - Pictogram

3   Jenny records the colours of cars passing her school one day.
The results are shown in the table.

Colour	Frequency	Pie chart sector angle
Silver	5	
Black	8	
Red	3	
White	2	

a   Copy and complete the table.   [2]

b   Copy and complete the pie chart.

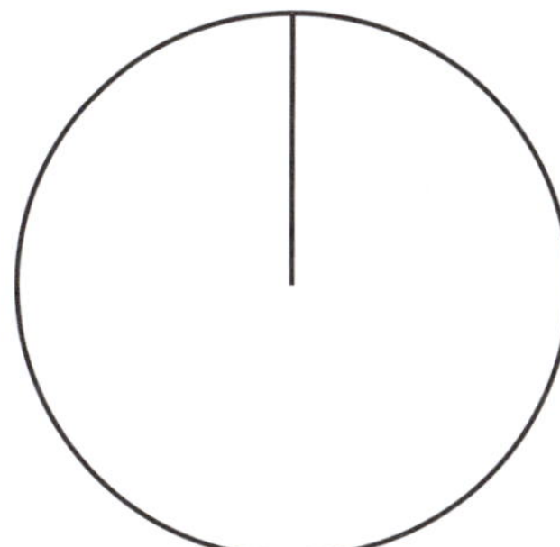

[2]

[Total: 4]

4   Craig asks some to students choose their favourite subject from drama, art,
music or design. The pie chart shows the results.

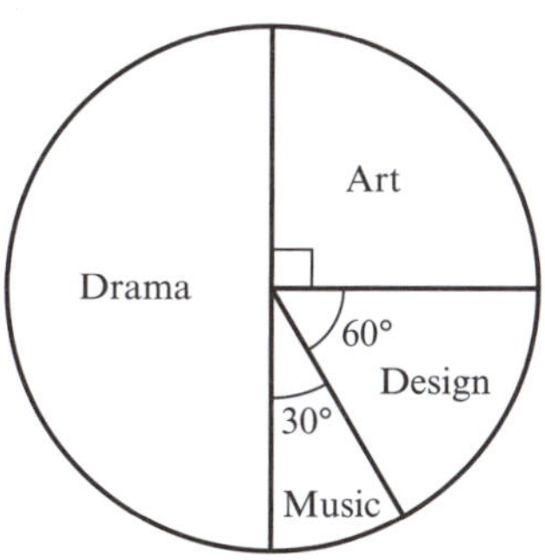

a   Write down the percentage of students who chose art.   [1]

b   Sarima says, 'I do not know how many people chose drama, but I do
know it is an even number.' Explain how Sarima knows this.   [1]

c   Craig now tells Sarima that 24 students chose art.
Work out how many students chose music.   [2]

[Total: 4]

5 Li-Mei asks 50 students at his school which is their favourite subject.
The table shows the results.

Maths	Science	History	Art
12	15	10	14

Copy and complete the pictogram.

Maths	⊕ ⊕ ⊕
Science	
History	
Art	

Key: ⊕ Represents 4 people

[2]

[Total: 2]

≪ RECALL AND CONNECT 2 ≪

What is the name for a line from the centre of a circle to the circumference?

What total do the angles around a point add up to?

SELF-ASSESSMENT CHECKLIST

Let's revisit the Knowledge and Exam skills focus for this chapter.
Decide how confident you are with each statement.

	Now I can	Show it	Needs more work	Almost there	Confident to move on
1	classify different types of data	Check that you can recall the definitions of numerical data, categorical data, continuous data, discrete data, primary data and secondary data.			
2	collect data in a tally table or frequency table	Draw a grouped frequency table to collect data on people's heights between 1.4 m and 1.8 m.			
3	organise data in a two-way table	Answer Question 4 in Section 4.2 correctly.			

CONTINUED

	Now I can	Show it	Needs more work	Almost there	Confident to move on
4	organise data using a stem-and-leaf diagram	Look back at Question 2 in Section 4.2. Create a stem-and-leaf diagram to represent the data.			
5	draw a pictogram to display data	Draw a pictogram to represent this data. Number of coloured pens = 4 blue, 2 red, 9 black.			
6	draw a bar chart to display data	Draw a bar chart to represent this data. Number of coloured pens = 4 blue, 2 red, 9 black.			
7	draw a pie chart to display data	Work out the angles in a pie chart for this data. Number of coloured pens = 4 blue, 2 red, 9 black.			
8	answer questions about a chart or stem-and-leaf diagram	Answer at least one exam-style question or real past exam question correctly using this skill.			
9	write a good answer to a drawing a chart or graph question	Write two things to remember when drawing stem-and-leaf diagrams.			
10	understand the command words 'explain' and 'state'.	What is the difference between 'explain' and 'state'?			

Exam practice 1

This section contains past paper questions from previous Cambridge exams, which draw together your knowledge on a range of topics that you have covered up to this point. These questions give you the opportunity to test your knowledge and understanding.

The following question has an example student response and commentary provided. Work through the question first, then compare your answer to the sample response and commentary. Are your answers different to the sample responses?

1   By writing each number in the calculation correct to 1 significant figure, find an estimate for the value of

$$\frac{27 - 2.3^2}{845.4 \times 0.048}$$

[2]

Cambridge IGCSE Mathematics (0580) Paper 12 Q18, June 2022   **[Total: 2]**

Example student response	Commentary
$\dfrac{30 - 2^2}{850 \times 0.05}$ $=\dfrac{30 - 4}{42.5}$	The student has not rounded one of the numbers to 1 significant figure. Rounding at least three of the numbers correctly, as here, would score 1 mark.
$\dfrac{26}{42.5} = 0.612$ (to 3 significant figures)	The student has used a calculator to work this out, instead of rounding and estimating. The answer is incorrect because of the incorrect rounding at the start. This would not gain any marks. **This answer scores 1 out of 2 marks.**

The following question has an example student response and commentary provided. Work through the question first, then compare your answer to the sample response and commentary. Are your answers different to the sample responses?

2

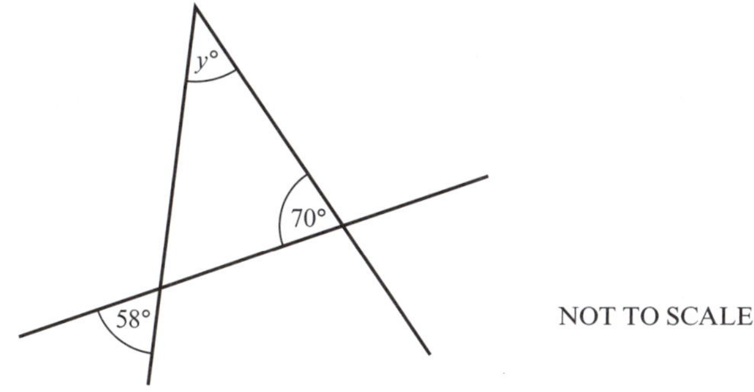

The diagram shows three straight lines.
Find the value of y.
Write down the geometric properties needed to find the value of y. [3]

Cambridge IGCSE Mathematics (0580) Paper 32 Q5b, June 2024 **[Total: 3]**

Example student response	Commentary
$y = 180 - 70 - 58 = 52°$ Angle sum of a triangle = 180°	The student has correctly found the value of y. This scores 1 mark. The student has written down one geometric property used to find the value of y. This scores 1 mark. To score the final mark, the student would have needed to write down the geometric reason they used to find the 58° angle. **This answer scores 2 out of 3 marks.**

The following question has an example student response and commentary provided.
Work through the question first, then compare your answer to the sample response and
commentary. Are your answers different to the sample responses?

3 In a league, teams gain 4 points for each win, 2 points for each draw and
bonus points.

A team has x wins, y draws and b bonus points.

Write down an expression, in terms of x, y and b, for the total number of points
the team has. [2]

Cambridge IGCSE Mathematics (0580) Paper 12 Q15, November 2024 **[Total: 2]**

Example student response	Commentary
$4x + 2y + 2b$	The student has found two correct terms. This scores 1 mark. To score the final mark, the student needs to write an expression with all three terms correct. **This answer scores 1 out of 2 marks.**

Now that you have read the commentary to the previous question, here is a similar question that you should attempt. Use the information from the previous response and commentary to guide you as you answer.

4 **a** The total cost of n bags of flour is $\$d$.
Write down an expression for the cost of one bag of flour. [1]

   b A bag of rice costs $\$r$ and a bag of almonds costs $\$a$.
Pedro buys x bags of rice and y bags of almonds.
Write down an expression for the change that Pedro receives from a \$20 note. [2]

Cambridge IGCSE Mathematics (0580) Paper 12 Q12, June 2022   [Total: 3]

The following question has an example student response and commentary provided. Work through the question first, then compare your answer to the sample response and commentary. Are your answers different to the sample responses?

5   Calculate the interior angle of a regular 9-sided polygon. [2]

Cambridge IGCSE Mathematics (0580) Paper 12 Q15, November 2023   [Total: 2]

Example student response	Commentary
$(9 - 2) \times 180° = 1260°$	The student has successfully found the sum of the interior angles of a 9-sided polygon, but they have not read the question correctly as they needed to calculate the value of one interior angle. **This answer scores 0 out of 2 marks.**

The following question has an example student response and commentary provided. Work through the question first, then compare your answer to the sample response and commentary. Are your answers different to the sample responses?

6 20 students choose their favourite science subject.
The results are shown in the bar chart.

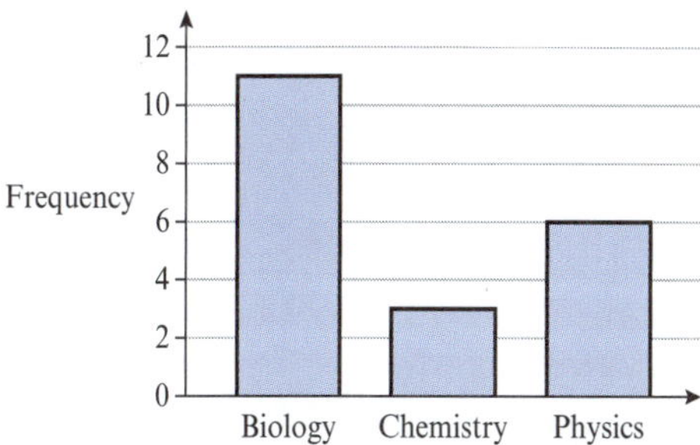

a Work out how many more students choose Biology than Physics. [1]

b Write down the fraction of students whose favourite science subject
is Chemistry. [1]

c The results are to be shown in a pie chart.

    i Complete the table.

Favourite science	Frequency	Pie chart sector angle
Biology		
Chemistry		
Physics		

[3]

    ii Complete the pie chart. [Use Figure 1 in the Past Paper Practice
Questions Resource Sheet.]

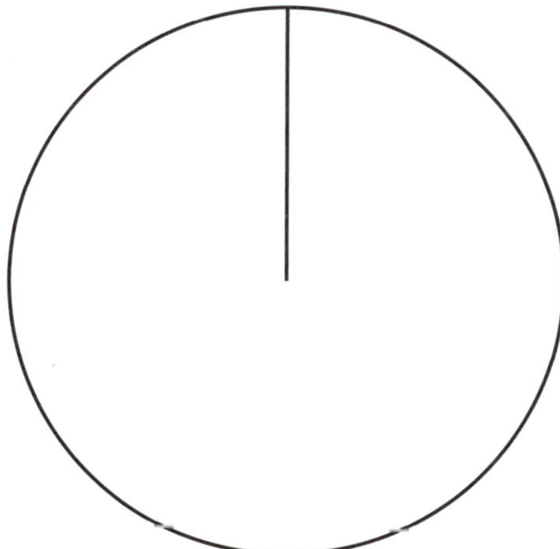

[2]

Cambridge IGCSE Mathematics (0580) Paper 32 Q1a, b, e, March 2021

[Total: 7]

Example student response	Commentary
a 2.5	The student has not used the vertical scale on the graph and they have not checked their answer in the context of the question: the number of people has to be a whole number. ***This answer scores 0 out of 1 mark.***
b 3 students choose Chemistry 20 students in total	The student has done some working, but they have not written the fraction, which is what the question asks for. This would score 0 marks. ***This answer scores 0 out of 1 mark.***
c i <table><tr><td>Favourite science</td><td>Frequency</td><td>Pie chart sector angle</td></tr><tr><td>Biology</td><td>11</td><td>200°</td></tr><tr><td>Chemistry</td><td>3</td><td>54°</td></tr><tr><td>Physics</td><td>6</td><td>108°</td></tr></table>	The student has calculated two angles correctly. This scores 2 marks. To score all three marks, they need to have all three angles correct. ***This answer scores 2 out of 3 marks.***
c ii 54° 108°	The student has drawn the angles accurately. They did not need to label the sizes of the angles, but they should have labelled the sections of the pie chart so it is clear which section represents which science. ***This answer scores 1 out of 2 marks.***

7   Now that you've gone through the commentary, try to write an improved answer
     to the parts of the question where you lost marks. This will help you check
     if you've understood why each mark has (or has not) been allocated. Use the
     commentary to guide you as you answer.

5 Fractions, percentages and standard form

When you read an examination question, look carefully at the command word used. It is important to understand what each command word means and what it is asking you to do. In this chapter, look out for the questions containing the command words 'write' and 'work out'.

Write	give an answer in a specific form.
Work out	calculate from given facts, figures or information with or without the use of a calculator.

When an examination question uses the command word 'write', you should check the question to find out what form to give your answer in. For example, when answers involve fractions, you are usually asked to write your answer in the simplest form. When dealing with very large or very small numbers, you are often asked to write your answer in standard or ordinary form.

If an examination question uses the command words 'work out', you should use information given in the question to find the answer. You can be asked 'work out' questions on both the calculator paper and the non-calculator paper. If you have used a calculator to find the answer, remember to include your working in the answer, as you could still score marks for a correct method or working, even if your final answer is incorrect.

Fractions, percentage and standard form questions can appear on the non-calculator paper. When you are revising and completing the exercises in this chapter, practise working out the answers without a calculator and find which methods work best for you. Once you have completed the questions, you can go back and check your answers with a calculator.

5.1 Revisiting fractions and 5.2 Operations on fractions

UNDERSTAND THESE TERMS

- Equivalent fraction
- Common denominator
- Simplest form
- Mixed number

1. Find two equivalent fractions for each of the following.

   a $\dfrac{6}{7}$ b $\dfrac{63}{81}$ c $\dfrac{13}{5}$

2. Convert these fractions into equivalent fractions with denominator 100.

   a $\dfrac{2}{5}$ b $\dfrac{4}{25}$ c $\dfrac{1}{8}$ d $\dfrac{13}{20}$ e $\dfrac{80}{200}$

3. Convert these to fractions into their simplest form.

   a $\dfrac{54}{81}$ b $\dfrac{26}{52}$ c $\dfrac{5}{195}$ d $\dfrac{16}{64}$ e $\dfrac{125}{175}$

4. Evaluate the calculations. Give your answers in their simplest form.

   a $4 \times \dfrac{3}{7}$ b $\dfrac{5}{8} \times \dfrac{14}{15}$ c $1\dfrac{1}{5} \times \dfrac{7}{8}$ d $1\dfrac{1}{3} \times 2\dfrac{2}{5}$

5. Evaluate the calculations. Give your answers in their simplest form.

   a $\dfrac{5}{9} + \dfrac{3}{9}$ b $\dfrac{7}{12} - \dfrac{1}{4}$ c $2\dfrac{3}{8} - \dfrac{1}{2}$ d $\dfrac{7}{11} + \dfrac{2}{3}$

6. Evaluate the calculations. Give your answers in their simplest form.

   a $\dfrac{3}{5} \div 3$ b $2 \div \dfrac{3}{4}$ c $\dfrac{5}{9} \div \dfrac{1}{12}$ d $3\dfrac{4}{5} \div 2\dfrac{3}{8}$

7. Evaluate the calculations. Give your answers in their simplest form.

   a $\dfrac{2}{3} + \left(\dfrac{4}{5} \times \dfrac{5}{8} \right)$ b $3\dfrac{3}{4} - 3\dfrac{1}{2} + \dfrac{4}{7}$

8. Alisha cut a $1\dfrac{1}{2}$ m length of ribbon from a $2\dfrac{3}{8}$ m long ribbon to wrap a gift.

   How much ribbon is left? Write your answer as a fraction in its simplest form.   [3]

   [Total: 3]

9. A rectangular picture frame is $1\dfrac{1}{4}$ cm long and $2\dfrac{2}{3}$ cm wide.

   Work out the area of the picture frame.
   Write your answer as a fraction in its simplest form.   [3]

   [Total: 3]

10 In an amusement park, $\frac{3}{8}$ of the rides are for people who are at least 120 cm tall.

The amusement park has 104 rides.
Work out how many rides are available for those under 120 cm. [1]

[Total: 1]

11 In a marathon, $\frac{4}{7}$ of the people who entered finished the race.

364 people finished the marathon.
How many people entered the marathon? [2]

[Total: 2]

12 In a science experiment, 0.4 ml of acid is taken from a bottle containing 5 ml of acid.
Write the amount taken as a fraction of the bottle in its simplest form. [2]

[Total: 2]

13 A tank is $\frac{5}{8}$ full of water. When 120 litres of water are drained from

the tank, it is $\frac{1}{4}$ full.

Calculate the total capacity of the tank. [3]

[Total: 3]

14 A gardener uses $\frac{2}{5}$ of her land to grow vegetables. She uses $\frac{1}{3}$ of the remaining

land to grow flowers. What fraction of the total land is still available? [3]

[Total: 3]

⟪ RECALL AND CONNECT 1 ⟪

Find the LCM of 5 and 8. Find the HCF of 24 and 40.

How can you use the LCM to find equivalent fractions and solve $\frac{2}{5} + \frac{3}{8}$?

REFLECTION

How confident did you feel answering the non-calculator questions without a calculator? Are there any particular methods you used that helped you?
Did you check your answers? Were there any that you got wrong? Look at the mistakes that you made. What could you do to reduce the number of mistakes you may make in the future?

5.3 Percentages

1 Convert

    a   37.5% into a fraction   **b** $\frac{3}{48}$ into a percentage

    c   0.86 into a percentage.

2 Express 2.7 as a percentage of 48.

3 Calculate

   a 12% of 78   **b** 1.5% of 550   **c** 110% of 25

4 In a chemical reaction, the initial mass of a substance is 0.12 grams.
After the reaction, 0.02 grams of the substance remain.
Calculate the percentage decrease of the mass of the substance.

5 A sugar factory increased its production from 400 tonnes per year to 700 tonnes
per year. Find the percentage increase of sugar production.

6 Increase 67 by 15%.

7 Decrease 135 by 20%.

8 Zuri sells cakes for $12 each. The cost to make one cake is $7.50.

   a Work out her percentage profit. [2]

   b The cost to make each cake increases to $8.50.
Work out the new selling price if Zuri wants to make the same
percentage profit. [2]

[Total: 4]

9 A factory finds that 1.5% of the toys it makes are faulty.
They produce 2600 toys.
Work out how many are not faulty. [2]

[Total: 2]

10 Kotaro ordered a bowl of noodles at a restaurant.
The price of noodles on the menu is $4.20. The restaurant also charges
a service charge.
Kotaro paid $4.83 for the noodles.
Work out the percentage service charge.
Give your answer to the nearest whole percent. [1]

[Total: 1]

11 A 350 ml bottle of lemonade contains 17.5 ml of lemon juice.
Work out the amount of lemon juice as a percentage of the volume of
the lemonade. [2]

[Total: 2]

12 Tamara used up 27 GB of a 512 GB memory card.
After uploading pictures and videos, 479.4 GB space remained.
Work out the percentage increase of used space on the memory card.
Give your answer to the nearest whole percent. [3]

[Total: 3]

≪ RECALL AND CONNECT 2 ≪

   a Multiply $\dfrac{7x}{3} \times \dfrac{2x}{y}$.

   b Simplify $21h^2k^2 \div 3h$.

5.4 Standard form

UNDERSTAND THIS TERM

- Standard form

1 Which of these numbers is in standard form?

    a 0.27×10^5 **b** 10.2×10^{-2} **c** 7.26×10^2 **d** 0.000172

2 Write each of the following numbers in standard form.

    a 2780 000   **b** 0.0000000835

    c 1350   **d** 0.000991

3 Write each of the following as an ordinary number.

    a 1.12×10^3 **b** 9.08×10^{-4} **c** 5.561×10^{-5} **d** 7.295×10^4

4 1 micrometre is equal to 0.001 millimetres.
    The diameter of a microorganism is 0.2 micrometres.
    Write the diameter in millimetres using standard form.

5 Find the answers to these calculations.

    a $(3.24 \times 10^7) \times (1.57 \times 10^2)$ **b** $(5.92 \times 10^{-3}) \times (2.13 \times 10^{-2})$

    c $(7.49 \times 10^5) \div (4.81 \times 10^3)$ **d** $(6.35 \times 10^{-4}) \div (8.02 \times 10^{-3})$

6 The side length of a square-shaped microchip is 0.001079 m.

    a Write this length in standard form.   [1]

    b Calculate the area of the microchip in m².
        Give your answer in standard form correct to 4 significant figures.   [2]

                                                                  [Total: 3]

7 An aeroplane can travel a distance of (2.47×10^8) metres in (1.06×10^3) seconds.
    Work out the speed of the aeroplane in metres per second.
    Give your answer in standard form correct to 2 significant figures.   [3]

                                                                      [Total: 3]

8 The size of a microparticle is approximately (4.5×10^{-2}) mm long and
    (7×10^{-2}) mm wide. Work out the area of the microparticle in
    standard form.   [1]

                                                                      [Total: 1]

9 A cuboid is 23 nanometres long, 17 nanometres wide and 31 nanometres high.

    a 1 nanometre = 0.000000001 m.
        Write this in standard form.   [1]

    b Work out the volume of the cuboid in m³.
        Write your answer in standard form.   [2]

                                                                     [Total: 3]

10 The table shows the distances from Earth to two stars.

Star	Distance from Earth
Sirius	81 000 000 000 000 km
Betelgeuse	6100 000 000 000 000 km

   a Write each distance in standard form. [2]

   b How many times farther away from Earth is Betelgeuse than Sirius?
Give your answer to the nearest whole number. [2]

[Total: 4]

≪ RECALL AND CONNECT 3 ≪

Use the laws of indices to calculate the following.

a $10^2 \times 10^5$ **b** $10^4 \div 10^6$ **c** $10^7 \times 10^{-2}$ **d** $10^{-2} \div 10^{-3}$

SELF-ASSESSMENT CHECKLIST

Let's revisit the Knowledge and Exam skills focus for this chapter.
Decide how confident you are with each statement.

	Now I can	Show it	Needs more work	Almost there	Confident to move on
1	find equivalent fractions	Write down a fraction and swap with a partner. List three equivalent fractions to your partner's fraction.			
2	simplify fractions	Write down the steps to simplify a fraction. Use them to simplify $\frac{84}{126}$.			
3	add, subtract, multiply and divide fractions and mixed numbers	Pick two fractions or mixed numbers. Find their sum, difference, product and quotient.			
4	find fractions of numbers	What is $\frac{4}{5}$ of 225?			
5	find a percentage of a number	Think of a number. Calculate **a** 20% **b** 65% **c** 72% of your number without a calculator.			

CONTINUED

	Now I can	Show it	Needs more work	Almost there	Confident to move on
6	find one number as a percentage of another	Find 75 as a percentage of 235.			
7	calculate percentage increases and decreases	A smartphone was $720 when it was first released. After 4 years, the price is $340. What is the percentage decrease in price?			
8	increase and decrease by a given percentage	Find the price of three items in your local shop. Calculate the new price if they were reduced by 20%. Calculate the new price if their prices were increased by 15%.			
9	use standard form	Pick a planet. Find its diameter and write it in ordinary and standard form. Pick a microorganism. Find its diameter and write it in ordinary and standard form.			
10	calculate with values in standard form	Calculate $(4.34 \times 10^{12}) \div (1.23 \times 10^{7})$.			
11	understand the command word 'write' and answer 'write' questions	Look through the exercises in the chapter. Make a list of the different forms you could be asked to write your answers.			
12	understand the command words 'work out' and answer 'work out' questions	Work out the value of 67 after an increase of 12.5%. A student gave the answer: 75.4. How could their answer be improved?			
13	answer fraction, percentage and standard form questions without a calculator.	Check your answers to all the non-calculator questions in this chapter. If you made any mistakes, try them again.			

6 Equations, factors and formulae

When you read an examination question, look carefully at the command word used. It is important to understand what each command word means and what it is asking you to do. In this chapter, look out for the questions containing the command words 'show (that)'.

Show (that)	provide structured evidence that leads to a given result.

If an examination question uses the command words 'show' or 'show that', usually you will be given the result and you will need to give your reasons and working to demonstrate that the result is correct. For a 'show (that)' question, marks will be awarded for the reasons and evidence you give, so it is important to write down all your working.

In earlier chapters you have seen topics such as directed numbers and working with algebraic expressions. Many of the skills from these topics are useful when working with equations and formulae. As you work through the chapter, think about how different questions link to other topics you have already learned, as well as how the skills in this chapter may apply to topics later in the book.

6.1 Solving equations

1 Solve the following.

  a $5x = -30$ **b** $3a - 8 = 7$ **c** $10 - 4m = -2$

2 Solve the following.

  a $5x + 7 = 9x - 3$ **b** $6 - 3k = k - 14$ **c** $\frac{1}{2}p + 5 = \frac{1}{4}p + 7$

3 Solve the following.

  a $3(2x + 7) = 12$ **b** $-3(2q - 5) = 21$ **c** $\frac{1}{3}(4r - 1) = 5$

4 Solve the following.

  a $2(x + 1) = 3(x - 1)$

  b $6h - (2h + 9) = 1 - (10 - 3h)$

  c $3(2m - 1) - m = \frac{1}{2}(7 - 3m)$

5 Solve the following.

  a $\dfrac{3b - 1}{2} = 7$ **b** $\dfrac{4v - 1}{3} = -7$ **c** $\dfrac{t + 1}{2} = \dfrac{3}{2}$

6 A student wrote these steps to solve $4(x + 1) = 12$.

$$4(x + 1 - 1) = 12 - 1$$
$$4x = 11$$
$$x = \frac{11}{4}$$

  a Explain what mistake this student has made.

  b Write the correct solution to the equation.

7 In a game show, every correct answer is awarded 100 points, while 50 points are deducted for every incorrect answer.
c represents the number of questions answered correctly.
i represents the number of questions answered incorrectly.

  a Write an expression for the number of points, p, scored in terms of c and i.   [2]

  b Farida got 4 questions incorrect and scored 900 points. Show that Farida answered 11 questions correctly.   [3]

                    [Total: 5]

8 A rectangular room has a perimeter of $46\,\text{m}$.
The room has length $(4x + 3)\,\text{m}$ and width $(3x - 1)\,\text{m}$.

  a Write an equation for the perimeter of the room in its simplest form.   [2]

  b Solve the equation to find the length and width of the room.   [3]

                    [Total: 5]

9 A taxi charges a fixed cost of $10.00 and a variable cost of 50 cents per km.
A passenger travelled x km.

  a Write an equation for M, the amount that the passenger must pay.   [1]

  b Show that the distance is $180\,\text{km}$ if the passenger paid $100.   [1]

                    [Total: 2]

10 Aulia is three times as old as her brother, Baqi.
    In four years' time, Aulia's age will be exactly double Baqi's age.

   a   Let x be Baqi's current age. Write an equation in terms of x to
       represent the information given.   [1]

   b   Solve your equation to find Baqi's current age.   [3]

   c   Find Aulia's current age.   [1]

                                                                  [Total: 5]

11 Alina is comparing cell phone plans from two providers, Telstar and Comlink.
    Telstar offers a plan that costs \$30 per month plus 10 cents per text.
    Comlink offers a plan that costs \$45 per month plus 5 cents per text.
    x represents the number of texts sent.

   a   Write an expression to represent the cost for each provider.   [2]

   b   Show that the two plans cost the same when 300 texts are sent.   [2]

                                                                  [Total: 4]

《 RECALL AND CONNECT 1 《

Expand and simplify $2(3x + 1) - 3(3 - 2x)$.

REFLECTION

Look back at the 'show (that)' questions. Was there anything you struggled with
when answering those questions? How could you use the information given in
the question to make sure you have shown the correct steps?

6.2 Factorising algebraic expressions

UNDERSTAND THESE TERMS

- Factorisation
- Subject

1   Factorise the following fully.

   a $6x - 18$ b $3s - 6r + 12t$ c $2a - 6b + 16c$
   d $\dfrac{1}{2}h - \dfrac{3}{2}k$ e $\dfrac{1}{4}p + \dfrac{1}{2}q$

2   Factorise the following fully.

   a $21x^3y - 28x$ b $28g^2h - 35gh^3$ c $24mn^3 + 36m^2n$
   d $2pqr - p^2r$ e $5s^2t^2 + 2st^2$

3   Factorise the following fully.

   a $2x^2y^3 + 4x^2y^2$ b $6p + 2p^2$
   c $6m + 3mn + 6$ d $2d^2t - 6dt + 8d$

4   Look at the shape.

   a   Write an expression for the perimeter of the shape.   [1]

   b   Factorise your expression.   [2]

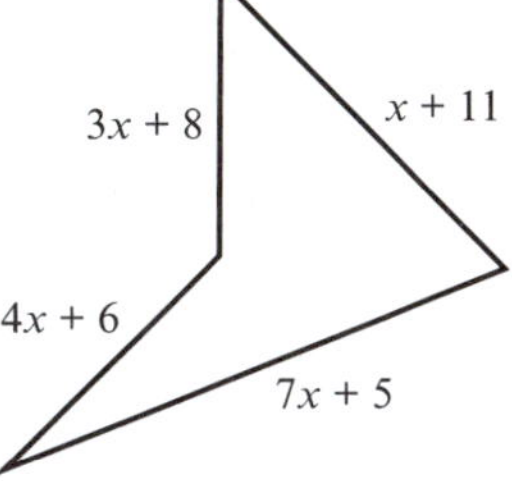

[Total: 3]

5   A rectangular picture frame in has length $(2x + 6)$ cm and width $(x + 3)$ cm.

   a   Show that the perimeter is $(6x + 18)$ cm.   [2]

   b   Fully factorise $6x + 18$.   [1]

[Total: 3]

6 $K = 3v^2 - 12v$

   a   Fully factorise $3v^2 - 12v$.   [1]

   b   Work out K when $v = 5$.   [1]

[Total: 2]

> ## ≪ RECALL AND CONNECT 2 ≪
>
> **a**   Express the number 630 as a product of its prime factors.
>
> **b**   The area of a rectangle is 64 cm².
> Work out each possible length-width combination, given that both values are integers.

6.3 Rearranging formulae

1   Rearrange $\dfrac{2m}{n} = q$ to make m the subject.

2   Rearrange $ax - y = b$ to make x the subject.

3   Rearrange $2ghk = r$ to make h the subject.

4   Make n the subject of each formula.

   a $V = 3n + t$ **b** $R = 2(n - m)$

5   The formula for the area of a trapezium is given by $A = \dfrac{1}{2}(a + b)h$,

   where a and b are the lengths of the parallel sides, and h is the height.
   Rearrange the formula to make a the subject.   [3]

[Total: 3]

6 $E = \frac{1}{2}mv^2$

    a Rearrange the formula to make m the subject. [1]

    b Calculate m when $E = 12\,500$ and $v = 10$. [1]

[Total: 2]

7 $c = a + 2ab$

    Rearrange the formula to make a the subject. [2]

[Total: 2]

REFLECTION

Look back through the exercises. What skills from other topics have you used? Can you see how these skills link with the maths in this chapter?

Are there any methods from this chapter that you may need in future topics? Do you feel confident with these methods?

SELF-ASSESSMENT CHECKLIST

Let's revisit the Knowledge and Exam skills focus for this chapter. Decide how confident you are with each statement.

	Now I can	Show it	Needs more work	Almost there	Confident to move on
1	solve a linear equation	Make up a linear equation by thinking of a number and applying two operations to it. Swap your equation with a partner and solve their equation.			
2	factorise algebraic expressions	Fully factorise $3ax - 4ay + 6ax - 8ay$.			
3	rearrange a formula to change the subject	Look up some formulae from your coursebook or from other subjects. Pick three formulae and rearrange them to change the subjects.			
4	understand the command word 'show (that)' and answer 'show (that)' questions	Write a list of things to remember when answering a 'show (that)' question.			
5	make connections with other topics.	Make a list of other topics that you used while answering the questions in this chapter.			

7 Perimeter, area and volume

KNOWLEDGE FOCUS

In this chapter you will answer questions on:

- calculating areas and perimeters of two-dimensional shapes
- calculating areas and perimeters of shapes that can be separated into two or more simpler shapes
- calculating areas and circumferences of circles
- calculating areas and perimeters of circular sectors
- using nets for three-dimensional solids
- calculating volumes and surface areas of three-dimensional solids.

EXAM SKILLS FOCUS

In this chapter you will:

- show that you understand the command word 'calculate' and can answer 'calculate' questions
- keep track of time when working on questions.

When you read an examination question, look carefully at the command word used. It is important to understand what each command word means and what it is asking you to do. In this chapter, look out for the questions containing the command word 'calculate'.

| Calculate | work out from given facts, figures or information. |

If an examination question about perimeter, area or volume uses the command word 'calculate', you should look for any information given in the question or an accompanying diagram that you can use to find the answer. You will usually need to substitute any values you are given into a formula and work out the result. You should remember to include all your working. Write down the values of the variables you are using and any formulas that you are applying.

When you are working through an examination, it is important to make sure that you are keeping time so that you will be able to attempt all the questions. One way to do this is to allow one minute per mark. If you find yourself spending more than 5 minutes on a question worth 5 marks then you might be doing more work than necessary. It is also important to try to leave some time at the end to go back and check through your answers. As you work through the Examination skills focus questions in this chapter, try to complete them within a time limit.

7.1 Perimeter and area in two dimensions

1 Find the perimeter of each shape.

a

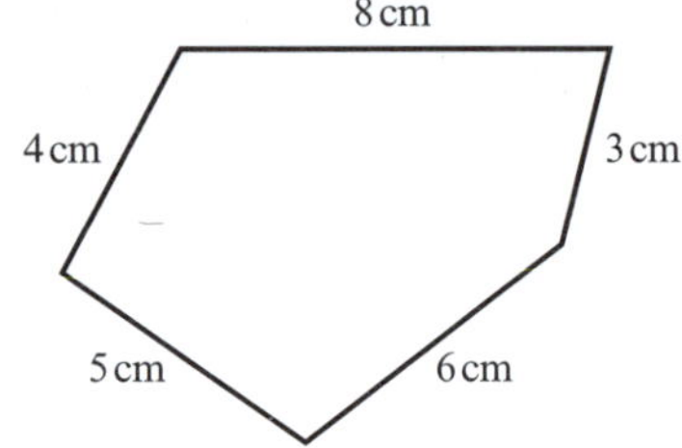

b

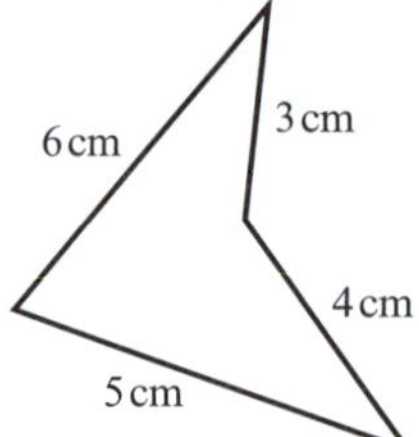

c

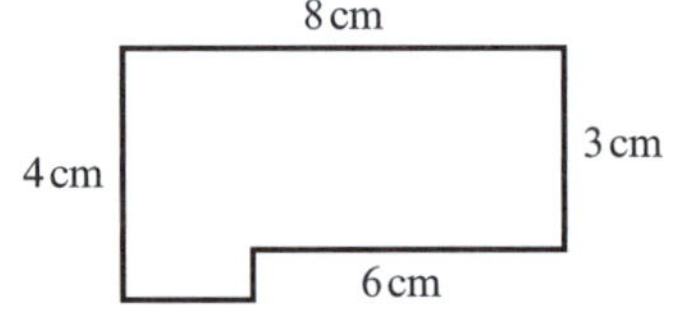

2 Find the area of each shape.

a

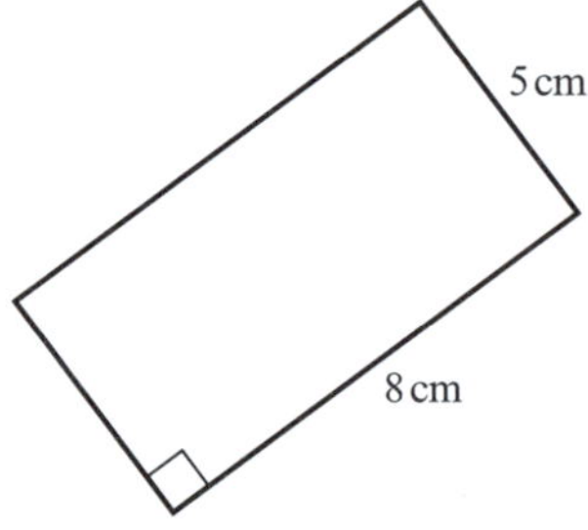

b

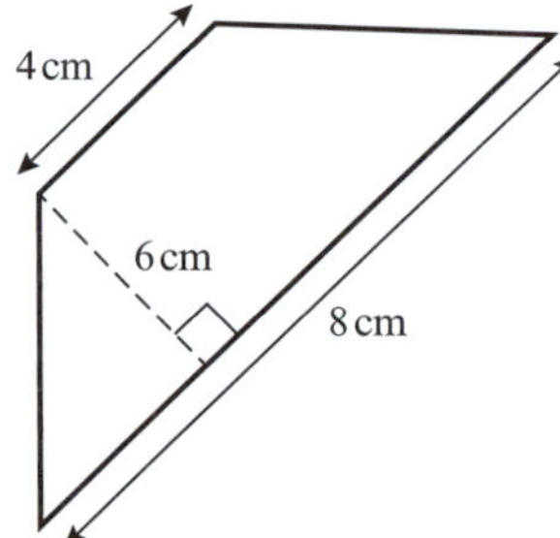

c

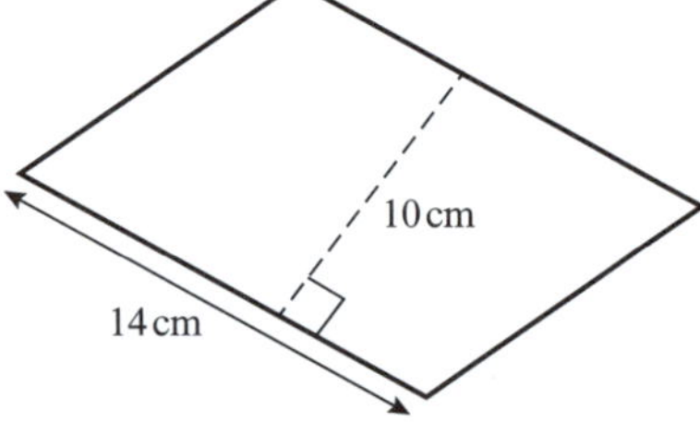

3 Find the area of the compound shape made from a semicircle and a trapezium.

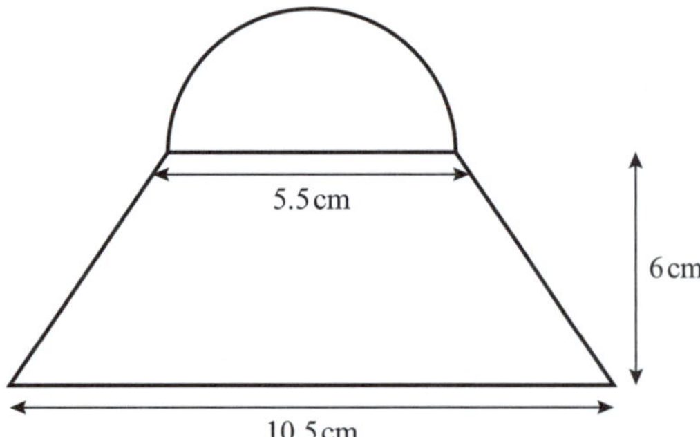

4 This shape has four identical triangles attached to each side of a square.
Find the total area of the shape.

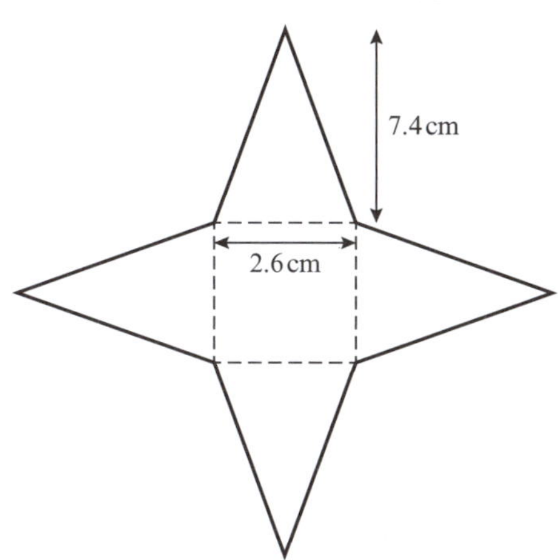

5 Find the exact perimeter and area of each shape.

a

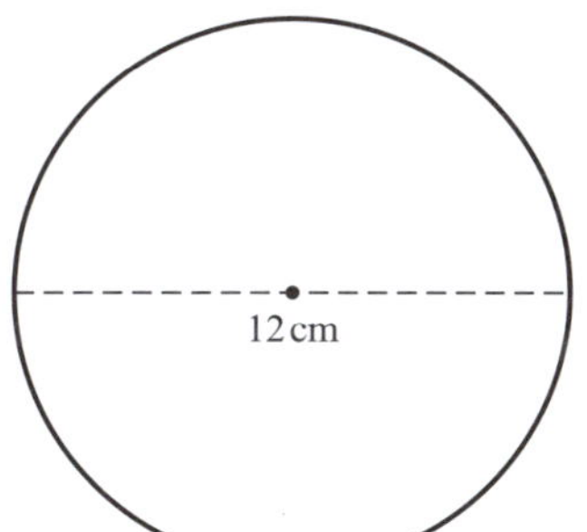

b

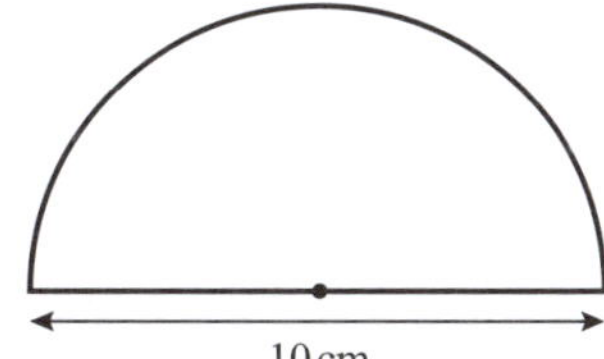

c

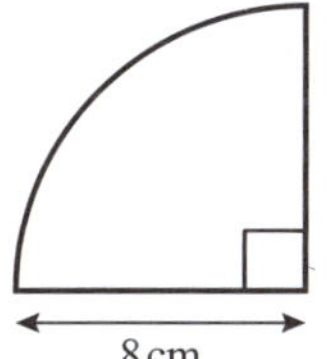

d

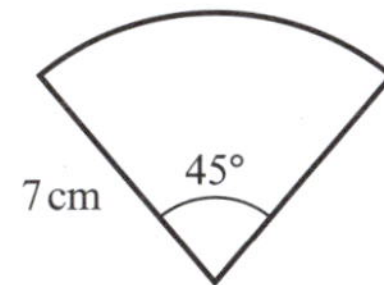

e

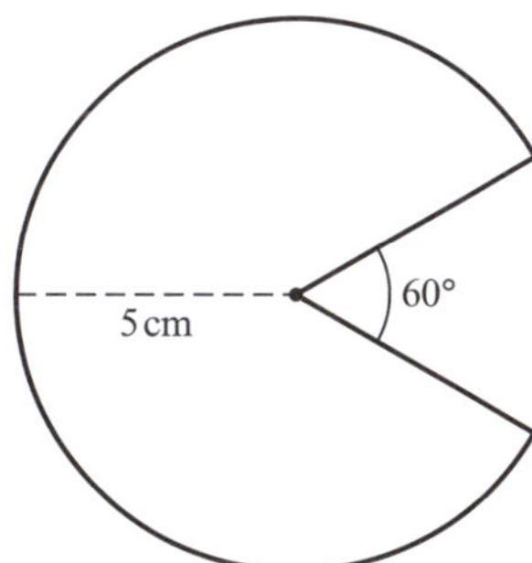

6 Find the shaded area of each shape.

a

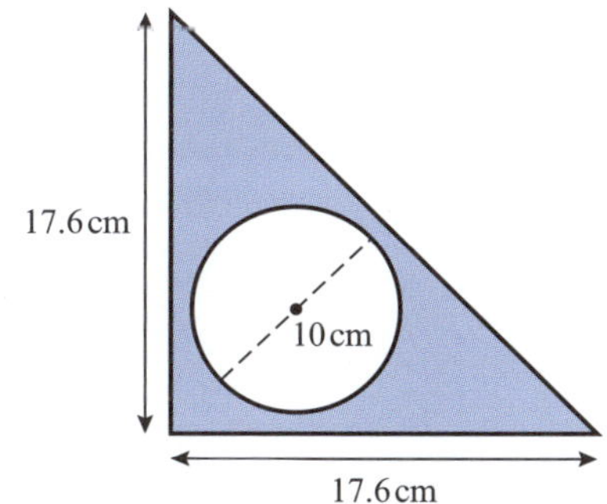

b

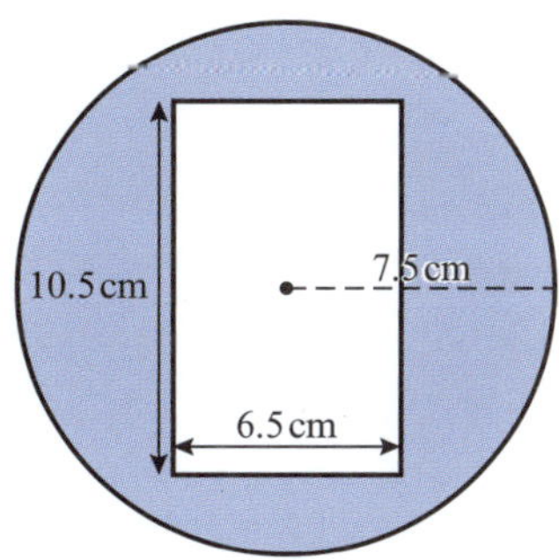

7 Lia builds a frame in the shape of an isosceles trapezium.
The base of the trapezium is 14 cm, and the length of the top is
half the length of the base.

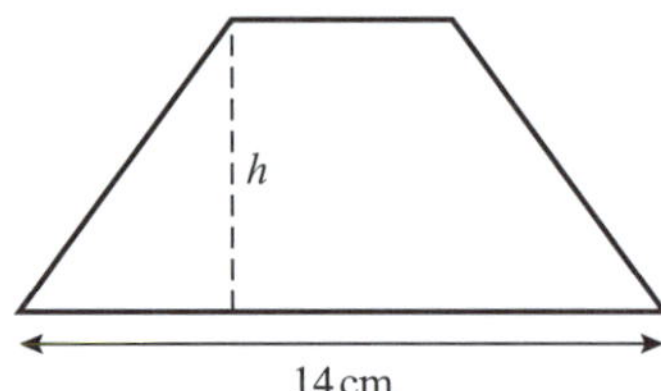

The area of the trapezium is 89.25 cm².
Calculate the height, h. [2]

[Total: 2]

8 Elaine creates this design for a ticket.
She cuts two quarter-circles from the corners of a rectangle.

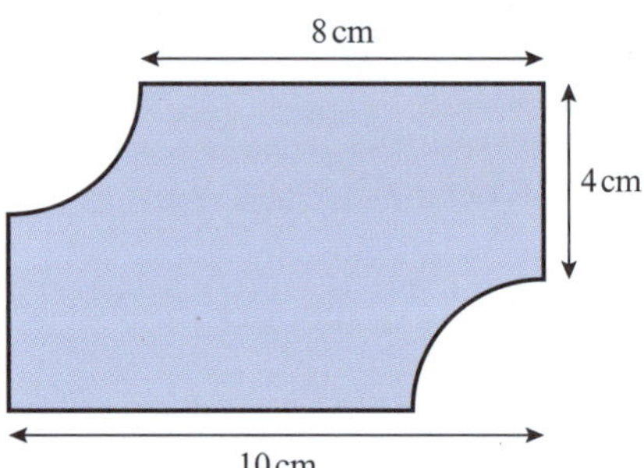

a Calculate the perimeter of the ticket.
Give your answer to the nearest whole number. [4]

b Calculate the area of the ticket.
Give your answer to the nearest whole number. [4]

[Total: 8]

9 The congruent sides of an isosceles triangle are given as $2x - 7$ and $3x - 20$.

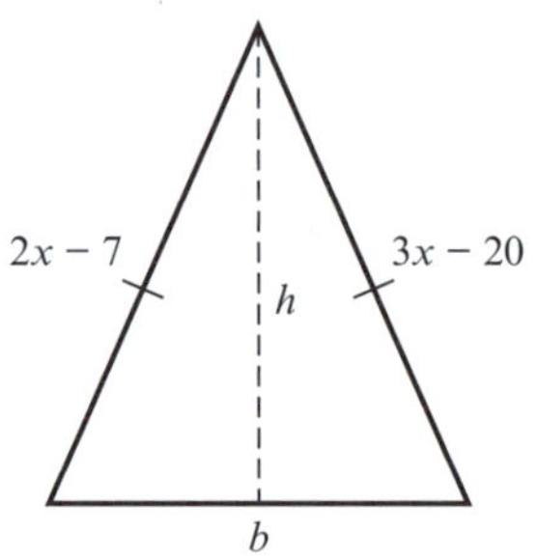

a Show that $x = 13$. [2]

b The triangle has a perimeter of 50 cm, and the area is 108 cm².
Find
  i b [3]
  ii h. [2]

[Total: 7]

10 Alejandro created the following design for a computer mouse manufacturer logo. The design is made of a combination of different shapes.

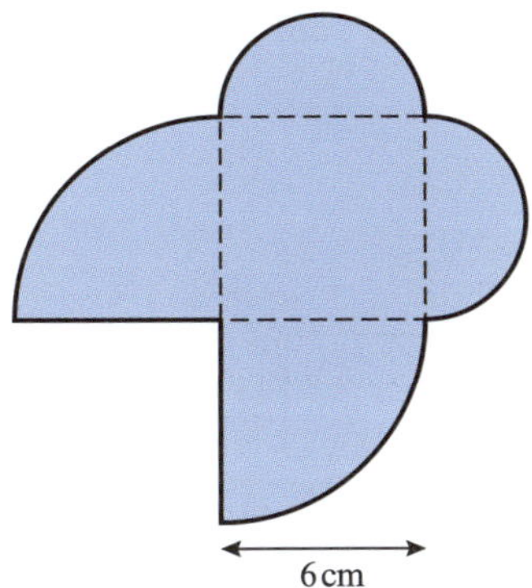

    a Calculate the area of the logo. [4]

    b Calculate the perimeter of the logo. [3]

[Total: 7]

≪ RECALL AND CONNECT 1 ≪

Express the area and perimeter of the rectangle in terms of x.

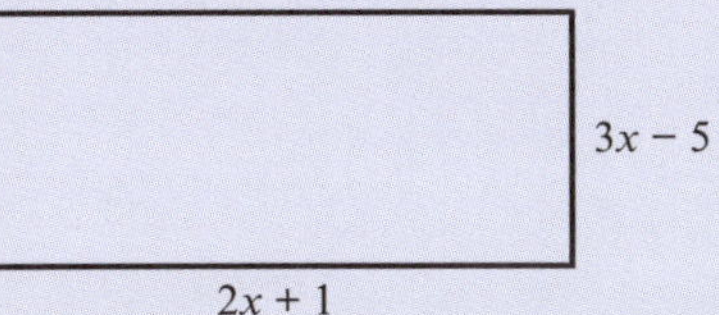

REFLECTION

The questions in this chapter use a lot of formulae. How well do you remember these formulae?

What can you do to help learn the different formulae? Check what formulae you need to remember and which you will be given in the examination.

7.2 Three-dimensional objects and
7.3 Surface areas and volumes of solids

UNDERSTAND THESE TERMS

- Net
- Face
- Vertex
- Surface area
- Volume
- Apex
- Slant height

1 Draw the net of this right-angled triangular prism on a 1 cm² grid.

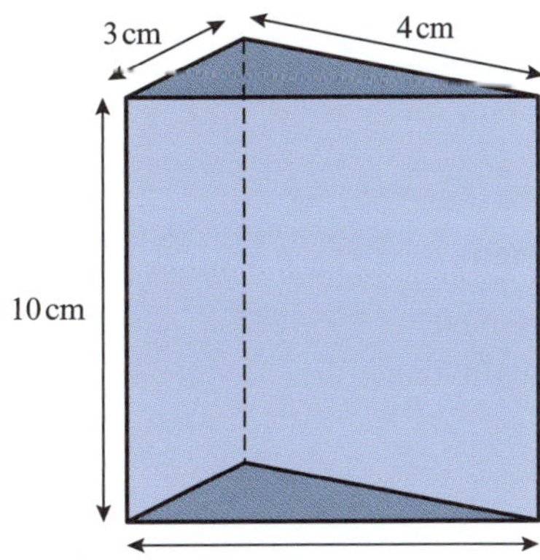

2 This is the net of a solid drawn on a 1 cm² grid.

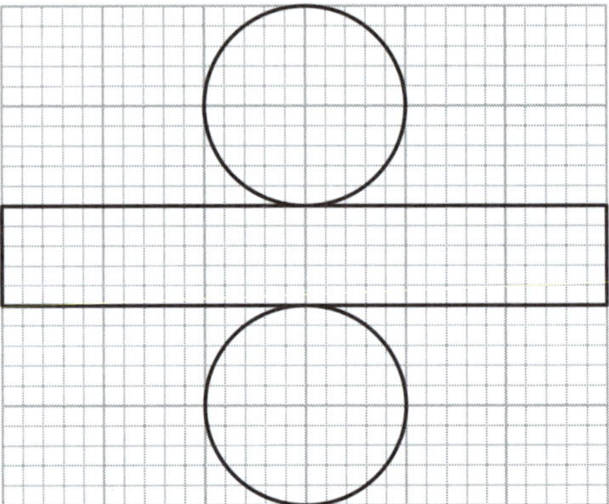

    a What is the name of the solid?

    b What is the radius of the circular face?

    c What is the distance between the two circular faces?

3 Look at this object.

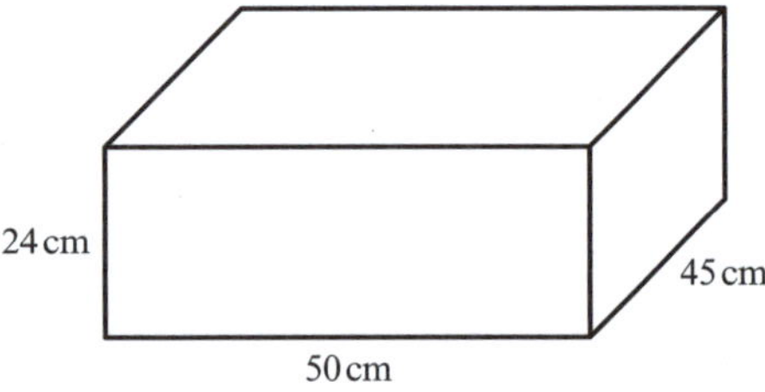

    a Find the volume.

    b Find the surface area.

4 John set up a tent in his backyard. The triangular part of the
tent is an equilateral triangle with side length 6 m and height 5.2 m.
The tent has a length of 12 m.

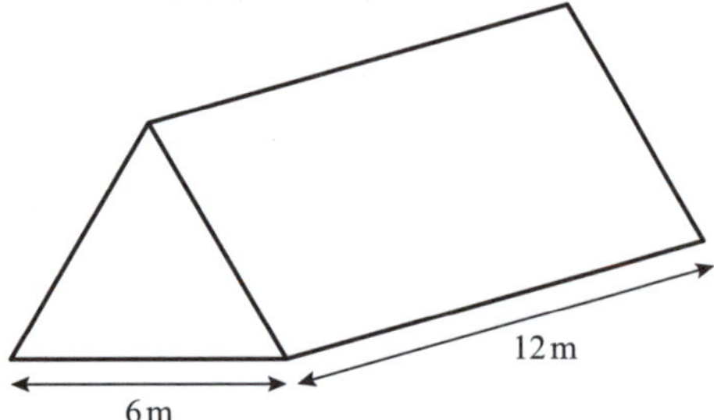

    a Find the volume of the tent.

    b The tent does not have a base.
       Find the surface area of the tent.

5   Cylinder *A* has the same volume as cylinder *B*.
Find *h*.

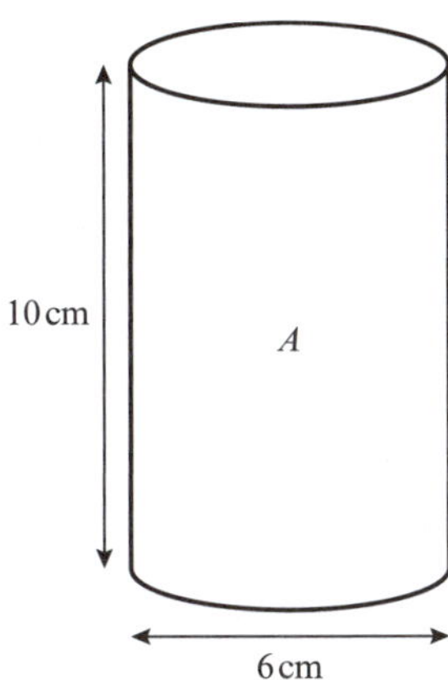
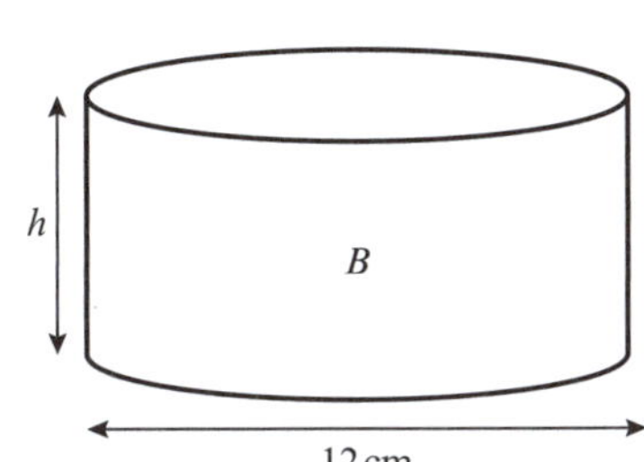

6   This cuboid has a circle cut out of the top face.
Find the surface area of the cuboid.

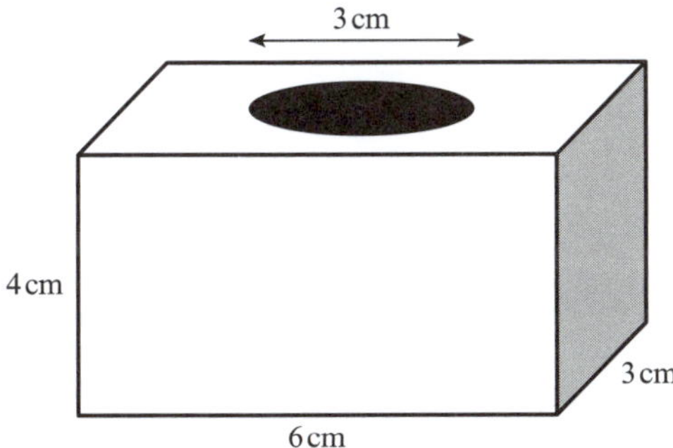

7   **a**   The Great Pyramid of Giza is approximately a square-based pyramid.
Each side of the base is 230 m long. The pyramid has a height of 147 m.
Find its volume.

   b   The Pyramid of Menkaure has a base area of 11 881 m².
It has a volume of 261 382 m³.
Find its height.

8   Genevieve is constructing a box and draws this net on a 1 cm² grid.

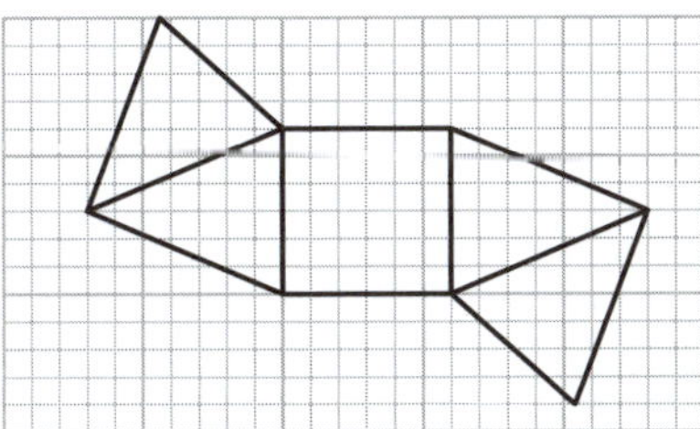

   a   What shape is Genevieve making?   [1]

   b   Calculate the surface area of the shape.   [3]

[Total: 4]

9 The diagram shows a triangular prism.

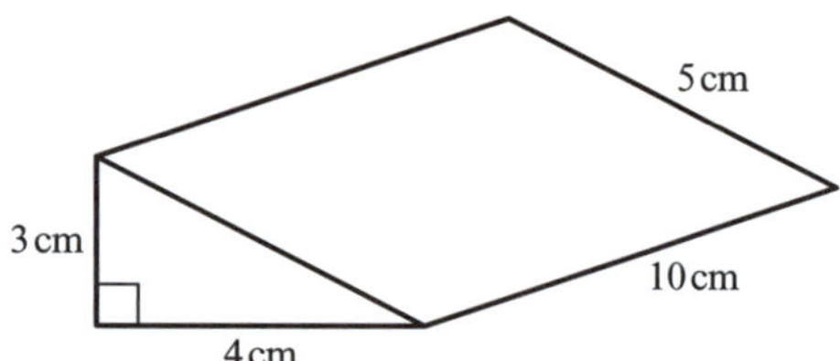

   a   Calculate the volume. [2]

   b   Calculate the surface area. [2]

[Total: 4]

10 An aquarium has dimensions 120 cm by 50 cm by 50 cm.

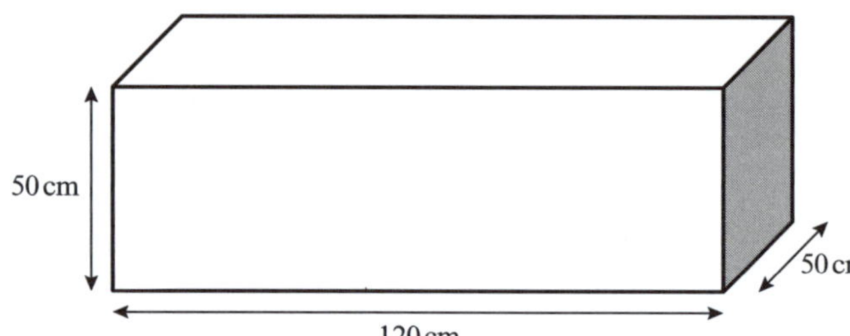

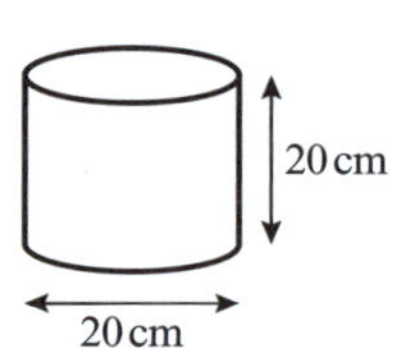

Chandra is using a cylindrical container to fill the aquarium with water.
The cylinder has height 20 cm and diameter 20 cm.
How many times will Chandra need to refill the container to completely
fill the aquarium? [3]

[Total: 3]

⟪ RECALL AND CONNECT 2 ⟪

Determine the angle of the sector.

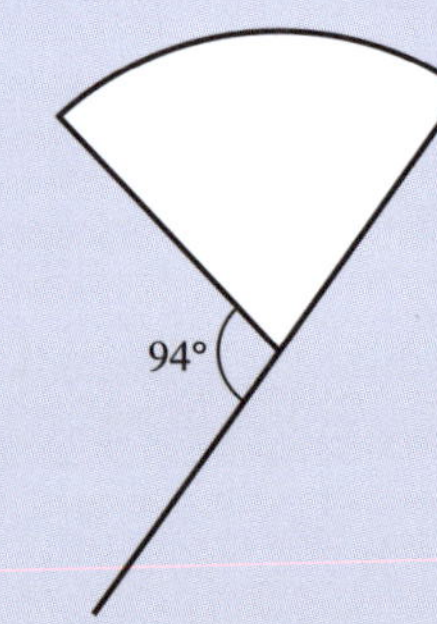

REFLECTION

How long did you spend on the exam skills questions? Did you give yourself
enough time to answer them? Were you able to stick to a time limit?

What could you do to improve your timings?

SELF-ASSESSMENT CHECKLIST

Let's revisit the Knowledge and Exam skills focus for this chapter.
Decide how confident you are with each statement.

	Now I can	Show it	Needs more work	Almost there	Confident to move on
1	calculate areas of two-dimensional shapes	Draw a trapezium. Swap with a partner. Calculate the area of your partner's trapezium.			
2	calculate perimeters of two-dimensional shapes	Calculate the perimeter. 3 cm, 5 cm, 8 cm, 5 cm, 3 cm			
3	calculate areas of shapes that can be separated into two or more simpler shapes	Calculate the area. 5 cm, 3 cm, 8 cm			
4	calculate perimeters of shapes that can be separated into two or more simpler shapes	Find the perimeter of the net in Section 7.2 Question 2.			
5	calculate areas of circles	Find the area of a circle with diameter 20 cm.			
6	calculate circumferences of circles	Find the circumference of a circle with radius 17 cm.			
7	calculate areas of circular sectors	Find the area of a sector with angle 30° and radius 7 cm.			
8	calculate perimeters of circular sectors	Calculate the perimeter of a sector with angle 30° and radius 7 cm.			
9	use nets for three-dimensional solids	Draw the net of a square-based pyramid.			
10	calculate volumes of cuboids, prisms and cylinders	Calculate the volume of a cylinder with radius 5 cm and height 7 cm.			

CONTINUED

	Now I can	Show it	Needs more work	Almost there	Confident to move on
11	calculate surface areas of cuboids, prisms and cylinders	A triangular prism has a triangular base. The base has a perimeter of 23.44 cm and an area of 15 cm². The prism has a height of 18 cm. Draw a diagram of the prism. Calculate the surface area.			
12	calculate volumes of pyramids, cones and spheres	Calculate the volume of a cone with base radius 3 cm and height 8 cm.			
13	calculate surface areas of pyramids, cones and spheres	Calculate the surface area of a sphere with radius 2 cm.			
14	understand the command word 'calculate' and answer 'calculate' questions	Make a list of information you might find in a 'calculate' question for each of the perimeter, area and volume.			
15	keep time.	Set yourself a time limit for one of the exam skills questions. Try to answer the question within the limit.			

8 Introduction to probability

In this chapter you will answer questions on:

* expressing probabilities mathematically

* calculating probabilities associated with simple experiments

* drawing and using sample space diagrams to help calculate probabilities

* identifying when events are independent or mutually exclusive.

In this chapter you will:

* show that you understand the command word 'explain' and can answer 'explain' questions

* understand what a good answer to a probability question looks like.

When you read an examination question, look carefully at the command word used. It is important to understand what each command word means and what it is asking you to do. In this chapter, look out for the questions containing the command word 'explain'.

Explain	set out purposes or reasons / make the relationships between things clear / say why and/or how and support with relevant evidence.

If an examination question uses the command word 'explain', you will need to write reasons and provide evidence to support those reasons. In a probability question, you could be asked to explain why something is true or false. You may need to remember and give facts or use figures you have worked out to support your answer.

Whenever you are answering an examination question, you should always try to write down all your working as well as your final answer, including all the steps you took. When answering probability questions, you could be asked to give your answer in different forms, such as fractions, decimals or percentages. Make sure you check how you should give your answer. For example, you may need to convert some values to a different form in your final answer.

8.1 Understanding basic probability

<table>
<tr><td>UNDERSTAND THESE TERMS</td></tr>
</table>

- Probability
- Event
- Relative frequency
- Experimental probability
- Theoretical probability
- Trial

1 **a** What is the probability of an impossible event?

    b What is the probability of a certain event?

2 The probability it will rain is 0.35. What is the probability that it won't rain?

3 Kai collected data on the colour of cars passing through the street in front of his house.
He counted 250 cars altogether. 20 of the cars were red.
Estimate the probability that the next car passing through will be red.

4 A set of twenty number cards contains the numbers 1 to 20.
If a card is chosen at random, find the probability of choosing

    a an odd number   **b** a prime number

    c a multiple of 3.

Give your answers as fractions.

5 A traffic survey was conducted to record the number of people in each car.
1000 cars were surveyed, and the results were presented in a bar chart.

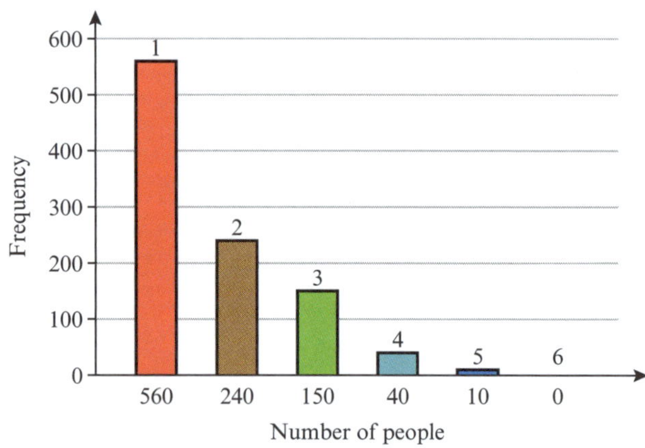

    a Find the relative frequency of a car with 1 person.

    b Find the relative frequency of a car with fewer than 3 people.

    c The next day, 500 cars are surveyed. How many would you expect to have 4 people?

6 The table below shows the different human blood types and the proportion of people in a population who are of that type.

Blood type	O+	O−	A+	A−	B+	B−	AB+	AB−
Percentage of population	37.4%	6.6%	35.7%	6.3%	8.5%	1.5%	3.4%	0.6%

    a Use the table to determine which blood type is the rarest.

    b What is the relative frequency of a person with blood type AB−?

    c How many people with blood type B+ do you expect in a population of 33 400?

7   Pia attempted to flip a bottle so that it lands standing upright.
She made 50 attempts and was successful 35 times.

    a   Calculate the probability that Pia was successful.
Give your answer as a fraction.   [2]

Pia tried again and made 80 attempts.

    b   Find the expected number of times she was not successful.   [2]

[Total: 4]

8   When you toss a coin, you would expect to get a head half of the time.
Fatima says, 'If I flip a coin 20 times, it will land on heads 10 times.'
Is Fatima correct?
Explain your answer.   [1]

[Total: 1]

9   Aisyah conducted a survey to find out the number of mobile phones owned by
households in her neighbourhood. The results are shown in the table.

Number of mobile phones	0	1	2	3	4	5
Frequency	3	5	8	10	13	7

    a   How many households did Aisyah survey?   [1]

    b   Calculate the relative frequency of a household owning at least one
mobile phone.   [2]

    c   If another household is surveyed, explain why you would expect
it is more likely they own three or more mobile phones.   [2]

    d   Another 100 households are surveyed.
How many would you expect to have no mobile phones?
Give your answer to the nearest whole number.   [3]

[Total: 8]

10   A bag contains tiles marked with the letters A, E, I, O or U.
The number of each tile is shown in the table.

A	E	I	O	U
5	12	9	8	4

    a   What is the probability of picking a tile randomly from the bag and
getting 'A'?   [1]

    b   What is the probability of not getting an 'A'?   [1]

    c   Explain why you are most likely to pick an 'E' compared to other vowels.   [1]

[Total: 3]

≪ RECALL AND CONNECT 1 ≪

The probability of an event can be expressed as a fraction.

How is probability related to the part-of-a-whole concept of fractions?

8.2 Sample space diagrams

<table>
<tr><td>

UNDERSTAND THESE TERMS

- Outcome
- Bias
- Sample space
- Sample space diagram

</td></tr>
</table>

1 Three runners, Alisha, Bao and Chiara, are running a race.
List all the possible outcomes for first, second and third place.

2 Usman has a six-sided die numbered 1–6 and a four-sided die numbered 1–4.
Both dice are unbiased. He throws each die and finds the sum of the numbers.

    a Draw a sample space diagram to show all possible outcomes.

    b Find the probability, in simplest fraction form, that

        i the sum is 5   **ii** the sum is less than or equal to 4

        iii the sum is greater than 8   **iv** the sum is a prime number

        v the sum is odd.

3 A coin is tossed and a spinner with four equal sectors (numbered 1–4) is spun.

    a Draw a sample space diagram showing all possible outcomes.

    b Find the probability that the outcome is

        i a head and an odd number   **ii** a tail and a number greater than 1.

4 A fair spinner with four equal sections numbered 2, 4, 6 and 8 is spun.
An unbiased four-sided die with faces numbered 1, 3, 5 and 7 is thrown.
The two numbers are added together.

    a Draw a sample space to show the possible outcomes.   [2]

    b Work out the probability that the total is less than 6.
Give your answer as a fraction in its simplest form.   [1]

    c Work out the probability that the total is a prime number.
Give your answer as a fraction in its simplest form.   [1]

        [Total: 4]

5 A fair spinner has four equal sections numbered 1, 2, 3, 4.
A fair die has six faces numbered 1–6.
The spinner is spun and the die is rolled.
The two numbers are multiplied.

    • Julius wins if the result is odd.

    • Cleo wins if the result is even.

    a Copy and complete the table to show all the possible results.   [2]

Die

Spinner	1	2	3	4	5	6
1						
2						
3						
4						

    b Do Cleo and Julius have an equal chance of winning?
Explain your answer.   [2]

        [Total: 4]

6   Abbas and Mei are playing a game where they flip three coins.
If more heads than tails appear, Abbas wins. Otherwise, Mei wins.

    a   List the possible outcomes of the three flips.   [4]

    b   Do Abbas and Mei have an equal chance of winning?
Explain your answer.   [2]

[Total: 6]

8.3 Combining independent and mutually exclusive events

> **UNDERSTAND THIS TERM**
>
> • Combined events

1   A bag contains ten balls of which two are red, five are blue and three are green.
One ball is picked at random, recorded and then replaced. Then another ball is
picked at random and recorded. Calculate the probability that

    a   the first ball is red and the second ball is green

    b   the two balls are the same colour

    c   the two balls are a different colour

    d   neither ball is blue

    e   at least one ball is green.

2   Anjeli is preparing for the theory and practical tests for driving.

The probability she passes the theory test is $\frac{4}{5}$.

The probability she passes the practical test is $\frac{3}{4}$.

Assume the two tests are independent of each other.
Calculate the probability that

    a   Anjeli passes both tests

    b   Anjeli passes only one of the two tests

    c   Anjeli passes at least one of the two tests.

3   Two six-sided dice, *A* and *B*, are biased.

On die *A*, the probability of rolling a 6 is $\frac{1}{2}$.

On die *B*, the probability of rolling a 6 is $\frac{1}{3}$.

Both dice are rolled.

    a   Which die is more likely to land on a number less than 6?

    b   Calculate the probability of each of these outcomes.

        i   Rolling a number less than 6 on both dice.

        ii   Getting a sum of 12.

        iii   Only one die shows a 6.

4 A bag contains different coloured balls.
The table shows the probability of picking red, blue or green balls from the bag.

Colour	Probability
Red	$\dfrac{3}{10}$
Green	$\dfrac{2}{5}$
Blue	$\dfrac{1}{8}$

a Find the probability that a ball taken from the bag is not blue or green. [2]

A ball is picked from the bag and then replaced. Then another ball is picked.

b Find the probability that the first ball is red and the second ball is green. [2]

[Total: 4]

5 Kim throws two fair dice.

a Copy and complete the table to show all possible sums of the dice. [1]

Die 1

	1	2	3	4	5	6
1						
2						
3						
4						
5						
6						

Die 2

b Find the probability that the sum is 6. [1]

c Find the probability that both dice show odd numbers. [1]

d Are the events 'sum is 6' and 'both dice are odd' mutually exclusive?
Explain your answer. [1]

[Total: 4]

≪ RECALL AND CONNECT 2 ≪

Find the answers to these calculations. Simplify your answers as much
as possible.

a $\dfrac{5}{36} + \dfrac{3}{4}$ **b** $1 - \dfrac{1}{6}$ **c** $\dfrac{2}{3} \times \dfrac{5}{6}$

REFLECTION

Look back at your answers to the exam skills questions. How well do you think you answered the questions? Did you include all your working? Did you use evidence and reasons to answer the 'explain' questions? Could you improve any of your answers?

SELF-ASSESSMENT CHECKLIST

Let's revisit the Knowledge and Exam skills focus for this chapter.
Decide how confident you are with each statement.

	Now I can	Show it	Needs more work	Almost there	Confident to move on
1	express probabilities mathematically	Count the number of different types of items in your pencil case. Write down the probability of picking each item at random.			
2	calculate relative frequency	A 6-sided die is rolled 100 times and the frequencies of rolling each number are shown here. Number: 1, 2, 3 — Frequency: 10, 18, 24 Number: 4, 5, 6 — Frequency: 12, 17, 19 Calculate the relative frequency of rolling a 5.			
3	calculate expected outcome	A bag contains green and red counters. A counter is picked at random and replaced 20 times. A red counter is picked 15 times and a green counter is picked 5 times. How many green counters would you expect to pick if you picked a counter 100 times?			
4	draw a sample space	Draw a sample space diagram to show all the outcomes of rolling a die and flipping a coin.			

CONTINUED

	Now I can	Show it	Needs more work	Almost there	Confident to move on
5	use a sample space	Use your sample space diagram to calculate the probability of getting an even number and a head.			
6	identify when events are independent	State whether the following pairs of events are independent. i Event A: tossing a coin and getting heads, Event B: rolling a 6 on a six-sided die. ii Event A: drawing a red card first from a deck, Event B: drawing an ace second. iii Event A: rolling two dice and getting a sum of 6, Event B: rolling two dice and getting the same number on each.			
7	identify when events are mutually exclusive	State whether the following pairs of events are mutually exclusive. i Event A: rolling a die and get 2, Event B: rolling a die and get 5. ii Event A: drawing a red card from a deck, Event B: drawing a queen. iii Event A: picking a student who is left-handed, Event B: picking a student who has brown eyes.			
8	understand the 'explain' command word and answer an 'explain' question	Write some advice to help someone answer an 'explain' exam question.			
9	write a good answer to a probability question.	Choose a question from this chapter. Try to improve your original answer.			

This section contains past paper questions from previous Cambridge exams, which draw together your knowledge on a range of topics that you have covered up to this point. These questions give you the opportunity to test your knowledge and understanding.

The following question has an example student response and commentary provided. Work through the question first, then compare your answer to the sample response and commentary. Are your answers different to the sample responses?

1 Write these numbers in order, starting with the smallest.

$$\frac{3}{16} \qquad 18.7\% \qquad 0.19 \qquad \frac{9}{50}$$

[2]

Cambridge IGCSE Mathematics (0580) Paper 12 Q5, November 2023 [Total: 2]

Example student response	Commentary
$\dfrac{9}{50}, \dfrac{3}{16}$, 0.19, 18.7	This student has used the number 18.7, rather than converting 18.7% to its equivalent decimal. The first three values are in the correct order though, so this would get 1 mark. **This answer scores 1 out of 2 marks.**

The following question has an example student response and commentary provided. Work through the question first, then compare your answer to the sample response and commentary. Are your answers different to the sample responses?

2 a The length, l cm, of a pencil is 18 cm, correct to the nearest centimetre.
Complete the statement about the value of l.

.... $\leqslant l <$ .... [2]

 b i Write 9.314×10^5 as an ordinary number. [1]

 ii Calculate $(4.1 \times 10^{-3}) \times (8.9 \times 10^7)$.
Give your answer in standard form. [2]

 c Calculate $\sqrt{(8 + 4 \times 75^{0.6})}$ [1]

Cambridge IGCSE Mathematics (0580) Paper 12 Q18, November 2020 [Total: 6]

Example student response	Commentary
a $17.95 < l < 18.05$	This student did not understand finding the value correct to the nearest centimetre, and instead found the bounds for rounding to one decimal place. ***This answer scores 0 out of 2 marks.***
b **i** 0.00009314	This student has interpreted the power incorrectly. When the power of 10 is positive, this means the standard form represents a large number. ***This answer scores 0 out of 1 mark.***
ii 36.49×10^4	The student has correctly multiplied the two values together, however, they have not written their final answer in standard form. ***This answer scores 1 out of 2 marks.***
c $7.832\ldots$	The student has applied the order of operations correctly and has written the correct answer. ***This answer scores 1 out of 1 mark.***

The following question has an example student response and commentary provided.
Work through the question first, then compare your answer to the sample response and
commentary. Are your answers different to the sample responses?

3 **a** Expand and simplify.
$(x + 3)(x - 5)$ [2]

b Renuka's teacher asks her to factorise completely $8x^2 - 12x$.
Renuka writes $2x(4x - 6)$ as her answer.
Explain why she does not score full marks and give the correct answer. [2]

Cambridge IGCSE Mathematics (0580) Paper 12 Q23, March 2022 [Total: 4]

Example student response	Commentary
a $x^2 - 15$	This student has just multiplied out the pairs of first terms and last terms, rather than multiplying together all different pair combinations. ***This answer scores 0 out of 2 marks.***
b Renuka has not fully factorised the expression since there is a further factor of 2. $4x(2x - 3)$	The student has correctly spotted that $4x$ and -6 can also be divided by 2 and has explained this. They have correctly factorised the expression. ***This answer scores 2 out of 2 marks.***

Here is a similar question that you should attempt. Use the information from the previous response and commentary to guide you as you answer.

4 **a** $T = 5P + 3Q$
   Find the value of T when $P = 6$ and $Q = 8$.   [2]

   b   Simplify.
   $3a - 7b + 2a + 4b$ [2]

   c   Multiply out.
   $5(2x - 3y)$ [1]

   d   Solve.
   $5x - 1 = 3x + 19$ [2]

   e   Make t the subject of the formula $p = 5t - 3$.   [2]

Cambridge IGCSE Mathematics (0580) Paper 32 Q8a–e, June 2023   **[Total: 9]**

The following question has an example student response and commentary provided. Work through the question first, then compare your answer to the sample response and commentary. Are your answers different to the sample responses?

5 **a**

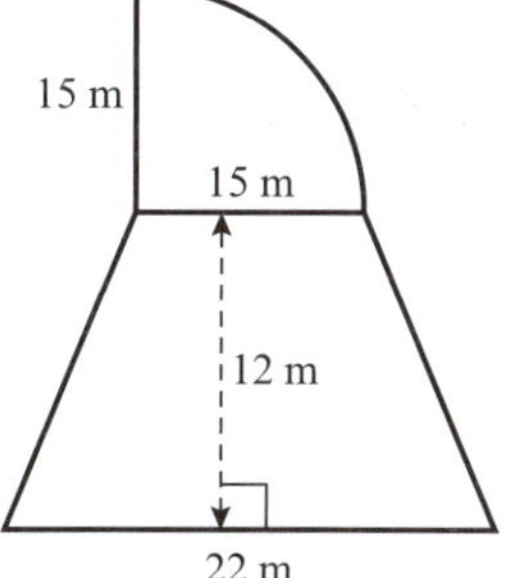

   The diagram shows a shape made from a quarter circle and a trapezium.
   Find the total area of this shape.   [4]

   b

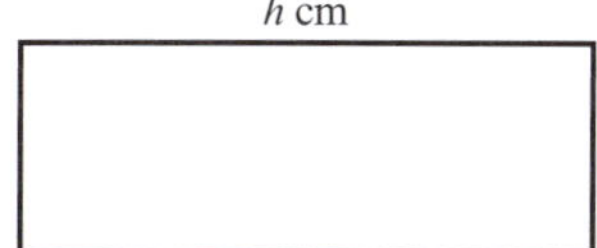

   The diagram shows a rectangle.
   The area of the rectangle is $387.1\,\text{cm}^2$.
   Find the value of h.   [2]

   c

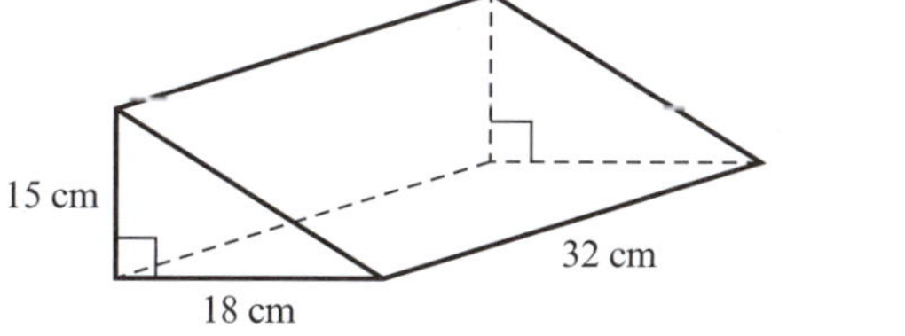

   The diagram shows a right-angled triangular prism.
   Find the volume of the prism.   [3]

Cambridge IGCSE Mathematics (0580) Paper 32 Q7, November 2021   **[Total: 9]**

Example student response	Commentary
a $\pi \times 15^2 = 706.858 \ldots$ $\left(\dfrac{15 + 22}{2} \times 12\right) = 222$ $706.858 + 222 = 928.86\,\text{m}^2$	This student has added together the area of a circle with radius 15 and the area of the trapezium. They forgot that a quarter circle would only be a quarter of the area of the full circle. The final answer is incorrect, but because some of the working is correct, this would score 2 marks. **This answer scores 2 out of 4 marks.**
b $2(15.8 + h) = 387.1$ $15.8 + h = 193.5$ $h = 177.75$	This student has mistakenly used 387.1 as the perimeter of the rectangle and has calculated h using the formula for the perimeter. **This answer scores 0 out of 2 marks.**
c $\dfrac{1}{2} \times 15 \times 18 \times 32 = 4320\,\text{cm}^3$	The student has correctly applied the formula for the area of a triangular prism. **This answer scores 3 out of 3 marks.**

Here is a similar question that you should attempt. Use the information from the previous response and commentary to guide you as you answer.

6   **a**   The diagram shows the net of a cuboid.

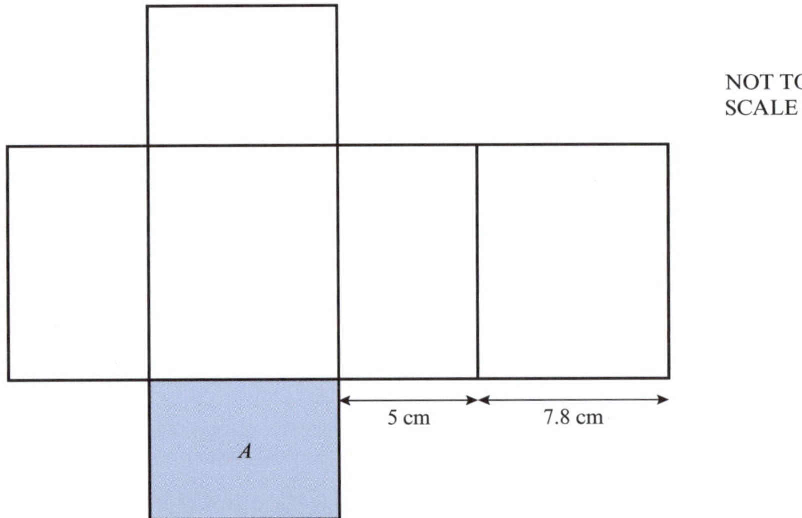

     i   Work out the area of the shaded rectangle, A.   [2]

     ii   The volume of the cuboid is $468\,\text{cm}^3$.
        Complete the statement.
        The dimensions of the cuboid are
        ………….. cm by ………….. cm by ………….. cm.   [2]

   b   A cylinder has a radius of $8\,\text{cm}$ and a height of $12\,\text{cm}$.
       Calculate, in terms of π, the volume of the cylinder.   [2]

c

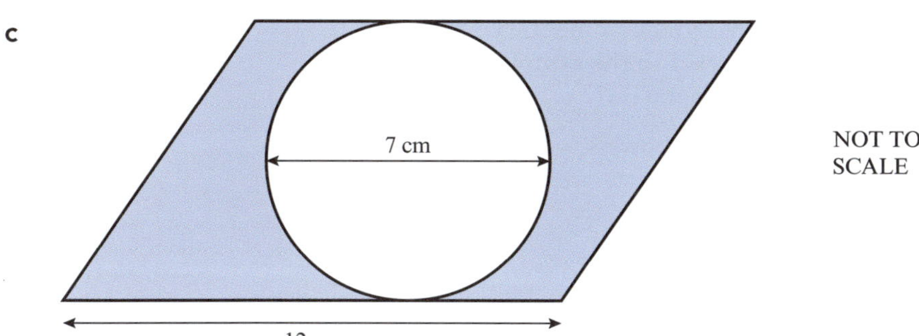

The diagram shows a circle with a diameter of 7 cm and a parallelogram with a base of 12 cm. The circle touches two of the sides of the parallelogram. Calculate the shaded area.   [3]

Cambridge IGCSE Mathematics (0580) Paper 32 Q4, June 2022   **[Total: 9]**

The following question has an example student response and commentary provided. Work through the question first, then compare your answer to the sample response and commentary. Are your answers different to the sample responses?

7   **a**

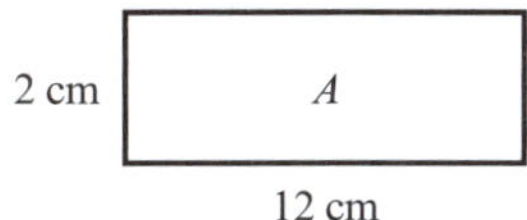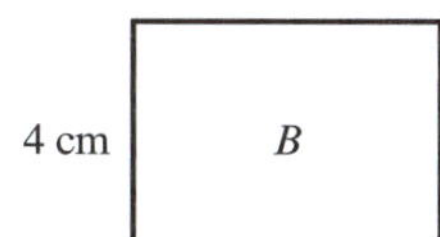

The area of rectangle A is equal to the area of rectangle B.
Work out which rectangle has the greater perimeter and by how much.   [4]

b   A circle has an area of 150 cm².
Calculate the radius of this circle.   [3]

Cambridge IGCSE Mathematics (0580) Paper 32 Q7a, b, November 2022   **[Total: 7]**

Example student response	Commentary
a Perimeter of $A = 2 \times (2 + 12) = 28$ cm $2:4 = 12:x$ so $x = 24$ Perimeter of $B = 2 \times (4 + 24) = 56$ cm $56 - 28 = 28$ cm B has the greater perimeter by 28 cm	This student has correctly calculated the perimeter of rectangle A, which would score 1 mark. They have not used the information in the question that A and B have the same area. Instead they have assumed B is an enlargement of A and have calculated the perimeter of B incorrectly. In order to get the remaining marks they would need to use the areas to calculate the side lengths of B. ***This answer scores 1 out of 4 marks.***
b radius is 47.75 cm	This student has used the formula for the area of the circle which would score 1 mark, however they have made a mistake in the final step and have forgotten to calculate the square root. ***This answer scores 1 out of 3 marks.***

The following question has an example student response and commentary provided.
Work through the question first, then compare your answer to the sample response and
commentary. Are your answers different to the sample responses?

8 Yasmin has 4 white flowers, 3 red flowers and x yellow flowers.
She picks a flower at random.
The probability that it is white is $\dfrac{1}{5}$.

Find the probability that it is yellow. [4]

Cambridge IGCSE Mathematics (0580) Paper 12 Q24, November 2021 [Total: 4]

Example student response	Commentary
$\dfrac{1}{5} = \dfrac{4}{4 + 3 + x}$ $7 + x = 20$ $x = 13$	This student has written a correct equation for the probability that a flower is white. This would score 1 mark. They have solved this equation and found that x would be 13. This would score 2 marks. The student has not read the question properly, though, and has not then found the probability that a flower picked at random would be yellow, so this would not score the final mark. ***This answer scores 3 out of 4 marks.***

Here is a similar question that you should attempt. Use the information from the
previous response and commentary to guide you as you answer.

9 The diagram shows a fair 8-sided spinner.

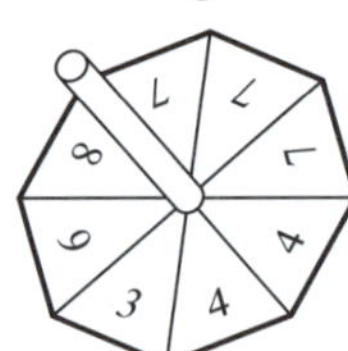

The numbers on the spinner are 3, 4, 4, 7, 7, 7, 8 and 9.

a The spinner is spun once.
Write down the probability that the spinner lands on

   i   the number 7 [1]

   ii   a number greater than 2. [1]

b The spinner is spun 160 times.
Work out the expected number of times the spinner lands on the number 7. [1]

Cambridge IGCSE Mathematics (0580) Paper 12 Q5, March 2020 [Total: 3]

9 Sequences, surds and sets

When you read an examination question, look carefully at the command word used. It is important to understand what each command word means and what it is asking you to do. In this chapter, look out for the questions containing the command words 'determine' and 'write down'.

Determine	establish with certainty.
Write down	give an answer without significant working.

When an examination question uses the command word 'determine', it is asking you to establish your answers with certainty. You need to give reasons or show the method that you are using, even if you are using a calculator. A 'determine' question will often award some marks for correct reasons or a correct method, even if the final answer is incorrect.

When an examination question uses the command word 'write down', it is asking for a brief, direct answer that you can find without doing much or any working.

> **REFLECTION**
>
> As you go through this chapter, think about the areas of your previous learning that link to this one. Are there any areas that you may need to go back and revise to feel more confident with this chapter?

9.1 Sequences

> **UNDERSTAND THESE TERMS**
>
> - Sequence
> - Term

1 Continue each sequence by writing the next three terms.

   a $2, 7, 12, 17, \ldots$ **b** $-4, 2, 8, 14, \ldots$

   c $11, 8, 5, 2, \ldots$ **d** $9, 8\frac{1}{5}, 7\frac{2}{5}, 6\frac{3}{5}, \ldots$

2 Describe the term-to-term rule for each sequence.

   a $2.5, 3.7, 4.9, 6.1, \ldots$ **b** $5, 10, 20, 40, \ldots$

   c $21, 7, \frac{7}{3}, \frac{7}{9}, \ldots$ **d** $3.63, 2.91, 2.19, 1.47, \ldots$

3 Continue each sequence by writing the next three terms.

   a $1.2, 0.6, 0.3, 0.15, \ldots$ **b** $4, 5, 7, 10, 14, \ldots$

   c $1, 8, 27, 64, \ldots$ **d** $2, 8, 18, 32, \ldots$

4 Consider the sequence

$6, 13, 20, 27, \ldots$

   a Find the nth term of the sequence.   [2]

   b Find the 20th term of the sequence.   [1]

   c Is the number 195 a term in the sequence? Explain your answer.   [2]

[Total: 5]

5 A sequence of shapes is made from squares.

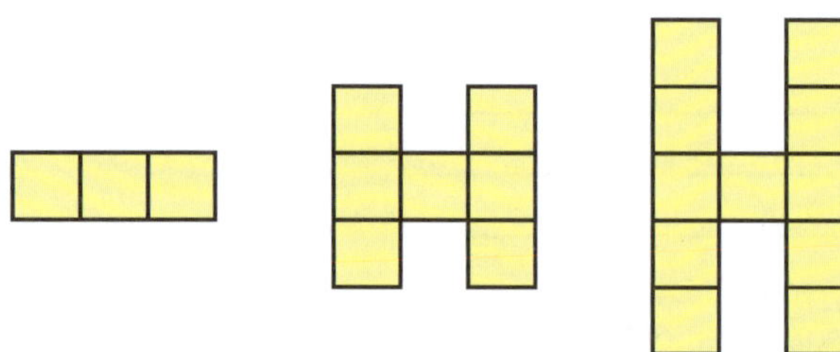

   a Draw the fourth shape in the sequence.   [1]

   b Write down the number of squares in the sixth shape.   [1]

   c Write an expression for the number of squares in the nth shape.   [1]

   d Use your formula to determine the number of squares in the 100th shape.   [1]

[Total: 4]

6 a Write down the first four terms of the sequence $n^2 - 2$. [2]

b Use your answer to part **a** to find an expression for the
nth term of the sequence
$1, -2, -7, -14, \ldots$ [2]

c Find an expression for the nth term of the sequence $2, 16, 54, 128, \ldots$ [1]

[Total: 5]

≪ RECALL AND CONNECT 1 ≪

Simplify the expressions

a $x^5 \times x^7$ b $35y^8 \div 7y^{-3}$ c $(5m^4)^3$

REFLECTION

What method did you use to answer Question 4c? Can you think of any different methods you could have used?

Are some methods better than others? When would each method be a more efficient option?

9.2 Rational and irrational numbers

1 State whether each number is rational or irrational.

a 1.375 b $\dfrac{\pi}{2}$ c -3.7

d $2\dfrac{4}{5}$ e 9.828282 f $\sqrt{49}$

g $\sqrt{75}$ h $\sqrt{12}$ i -5

UNDERSTAND
THIS TERM

- Terminating decimal

2 Write down an irrational number in the interval $10 < x < 20$. [1]

[Total: 1]

3 $\sqrt{a}$ and $b\pi$ are irrational numbers in the interval $3 < x < 7$,
where a and b are integers.

a Determine the minimum and maximum values of a. [2]

b List all the possible values of b. [2]

[Total: 4]

≪ RECALL AND CONNECT 2 ≪

a Write a formula for the diameter of a circle with circumference, C.

b The diameter of a circle is $\dfrac{2}{\pi}$.

Use a calculator to work out the circumference.

Is the circumference rational or irrational?

REFLECTION

How do you organise the definitions of mathematical terms to help you remember them?

Are you able to see connections between topics in definitions? How can you organise terms that connect to different topics to help you make connections between the different topics?

9.3 Sets

UNDERSTAND THESE TERMS

- Set
- Complement (of a set)
- Union
- Intersection
- Venn diagram
- Universal set

1 List all the members of each set.

   a {The set of odd numbers from 1 to 10}

   b {The set of prime numbers less than 10}

   c $\{x : x$ is a factor of 56$\}$

   d $\{x : x$ is a multiple of 4, $30 < x < 50\}$

2 $x = \{x : x$ is a natural number $1 \leqslant x \leqslant 12\}$

$A = \{x : x$ is a factor of 12$\}$ and $B = \{x : x$ is an even number less than 10$\}$.

Write down the members of each of the following sets.

   a B' **b** $A \cup B$ **c** $A \cap B$ **d** $A' \cap B$

3 The Venn diagram shows the sets A and B.

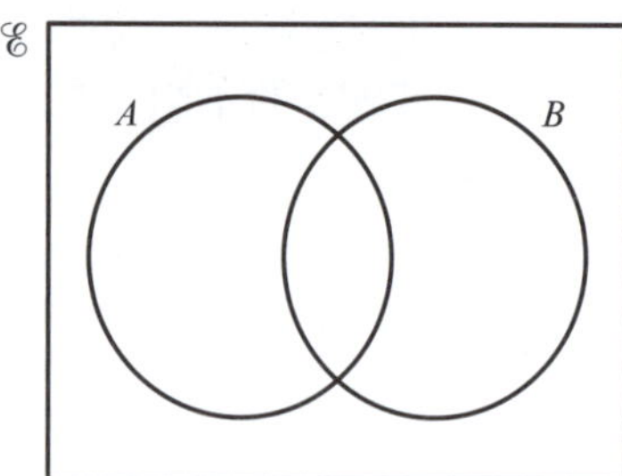

Copy the diagram and shade the regions given by

   a A' [1]

   b $A \cap B$ [1]

   c $A' \cap B'$ [1]

   d $A \cup B$ [1]

[Total: 4]

4 Use the Venn diagram to answer the questions.

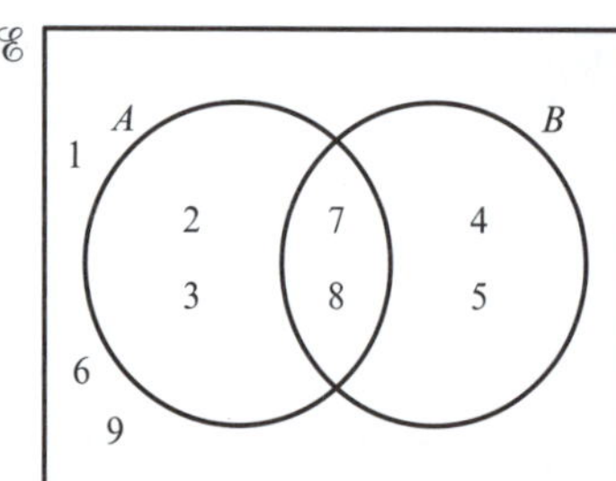

Write down the elements that belong to

a $A \cap B'$ [2]

b $A' \cup B$. [2]

Determine the value of

c $n(A \cup B)$ [1]

d $n(A' \cap B')$. [1]

[Total: 6]

5 $\mathscr{E} = \{x : x$ is a natural number, $1 \leqslant x \leqslant 15\}$

$P = \{1, 4, 6, 7, 12\}$

$Q = \{\text{factors of } 60\}$

Copy and complete the Venn diagram.

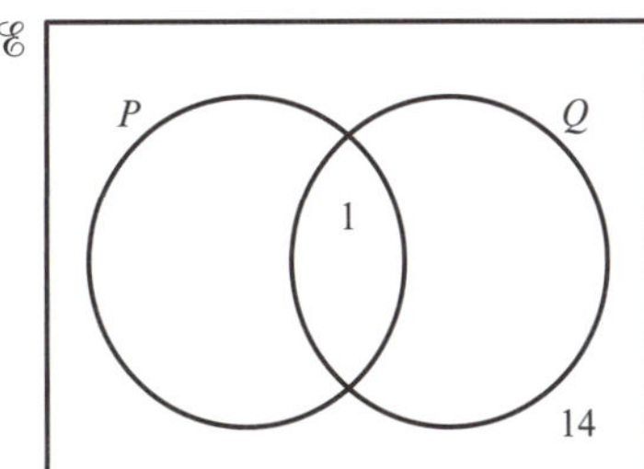

[3]

[Total: 3]

SELF-ASSESSMENT CHECKLIST

Let's revisit the Knowledge and Exam skills focus for this chapter.
Decide how confident you are with each statement.

	Now I can	Show it	Needs more work	Almost there	Confident to move on
1	describe the rule for continuing a sequence	Describe the term-to-term rule for the sequence 3, 7, 11, 15, …			
2	find the nth term of a sequence	Find the nth term of the sequence 5, 8, 11, 14, …			
3	use the nth term to find terms from later in a sequence	Find the 100th term of the sequence −4, 5, 14, 23, …			
4	generate and describe sequences from patterns of shapes	Here is a sequence made from dots. **a** Draw the fourth pattern. **b** Find an expression for the number of dots in the nth pattern.			

CONTINUED

	Now I can	Show it	Needs more work	Almost there	Confident to move on
5	distinguish rational and irrational numbers	Identify the irrational numbers from this list. $\frac{1}{3}, 9\pi, -2.1, \sqrt{81}, \sqrt{82}$			
6	use set language and notation to describe sets	$A = \{x : x$ is a factor of $15\}$ List the elements of A.			
7	find complements, unions and intersections of sets	$\mathscr{E} = \{x : x$ is an integer, $1 \leqslant x \leqslant 15\}$ $A = \{x : x$ is a factor of $15\}$ $B = \{x : x$ is a multiple of $3\}$ List the elements of **a** $A \cup B$ **b** $A \cap B$ **c** $A' \cup B$.			
8	represent sets and solve problems using Venn diagrams	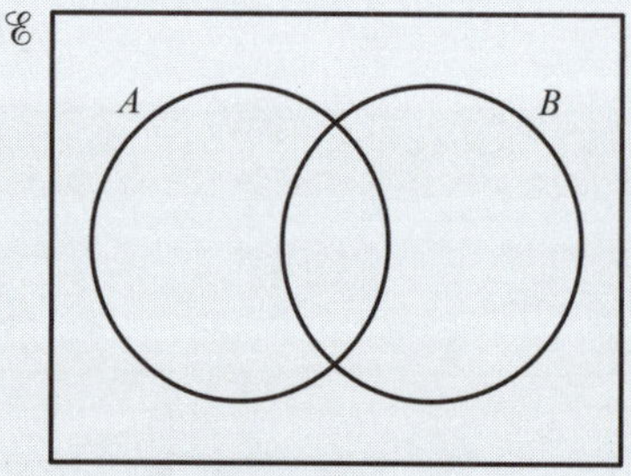 Make three copies of the Venn diagram and shade the regions **a** $A \cup B$ **b** $A \cap B$ **c** $A \cap B'$.			
9	understand the command words 'determine' and 'write down'	Explain how you might answer a 'determine' question differently to a 'write down' question.			
10	make connections between topics.	Look back through the exam skills questions in this chapter and write down a list of other topics that you used to answer them.			

10 Straight lines and quadratic equations

When you read an examination question, look carefully at the command word used. It is important to understand what each command word means and what it is asking you to do. In this chapter, look out for the questions containing the command words 'plot' and 'state'.

Plot	mark point(s) on a graph.
State	express in clear terms.

When you are answering examination questions with the command word 'plot', it is important that you mark points on a graph accurately. You should aim to have each point plotted to an accuracy of within half of the smallest square on the grid. In this chapter, you will need to plot points and draw a line through them using a straight edge.

When a question in the examination uses the command word 'state', it is asking for a brief, direct answer without explanation or detailed working. To answer a 'state' question, be concise and only include the information the question asks for. You may need to state the gradient or y-intercept of a line.

The examination will consist of a non-calculator paper and a calculator paper. The topics in this chapter could appear on either of those papers, so it is important to practise these skills without a calculator. The non-calculator paper may cause some anxiety if you are not used to answering without one. Practise answering the questions in this chapter without a calculator using written and mental methods, to help build your confidence for the non-calculator paper.

10.1 Straight-line graphs

1 Write down the equation of each line on this graph.

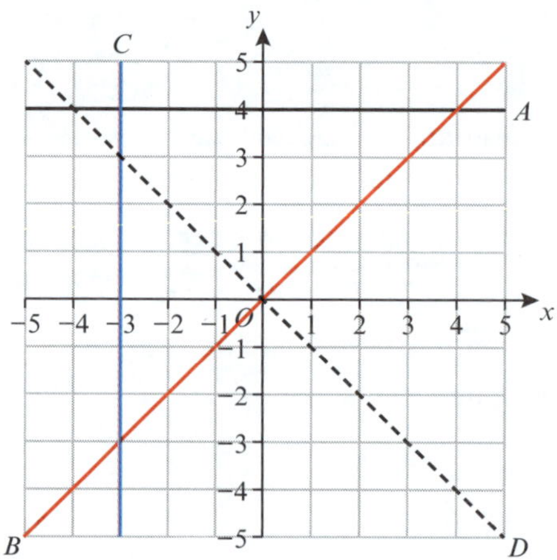

2 Find the gradient and y-intercept of each line.

  a $y = 2x + 5$ **b** $y = 3 - \dfrac{1}{2}x$ **c** $x + y = 7$ **d** $y - 2x - 3 = 0$

3 **a** Which two lines in question 2 are parallel?

    b Write the equation of a line parallel to $x + y = -8$.

4 **a** Copy and complete the table for line $y = 6 - 2x$.

x	−3	−2	−1	0	1	2	3
y							

                                                          [2]

    b Plot the line $y = 6 - 2x$ for x-values between −3 and 3 on a copy of the coordinate axes.

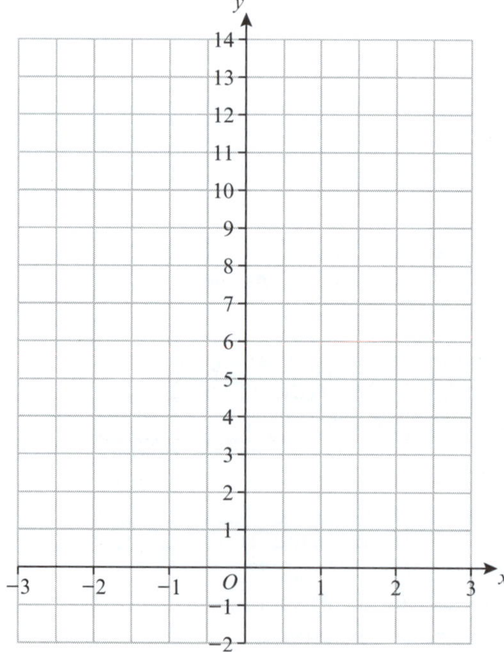

                                                         [2]

[Total: 4]

5   The graph shows the cost (y) of hiring a scooter for x hours.

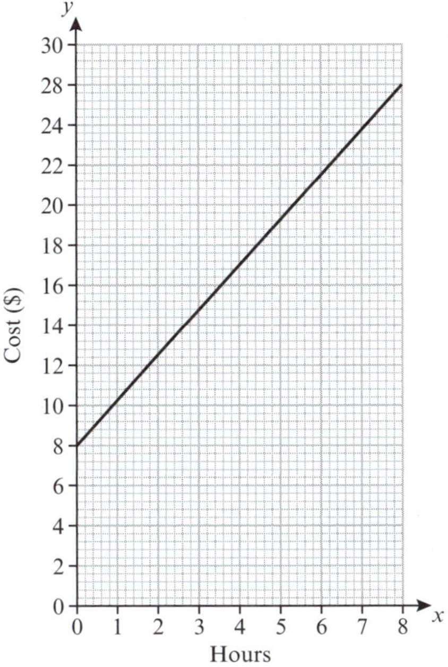

a   State the y-intercept of the line.   [1]

b   Find the gradient of the line.   [2]

c   State the equation of the line.   [1]

[Total: 4]

6   The graph shows the line L_1.

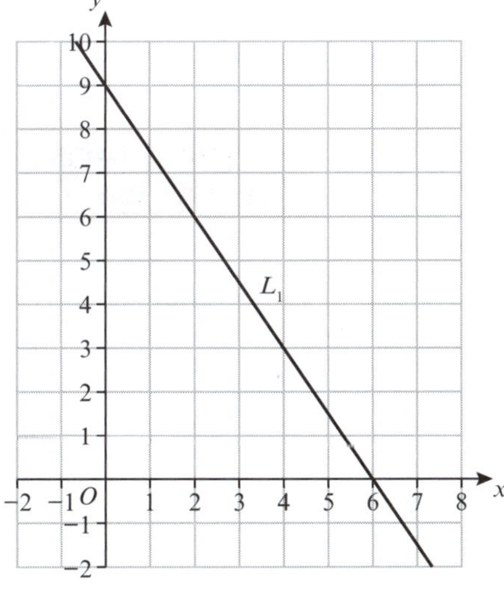

The line L_2 is parallel to L_1 and passes through $(-2, 2)$.
Find the equation of L_2 in the form $y = mx + c$.   [3]

[Total: 3]

7 The line $y = -3x + 24$ intersects the line $y = \frac{1}{2}x + 3$ at the point $(6, 6)$ and forms a triangle with the x-axis.

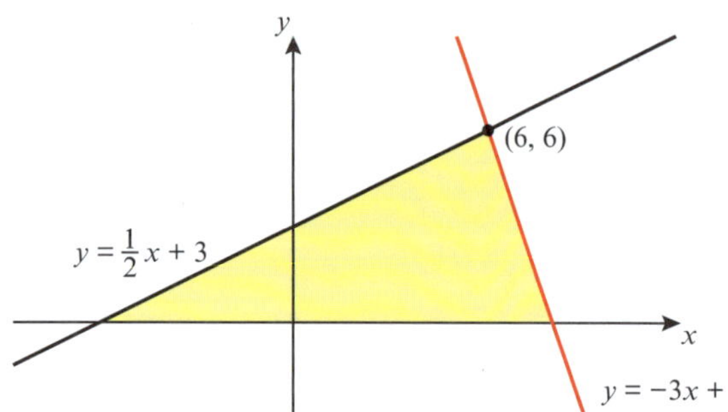

Calculate the area of the triangle. [4]

[Total: 4]

≪ RECALL AND CONNECT 1 ≪

The equation of a straight line can be written in the form $ax + by + c = 0$.

Find the value of y when $a = 4$, $x = 3$, $b = -5$ and $c = 22$.

REFLECTION

Question 5 was set in a context. How did the context relate to the information on the graph?

How can you use key information from a question in context to help answer the question?

10.2 Quadratic expressions and equations

UNDERSTAND THIS TERM

- Quadratic expression

1 Expand and simplify.

    a $(x + 1)(x + 5)$ **b** $(x - 3)(x + 2)$ **c** $(x - 6)(x - 5)$

2 Expand and simplify.

    a $(2x + 1)(2x + 3)$ **b** $(2x - 3)(x + 4)$ **c** $(3x - 2)(4x - 1)$

3 Expand and simplify.

    a $(x + 1)^2$ **b** $(2x - 5)^2$ **c** $(3x - 1)^2$

4   Write an expression for the area of each rectangle.

a

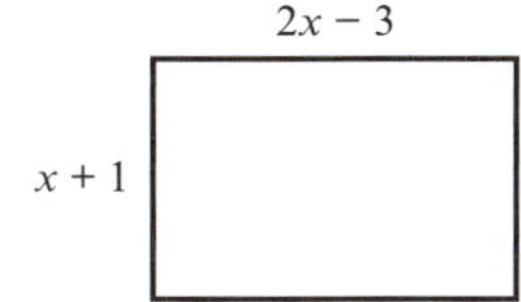

[2]

b

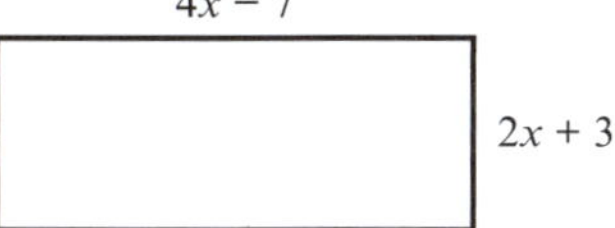

[2]

[Total: 4]

5   The diagram shows a shape made of rectangles.

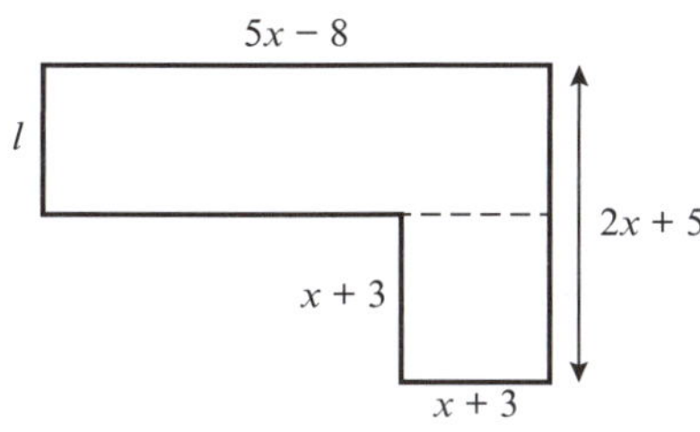

a   Show that the length marked l is $x + 2$.   [1]

b   Write an expression for the area of the shape.   [3]

[Total: 4]

6 $(x + 2)^2 = x^2 + 4x + 4$ and $(x − 3)^2 = x^2 − 6x + 9$.
Given that $x^2 + ax + 49 = (x \pm 7)^2$, state the value of a.   [1]

[Total: 1]

≪ RECALL AND CONNECT 2 ≪

Simplify $4(3x + 4) − 2(2x − 7)$.

REFLECTION

How confident did you feel answering the questions in this chapter without a calculator?

Are there any topics that you are worried about? What strategies could you use to help manage anxiety with these topics?

SELF-ASSESSMENT CHECKLIST

Let's revisit the Knowledge and Exam skills focus for this chapter.
Decide how confident you are with each statement.

	Now I can	Show it	Needs more work	Almost there	Confident to move on
1	recognise the equation of a straight line	Explain what the constants m and c represent in the equation $y = mx + c$.			
2	determine the equation of a line parallel to a given line	Write an equation of a straight line and swap with a partner. Write an equation of a straight line that is parallel to your partner's line.			
3	calculate the gradient of a line on a grid	Explain how to find the gradient of a straight line.			
4	expand products of algebraic expressions	Expand and simplify $(2a - 1)(3a + 1)$.			
5	understand the command word 'plot'	Complete a table of values for the line $y = 3x - 3$ for $x = 1, 2, 3, 4, 5$. Plot the points on a graph.			
6	understand the command word 'state'	State the gradient and y-intercept of the line $y = 5 - 7x$.			
7	use strategies to manage test anxiety.	Write a list of the topics that you find challenging and work with a peer to revise them.			

11 Pythagoras' theorem and similar shapes

When you read an examination question, look carefully at the command word used. It is important to understand what each command word means and what it is asking you to do. In this chapter, look out for the questions containing the command word 'calculate'.

Calculate	work out from given facts, figures or information.

When an examination question uses the command word 'calculate', you should use facts and figures given in the question to find the answer. The command word 'calculate' can be used on the non-calculator paper and does not mean you should use a calculator. However, if you are allowed to use a calculator, you should still show the method you are using. In the examination, a 'calculate' question will often have marks awarded for a correct reason or method, even if the final answer is incorrect.

When solving problems, it is important to set out your methods clearly and check that your answer is sensible in the context of the question. Show a clear, labelled diagram and state the correct rule first (Pythagoras' theorem or triangle similarity), then substitute the given values and show each step of your working logically. Write your final answer on the answer line provided to ensure the examiner can recognise your final answer.

11.1 Pythagoras' theorem

1   Find the length of the hypotenuse of each right-angled triangle.

 **a** 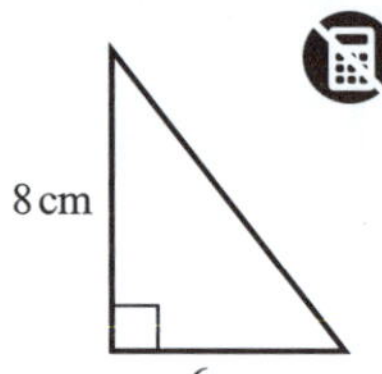 **b** 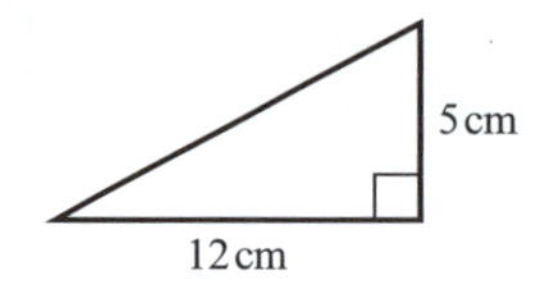 **c** 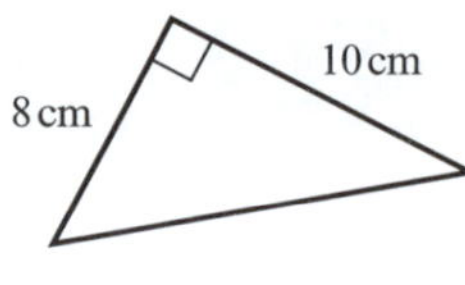

d 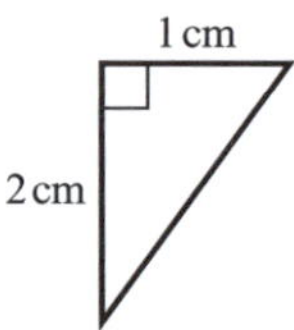 **e** 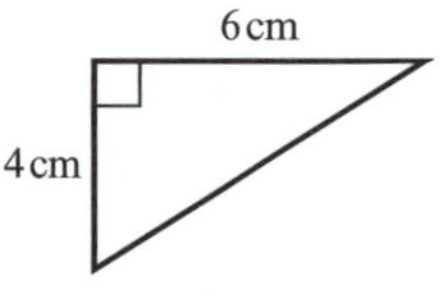 **f** 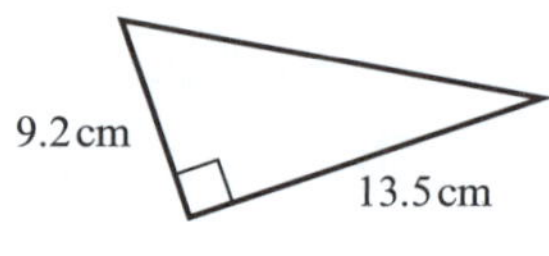

2   Find the missing length of each right-angled triangle.

 **a** 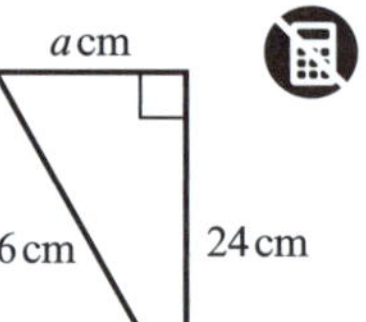 **b** 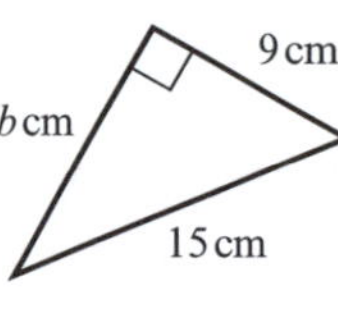 **c** 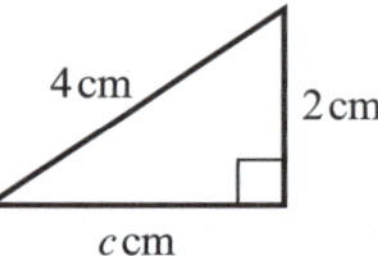

d 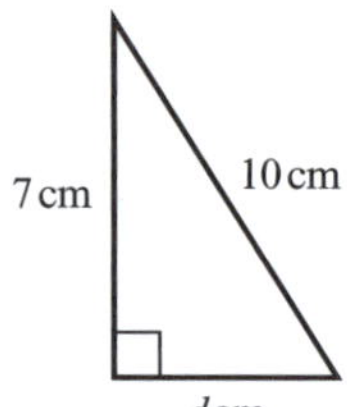 **e** 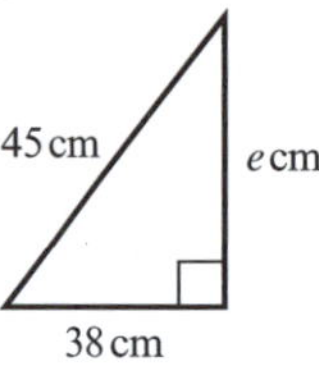 **f** 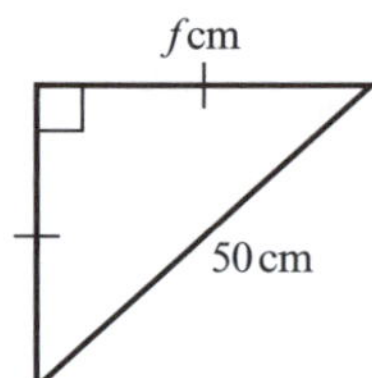

3   Show that this triangle has a right angle.

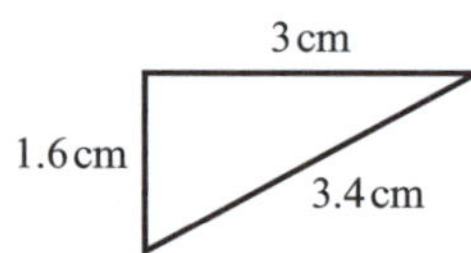

[2]

[Total: 2]

4   Calculate the diagonal of the rectangle.

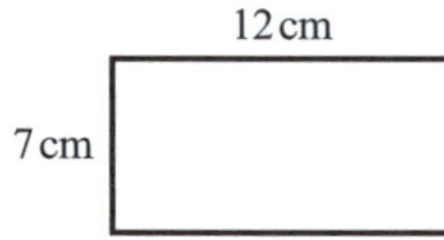

[2]

[Total: 2]

5   Calculate the area of the isosceles triangle.

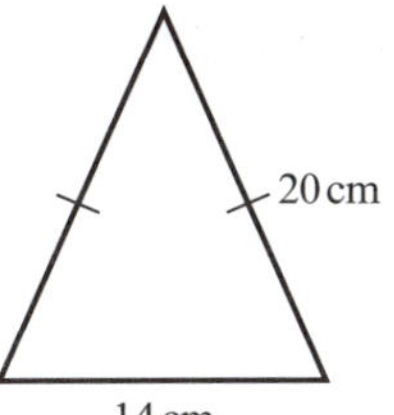

[3]

[Total: 3]

6   Calculate the length BC.

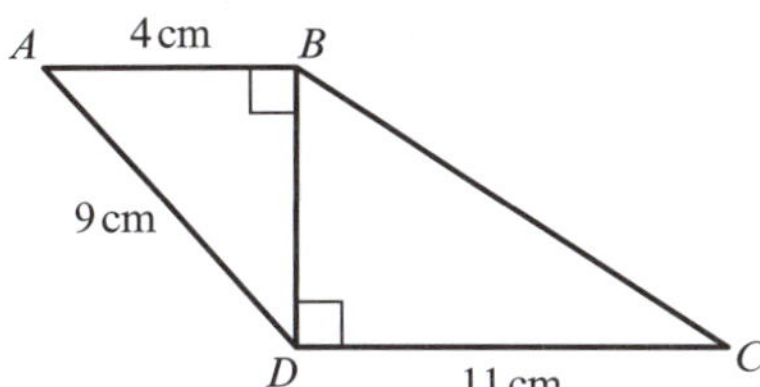

[4]

[Total: 4]

7   A regular hexagon with side length 4 cm is made from six identical equilateral triangles with side length 4 cm.

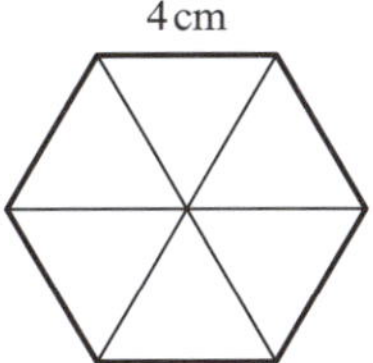

Calculate the area of the hexagon.

[5]

[Total: 5]

« RECALL AND CONNECT 1 «

Expand and simplify $(x + 1)^2 + (x + 3)^2$.

REFLECTION

What strategies do you prefer to use to remember formulae?

Are you confident when substituting into formulae? What could you do to increase your confidence with substituting?

Do you know which formulae are provided and which ones you will need to learn? Write a list of the formulae you need to learn and think of different methods you could use to help remember them.

11.2 Understanding similar triangles

UNDERSTAND THIS TERM

- Similar

1 Determine whether the triangles in each pair are similar.

a

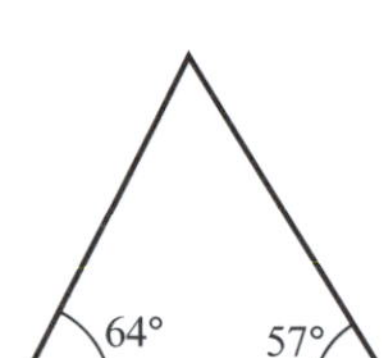
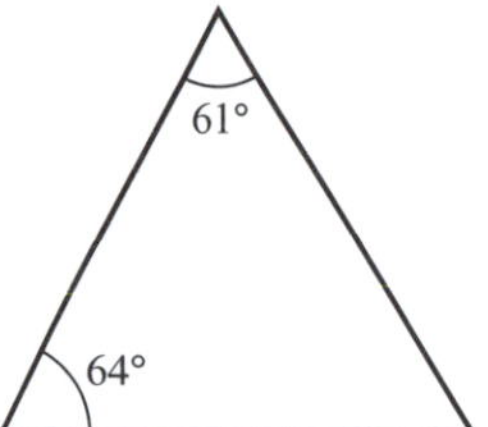

b

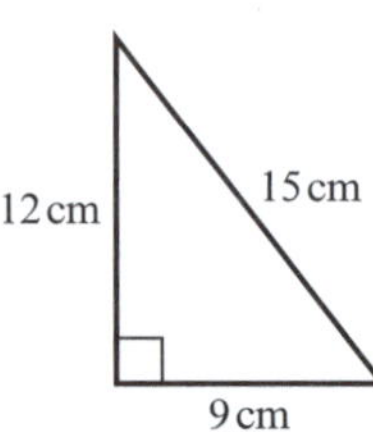
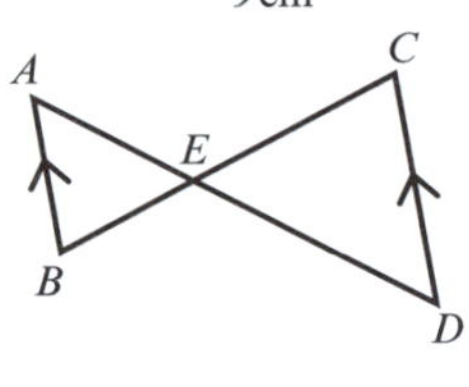

c

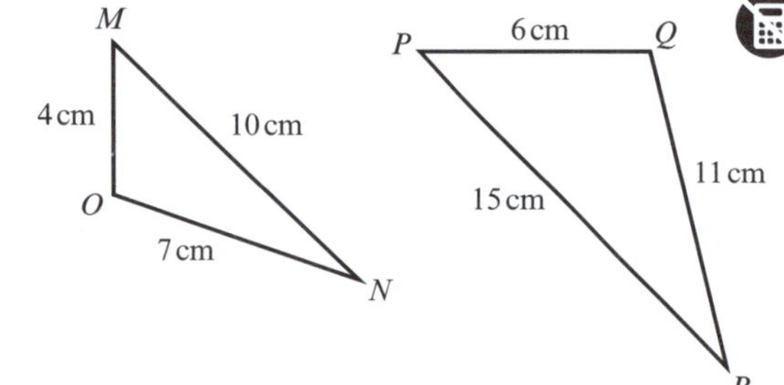

d

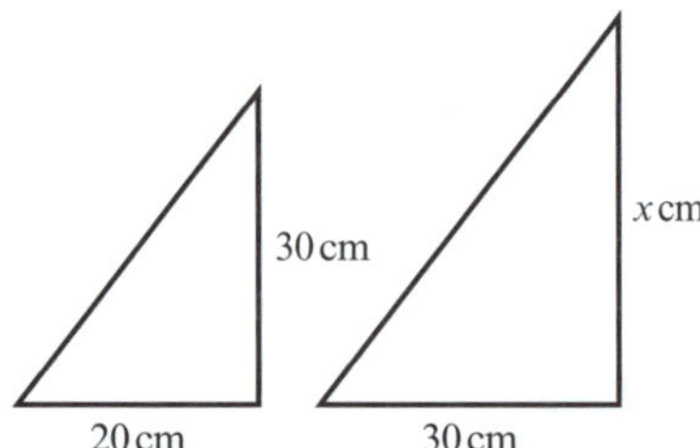

2 These two triangles are mathematically similar.

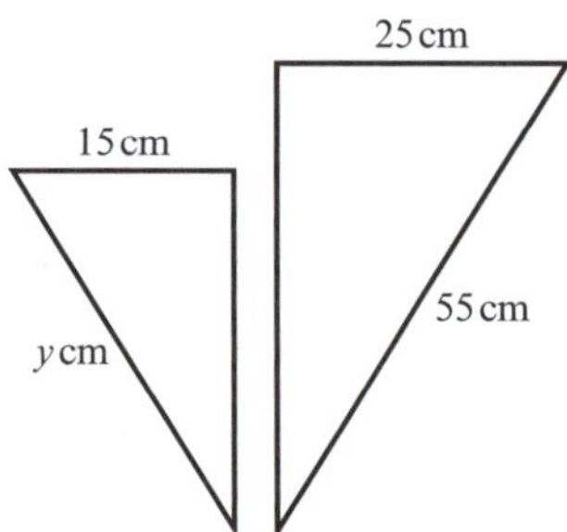

Calculate the length x. [2]

[Total: 2]

3 These two triangles are mathematically similar.

Calculate the length y. [2]

[Total: 2]

《 RECALL AND CONNECT 2 《

a   Find angle ABC, giving reasons for your answer.

b   Find angle BCE, giving reasons for your answer.

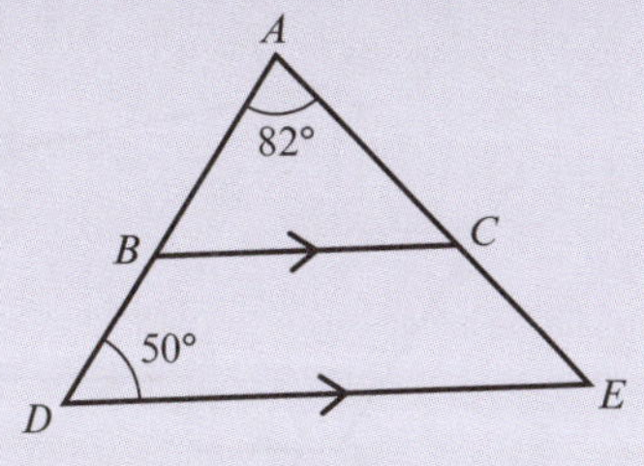

11.3 Understanding similar shapes and
11.4 Understanding congruence

UNDERSTAND THESE TERMS

- Congruent
- Scale factor

1   Determine whether the shapes in each pair are similar.

a

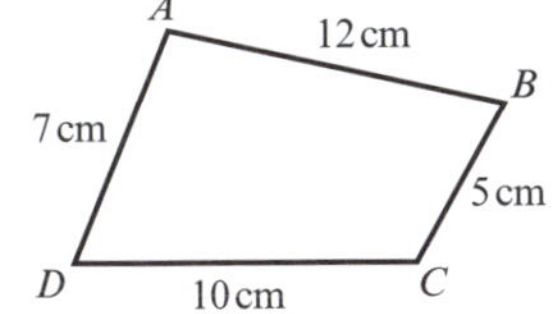

b

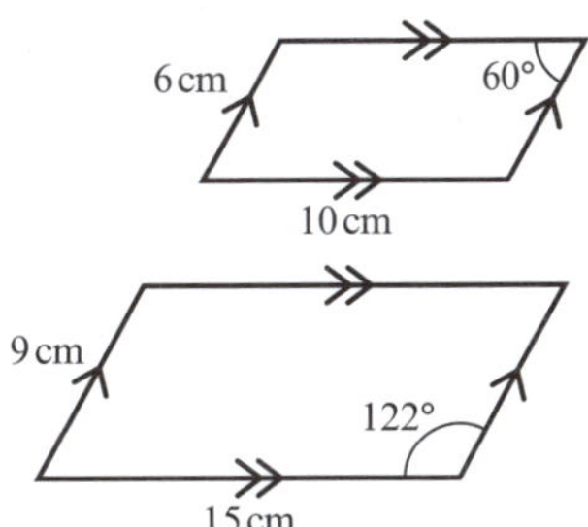

c

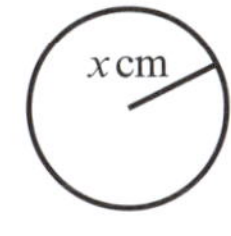 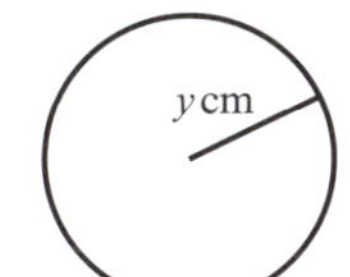

d

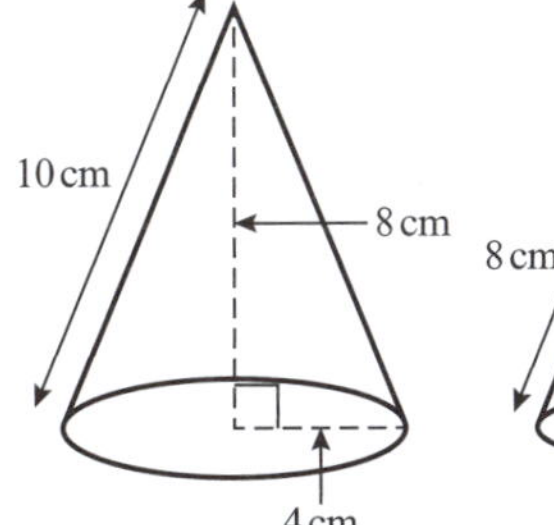 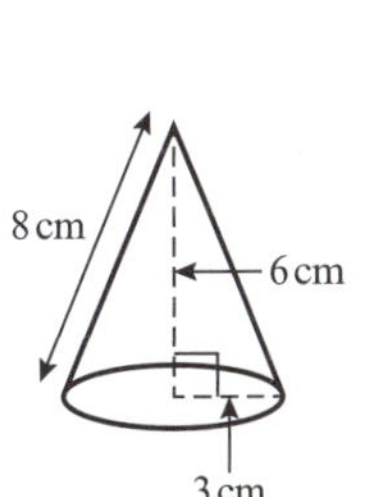

2   Write the pairs of shapes that are congruent.

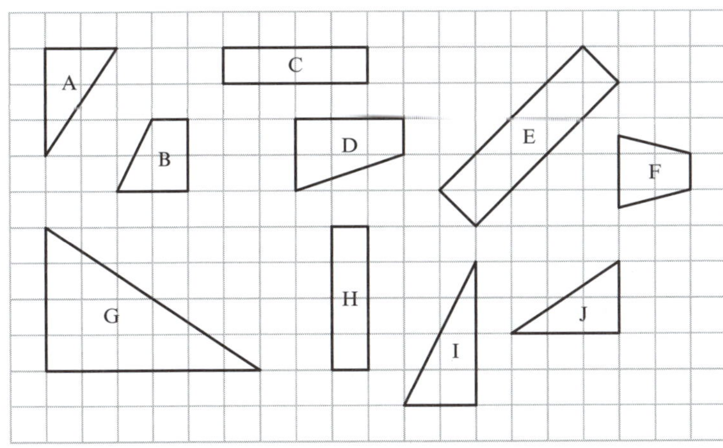

3 Shapes *X* and *Y* are congruent.

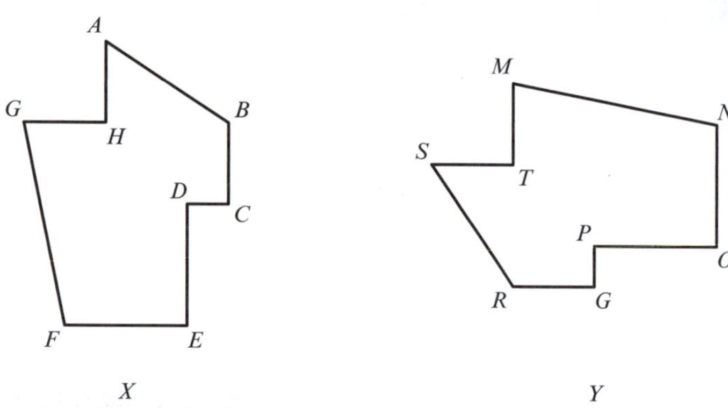

a Which angle of shape *Y* corresponds to angle *FGH*?

b Which angle of shape *X* corresponds to side *ST*?

4 Explain why these two cylinders are not mathematically similar.

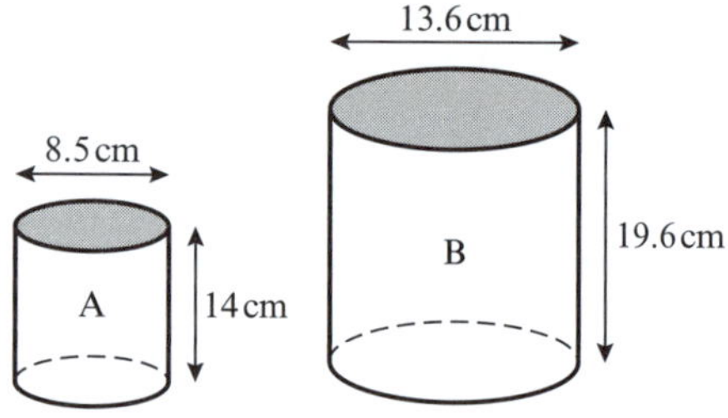

[2]

[Total: 2]

5 These rectangles are mathematically similar.

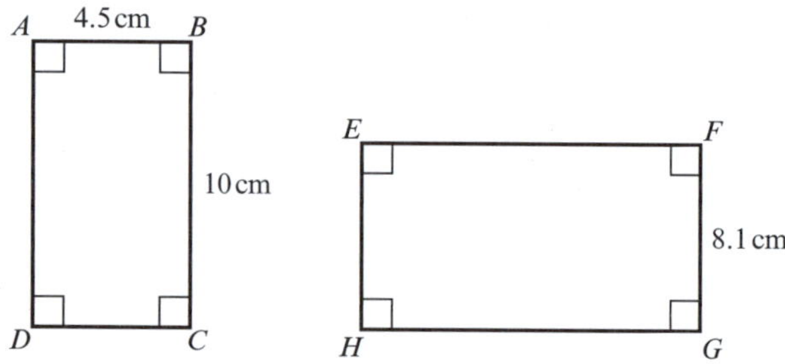

Calculate the length of

a *EF* [2]

b *EG*. [2]

[Total: 4]

6   *ACEG* is a rectangle drawn on a 1 cm square grid.

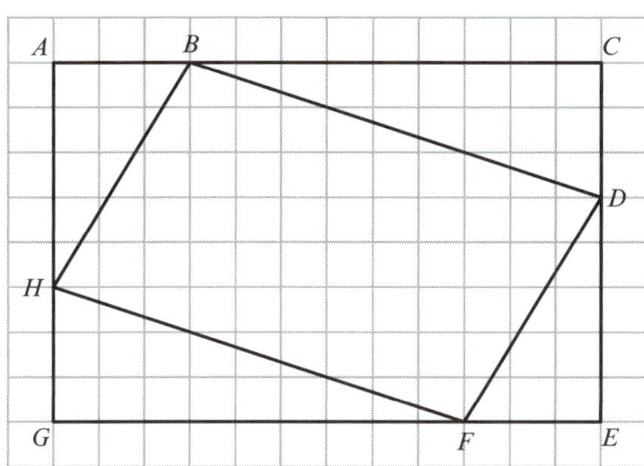

a   State which triangles are congruent.   [2]

b   State the geometric name of shape *BDFH*.   [1]

[Total: 3]

7   The diagram shows three congruent rectangular tiles placed together to form a larger rectangle.

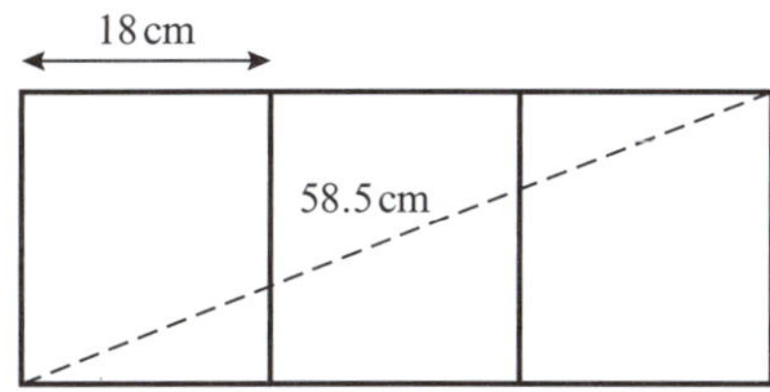

The width of one rectangular tile is 18 cm.
The diagonal of the larger rectangle is 58.5 cm.
Work out the length of one rectangular tile.   [3]

[Total: 3]

REFLECTION

How well do you think you answered the exam skills questions? Did you include your methods and working?

What could you do to improve the quality of your answers?

SELF-ASSESSMENT CHECKLIST

Let's revisit the Knowledge and Exam skills focus for this chapter.
Decide how confident you are with each statement.

	Now I can	Show it	Needs more work	Almost there	Confident to move on
1	use Pythagoras' theorem to find unknown sides of right-angled triangles	Find the missing side of the right-angled triangle. 52 cm, x cm, 20 cm			
2	use Pythagoras' theorem to solve problems	Find the height of an equilateral triangle with side length 7 cm.			
3	use properties of similar triangles to solve problems	Triangles DEF and GHI are mathematically similar. G, D, 10 cm, F 4 cm E, I 6 cm H Calculate the length of DE.			
4	find unknown lengths in similar figures	Pentagons A and B are mathematically similar. 4.8 cm, A, B, h, 3 cm, 15 cm Calculate the missing length h.			

CONTINUED

	Now I can	Show it	Needs more work	Almost there	Confident to move on
5	recognise whether shapes are congruent or not	Copy and complete the drawing of two congruent triangles.			
6	answer exam questions that use the command word 'calculate'	Write a question that uses the command word 'calculate'.			
7	write a good answer to an exam question about Pythagoras' theorem or similarity.	Pick one of the exam skills questions that you have already answered and improve your first answer.			

12 Averages and measures of spread

When you read an examination question, look carefully at the command word used. It is important to understand what each command word means and what it is asking you to do. In this chapter, look out for the questions containing the command words 'work out'.

Work out	calculate from given facts, figures or information with or without the use of a calculator.

When an examination question uses the command words 'work out', you should use information given in the question to find the answer. Many of the questions in this chapter will require a calculator. It is important that you show the method you are using, even if you are using a calculator, as you could still score marks for a correct method or working even if your final answer is incorrect.

Some statistics questions can be time consuming. It is important to manage your time effectively during an examination. You can use the number of marks as a guide for how long to spend on each question: aim to spend one minute per mark to ensure you are able to attempt every question and have some time at the end to check your answers.

12.1 Different types of average and 12.2 Making comparisons using averages and ranges

UNDERSTAND THESE TERMS

- Mean
- Mode
- Median
- Range

1 For each data set find
  i the mean
  ii the mode
  iii the median.

  a 5, 7, 1, 7, 7, 6, 5, 6

  b 80, 20, 60, 100, 80, 40, 50, 60, 80

  c 1.4, 0.8, 1.1, 2.0, 1.7, 0.5, 0.8

  d $9.35, $12.49, $2.49, $14.37, $16.88, $12.49, $19.05, $15.72

2 For each data set, find
  i the mean
  ii the range.

  a 8, 3, 6, 12, 26, 5, 4, 9

  b 45.6, 47.8, 39.2, 41.9, 53.7, 44.3

  c 7, −5, 2, −3, 11, −8, 14

3 For each data set, find
  i the median
  ii the range.

  a 15, 11, 6, 3, 14

  b 0.7, 0.3, 0.8, 1.3, 0.4, 1.1, 0.5

  c 345, 287, 296, 174, 338, 323

4 Five students take a test. The mean of their scores is 72.
Four of the students had the scores 70, 75, 68 and 74.
Work out the score of the fifth student.   [2]

[Total: 2]

5 The mean cost of eight concert tickets is $36.
A ninth ticket is bought for $45.
Work out the new mean cost of the nine tickets.   [2]

[Total: 2]

6 Two classes take a spelling test. Class A has 15 students, Class B has 10 students.
The mean of class A's scores is 19.
The mean of class B's scores is 21
Work out the mean score for all 25 students.   [3]

[Total: 3]

7 Find a set of five numbers that have a mean of 7, a median of 8 and a
mode of 10.   [3]

[Total: 3]

8 Two groups of ten students took a test.
Group A had a mean score of 69 and a range of 40.
The scores for Group B are given below.

40, 50, 60, 45, 55, 70, 65, 50, 75, 85

   a Work out the mean score for Group B. [2]

   b Work out the range of scores for Group B. [1]

   c Compare the performance of Group A and Group B in the test. [2]

[Total: 5]

9 The daily maximum temperatures (in °C) recorded in two cities
over 10 days are shown below.

City A: 15, 16, 14, 18, 19, 21, 20, 17, 18, 16

City B: 10, 12, 13, 14, 15, 15, 13, 12, 14, 16

   a Work out the mean temperatures for City A and City B. [4]

   b Determine the temperature ranges for City A and City B. [2]

   c Which city had more consistent weather conditions, A or B? [2]

[Total: 8]

10 A football coach recorded the number of goals scored in each match
by two players over seven matches.

Player A: 0, 1, 2, 1, 3, 2, 2

Player B: 1, 1, 0, 2, 1, 1, 3

   a Work out the median number of goals for each player. [3]

   b Write down the mode of the goals for each player. [2]

   c Determine the range of goals for each player. [2]

   d Compare the performance of the two players. [2]

[Total: 9]

REFLECTION

Did you check any of your answers at the end? How can you tell whether your
answer for the average is sensible?

Would you know how to spot if you had made a mistake on your calculator?
How would you know?

≪ RECALL AND CONNECT 1 ≪

These are the masses of some apples.

152 g, 146 g, 131 g, 147 g, 164 g, 169 g, 132 g, 142 g, 152 g,
134 g, 145 g, 133 g, 155 g, 133 g, 146 g, 147 g, 151 g

Draw a stem-and-leaf diagram to represent the data.

12.3 Calculating averages and ranges for frequency data

1   Find the mode of the data in each frequency table.

a

Number of siblings	Frequency
0	6
1	10
2	8
3	4
4	2

b

Number of pets	Frequency
0	6
1	7
2	9
3	1
4	5

c

Ages in ballet class	Frequency
9	8
10	5
11	8
12	3
13	2

d

Number rolled on a die	Frequency
1	22
2	19
3	18
4	26
5	17
6	14

2 The table shows how many books a group of students read over the summer holidays.

Books read	Frequency
1	2
2	5
3	3
4	2

a Calculate the mean number of books read. [3]

b Find the median number of books read. [2]

c Work out the range. [2]

[Total: 7]

3 The table shows the number of pets kept in different households.

Number of pets	Frequency
0	4
1	10
2	5
3	2
4	1

a Find the mean number of pets per household. [3]

b Find the median. [2]

c Work out the range. [2]

[Total: 7]

4 The stem-and-leaf diagram shows the ages of students.

1	5 6 8
2	0 2 3 9
3	1 4

Key: 1|5 represents 15 years

a Find the median age. [1]

b Work out the range of the ages. [2]

[Total: 3]

≪ RECALL AND CONNECT 2 ≪

The bar chart shows the number of goals scored in football matches across a season for a school league.

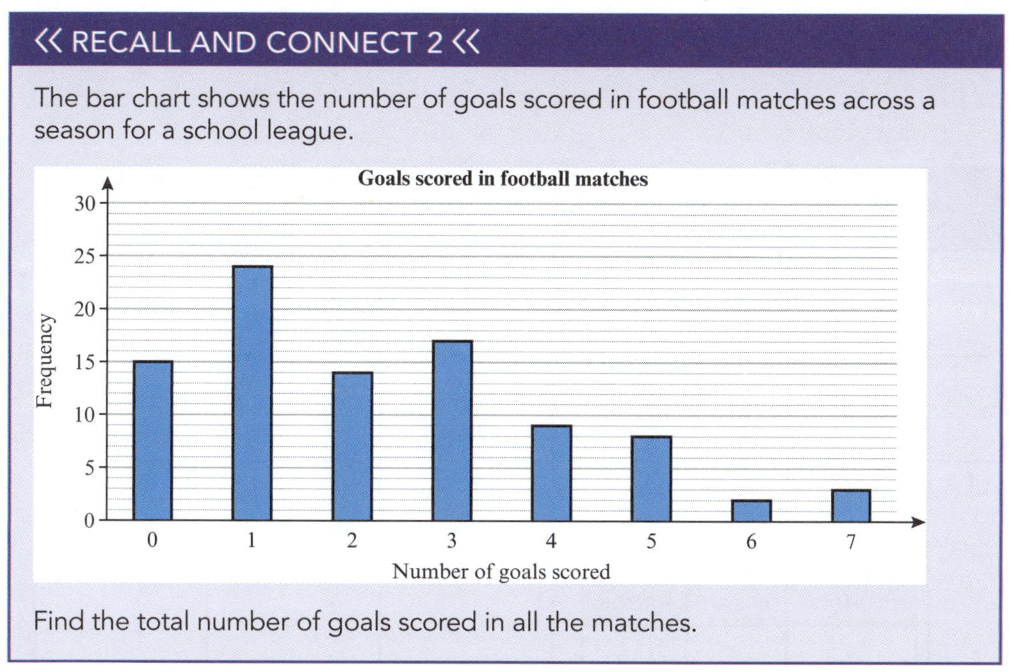

Find the total number of goals scored in all the matches.

REFLECTION

Did you remember how to read from a stem-and-leaf diagram?

How confident are you reading from different statistical diagrams and tables in order to calculate averages and range?

Write a list of different charts and diagrams and revise any that you feel less confident with.

SELF-ASSESSMENT CHECKLIST

Let's revisit the Knowledge and Exam skills focus for this chapter. Decide how confident you are with each statement.

	Now I can	Show it	Needs more work	Almost there	Confident to move on
1	calculate the mean, median and mode of sets of data	Write down nine values. Find the mean, median and mode of your values.			
2	calculate and interpret the range as a measure of spread	Find the range of the set of numbers you wrote down.			
3	interpret the meaning of average and range, and use them to compare sets of data	The reaction times (in seconds) were recorded for two students. 	Student	Mean	Range
---	---	---
A	0.49	0.4
B	0.52	0.4 | Use this information to compare their reaction times.			
4	calculate the average and range for frequency data	The stem-and-leaf diagram shows the number of books read by students over the summer holiday. 	0	3 5 9
1	0 2
2	1 3 4 6	 Key: 2|1 represents 21 books Find the median and range of the number of books read.			
5	understand the command words 'work out'	The heights of some plants are recorded in cm. 52, 29, 38, 82, 67, 59, 72, 47, 85 Work out the mean height.			
6	manage time during the examination.	Pick some exam skills questions and set yourself a time limit to complete them in.			
7	write a good answer to an exam question about Pythagoras' theorem or similarity.	Pick one of the exam skills questions that you have already answered and improve your first answer.			

Exam practice 3

This section contains past paper questions from previous Cambridge exams, which draw together your knowledge on a range of topics that you have covered up to this point. These questions give you the opportunity to test your knowledge and understanding.

The following question has an example student response and commentary provided. Work through the question first, then compare your answer to the sample response and commentary. Are your answers different to the sample responses?

1 A sequence of patterns is made using rectangular blocks.

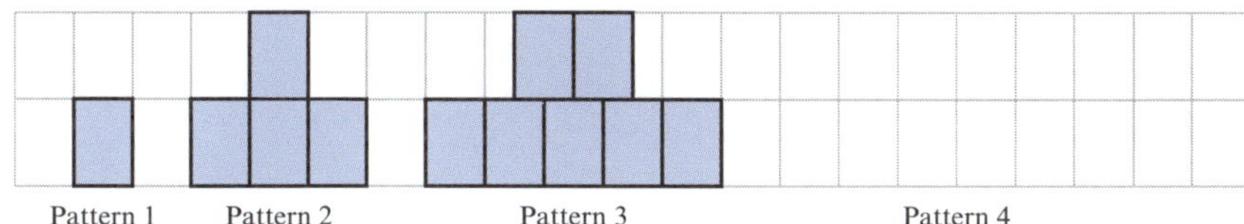

  a Draw Pattern 4.
  [Use Figure 2 on Past Paper Practice Questions Resource Sheet.] [1]

  b Complete the table.

Pattern number	1	2	3	4	5
Number of blocks	1	4	7		

  [2]

  c Find an expression, in terms of n, for the number of blocks in Pattern n. [2]

  d Tara wants to make one pattern in this sequence.
  She has 84 blocks.
  Work out the largest pattern number she can make and the number of blocks remaining. [4]

Cambridge IGCSE Mathematics (0580) Paper 32 Q9, June 2021 [Total: 9]

Example student response	Commentary
a	This is a correct response. *This answer scores 1 out of 1 mark.*
b 	Pattern number	1	2	3	4	5	 Number of blocks	1	4	7	10	13	 Each correct table entry would score 1 mark. *This answer scores 2 out of 2 marks.*
c $n + 3$	The student has written an expression describing the term-to-term rule instead of the position-to-term rule. *This answer scores 0 out of 2 marks.*

d $n + 3 = 84$ $n = 81$ 81st pattern with no blocks remaining.	The student has used their incorrect expression for the number of blocks in pattern n, but has used the correct method. Because the method is correct, this answer would score 1 mark. **This answer scores 1 out of 4 marks.**

The following question has an example student response and commentary provided. Work through the question first, then compare your answer to the sample response and commentary. Are your answers different to the sample responses?

2 135 girls are asked if they like soccer (S) and if they like hockey (H).
$n(S) = 53$, $n(H) = 68$ and $n(S \cup H) = 110$

    a Complete the Venn diagram. [Use Figure 3 on the Past Paper Practice Questions Resource Sheet.]

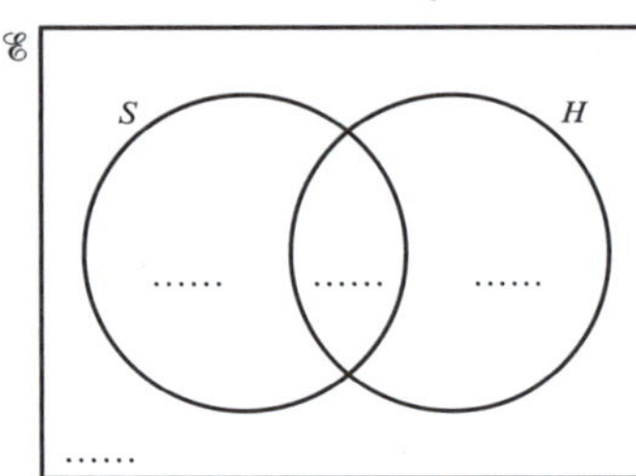

                                                 [3]

    b Write down $n(S \cap H)$ [1]

Cambridge IGCSE Mathematics (0580) Paper 32 Q7b, June 2021   **[Total: 4]**

Example student response	Commentary
a 38 15 53 29	The student has incorrectly subtracted 53 from 68 to find the value for the intersection. All the values in the Venn diagram are incorrect but the student has made sure that the total of each circle sums to 53 for soccer and 68 for hockey, so this would score 1 mark. **This answer scores 1 out of 3 marks.**
b 15	The student has used their incorrect values from the Venn diagram to answer the question. However, since they have chosen the value that corresponds to the correct section of the diagram they will score a follow-through mark for using their answer in a correct way. **This answer scores 1 out of 1 mark.**

The following question has an example student response and commentary provided. Work through the question first, then compare your answer to the sample response and commentary. Are your answers different to the sample responses?

3

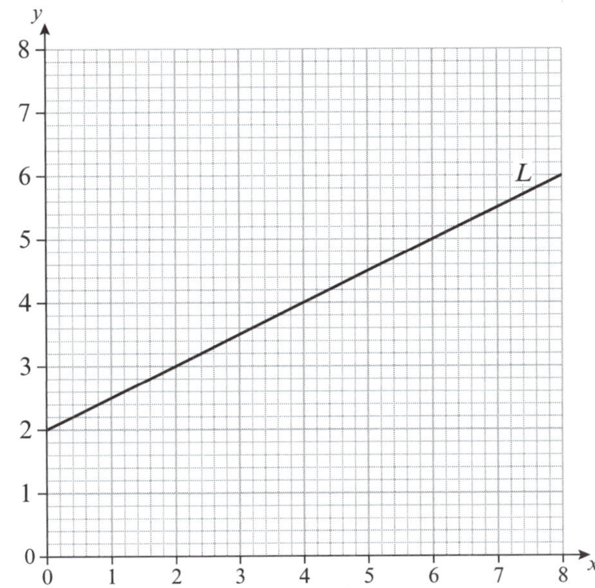

a Find the equation of line L in the form $y = mx + c$. [2]

b **i** Complete the table of values for $y = 8 - 2x$.

x	0	2	4
y		4	

[2]

   ii On the grid, draw the graph of $y = 8 - 2x$ for $0 \leqslant x \leqslant 4$.
   [Use Figure 4 on the Past Paper Practice Questions Resource Sheet.] [1]

c Find the coordinates of the point where line L intersects the graph of $y = 8 - 2x$. [1]

Cambridge IGCSE Mathematics (0580) Paper 32 Q8a, November 2024 [Total: 6]

Example student response	Commentary
a $\dfrac{8 - 0}{6 - 2} = \dfrac{8}{4} = 2$ $y = 2x + 2$	The student has not used the correct formula to find the gradient. Instead, they have used the formula $\dfrac{x\text{-change}}{y\text{-change}}$. The student has identified the correct y-intercept and written it in their equation, so this would score 1 mark. **This answer scores 1 out of 2 marks.**
	The student has completed the table correctly. They would score 1 mark for each correct value in the table. **This answer scores 2 out of 2 marks.**

b ii 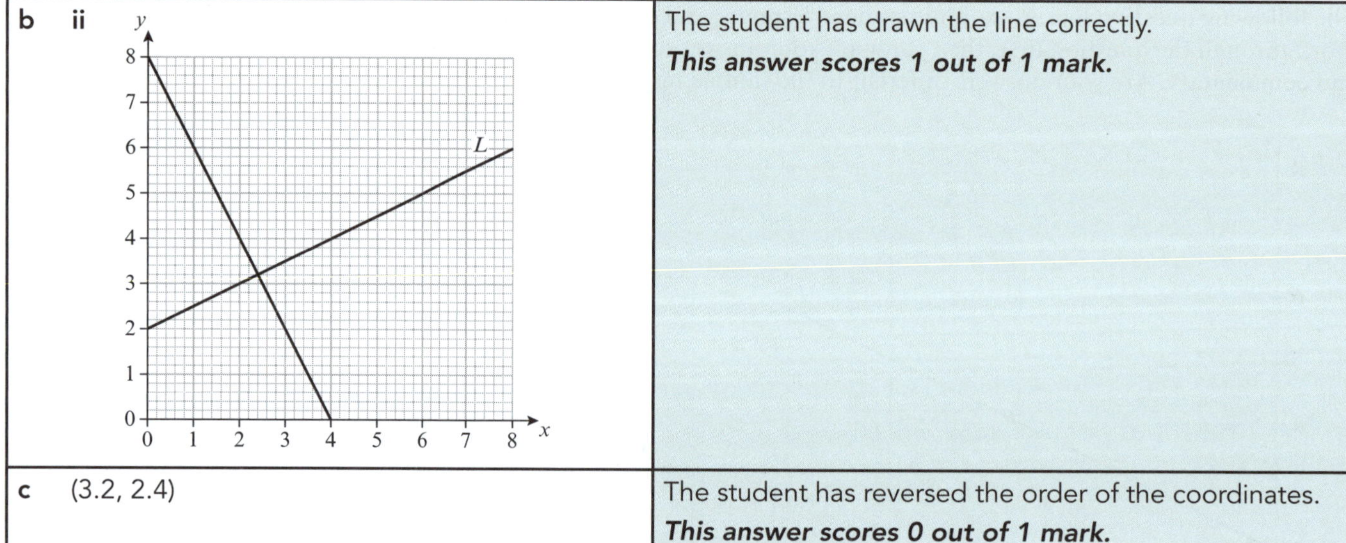	The student has drawn the line correctly. ***This answer scores 1 out of 1 mark.***
c (3.2, 2.4)	The student has reversed the order of the coordinates. ***This answer scores 0 out of 1 mark.***

The following question has an example student response and commentary provided.
Work through the question first, then compare your answer to the sample response and commentary. Are your answers different to the sample responses?

4

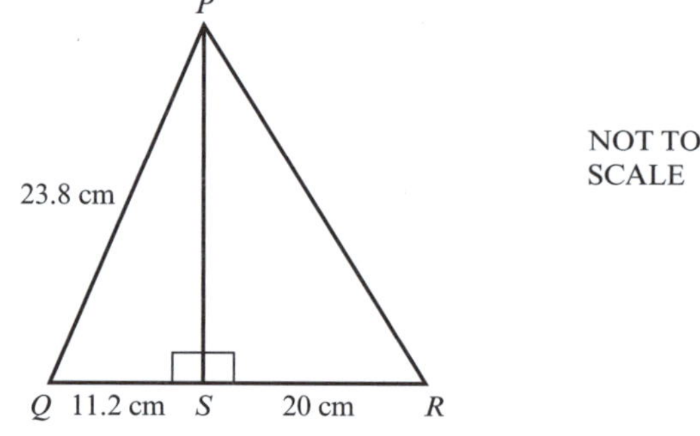

The diagram shows right-angled triangles PQS and PRS.
$PQ = 23.8$ cm, $QS = 11.2$ cm and $SR = 20$ cm.
Calculate PR.

[4]

Cambridge IGCSE Mathematics (0580) Paper 12 Q22b, June 2023

[Total: 4]

Example student response	Commentary
$PS^2 = 23.8^2 + 11.2^2$ $\quad = 691.88$ $PS = 26.30$ (2 d.p.) $PR^2 = 20^2 + 26.30^2$ $\quad = 1091.69$ $PR = 33.04$ cm (2 d.p.)	The student has not used Pythagoras' theorem correctly to find a short side of the triangle PQS. Although they have used their incorrect value of PS, they have used the correct method to find PR, so this would score 1 mark. ***This answer scores 1 out of 4 marks.***

The following question has an example student response and commentary provided.
Work through the question first, then compare your answer to the sample response and
commentary. Are your answers different to the sample responses?

5 **a** Here are the weekly wages, in dollars, of the ten workers in an office.

280	200	175	1180	95	182	238	256	194	250

     i   Find the median. [2]

     ii Calculate the mean. [2]

     iii For this office, explain why the mean is not a suitable average. [1]

  b The stem-and-leaf diagram shows the ages of the workers in a factory.

1	6	7	7	9	
2	2	3	4	6	8
3	0	2	3	6	9
4	1	4	4	8	
5	0	1	6	6	6	9
6	1	5	8		

Key : 2 | 3 represents 23

     i   Write down the mode. [1]

     ii Work out the range. [1]

Cambridge IGCSE Mathematics (0580) Paper 32 Q5, November 2020 [Total: 7]

Example student response	Commentary
a **i** $\dfrac{95 + 182}{2} = 138.5$	The student has not put the wages in order before finding the middle value. ***This answer scores 0 out of 2 marks.***
ii 280 + 200 + 175 + 1180 + 95 + 182 + 238 + 256 + 194 + 250 ÷ 10 = 2825	The student has tried to use the correct formula, however they have made a calculation error with the order of operations. ***This answer scores 0 out of 2 marks.***
iii The 1180 is an extreme value and makes the mean higher.	The student has written a correct reason. ***This answer scores 1 out of 1 mark.***
b **i** 6	The student has ignored the stem and has not used the key to understand the values in the diagram. ***This answer scores 0 out of 1 mark.***
ii 9 − 0 = 0	The student has ignored the stem and not used the key to understand the values in the diagram. ***This answer scores 0 out of 1 mark.***

The following question has an example student response and commentary provided.
Work through the question first, then compare your answer to the sample response and
commentary. Are your answers different to the sample responses?

6   The median of six numbers is 61.
Five of the numbers are 24, 43, 58, 71 and 85.
Work out the sixth number. [1]

Cambridge IGCSE Mathematics (0580) Paper 12 Q11, March 2023   [Total: 1]

Example student response	Commentary
$\dfrac{58 + 61}{2} = 59.5$	This student has used 61 as one of the numbers and calculated the median of the set 24, 43, 58, 61, 71 and 85, rather than working out what number should be added to the list to make a median of 61. ***This answer scores 0 out of 1 mark.***

Now that you have read the commentary to the previous question, here is a similar
question that you should attempt. Use the information from the previous response and
commentary to guide you as you answer.

7   Wilfred records his times, in seconds, for each of 5 laps.

59   74   69   63   65

After running a 6th lap his mean time is 67 seconds.
Find his time for the 6th lap. [3]

Cambridge IGCSE Mathematics (0580) Paper 32 Q3d, November 2021   [Total: 3]

13 Understanding measurement

When you read an examination question, look carefully at the command word used. It is important to understand what each command word means and what it is asking you to do. In this chapter, look out for the questions containing the command word 'give'.

Give	produce an answer from a given source or recall/memory.

If an examination question uses the command word 'give', you may have to recall a fact or information that you have learned and remembered. It could also mean that you need to provide your answer in a particular form or to a particular degree of accuracy. For example, the question may ask you to 'give your answer in centimetres'. This means that you may need to convert your answer into the units that are asked for. Make sure that you read the question carefully and check the format of your answer.

It is useful to understand what marks in the examination can be awarded for. When a question has multiple marks, this could be for different pieces of information you may need to include, or the marks could be given for correct working as well as the correct answer. For multi-mark questions, ensure your working clearly documents every step of your logic to secure full credit. Always double check that you have supplied all the information requested in the question.

13.1 Understanding units

UNDERSTAND THESE TERMS

- Conversion
- Metric

1 Convert these units.

    a $1\,km$ = ... m   **b** $100\,g$ = ... kg   **c** $20\,ml$ = ... litres

    d $1\,km^2$ = ... m^2 **e** $1\,cm^3$ = ... ml

2 Convert these lengths.

    a $378\,cm$ = ... m   **b** $2.78\,km$ = ... cm   **c** $5830\,mm$ = ... km

3 Convert these masses.

    a $179\,mg$ = ... g   **b** $6.14\,kg$ = ... g   **c** $0.89\,g$ = ... kg

4 A container has a capacity of $250\,cl$. Express the capacity of the container in

    a millilitres   **b** litres.

5 Olaf is comparing the sodium content of several snacks by creating the following table. Order the snacks from the least amount to the highest amount of sodium. [2]

Snack	A	B	C	D
Sodium content	3462 mg	3.49 g	0.0033 kg	3.5% per 100 g

[Total: 2]

6 A $500\,ml$ carton of milk has a mass of $516\,g$.
Work out the total mass of seven cartons of milk.
Give your answer in kilograms. [2]

[Total: 2]

7 Square floor tiles of side length $60\,cm$ are used to tile a room.
Work out the area of the room if 20 tiles are used.
Give your answer in m^2. [2]

[Total: 2]

8 Alina bought a 1.5 litre bottle of water and shared the water equally between 4 cups.
Work out the amount of water in each cup.
Give your answer in ml. [2]

[Total: 2]

≪ RECALL AND CONNECT 1 ≪

    a Write $127\,000$ in standard form.

    b Write 3.78×10^{-3} as an ordinary number.

    c Convert $3.78 \times 10^{-3}\,kg$ into grams.

> **REFLECTION**
>
> How do you remember the meanings of the prefixes of different units?
> How do you remember the rules for converting units?
>
> What methods do you prefer to use to help you to remember different rules and definitions?

13.2 Time

1   **a**   Convert 11.30 p.m. to the 24-hour clock.

   b   Convert 21:15 to the 12-hour clock.

2   Find the duration between 06:45 and 20:15.

3   This is the timetable for the Shinkansen (bullet train) between Tokyo and Shin-Hakodate.
From Tokyo to Shin-Hakodate.

Tokyo	Omiya	Sendai	Morioka	Shin-Aomori	Shin-Hakodate
-	-	-	-	06:32	07:34
-	-	-	06:54	07:56	08:58
-	-	06:40	07:59	09:04	10:01
06:32	06:57	08:05	08:50	9:51	10:53
08:20	08:43	09:51	10:31	11:20	12:17
09:36	09:59	11:07	11:47	12:36	13:33
10:44	11:09	12:17	13:05	13:59	15:01
12:20	12:45	13:53	14:37	15:31	16:30
13:20	13:45	14:53	15:37	16:45	17:47
14:20	14:15	15:53	16:37	17:32	18:29
15:30	15:45	16:53	17:37	18:41	19:44
17:20	17:45	18:54	19:37	20:42	21:44
19:20	19:45	20:54	21:38	22:32	23:29

From Shin-Hakodate to Tokyo.

Shin-Hakodate	Shin-Aomori	Morioka	Sendai	Omiya	Tokyo
06:39	07:43	08:43	09:29	10:39	11:04
07:38	08:37	09:41	10:29	11:39	12:04
09:35	10:39	11:43	12:29	13:39	13:04
10:53	11:52	12:45	13:29	14:39	15:04
12:48	13:52	14:44	15:30	16:39	17:04
13:39	14:38	15:44	16:29	17:39	18:04
14:48	15:52	16:44	17:29	18:39	19:04
16:20	17:22	18:10	18:55	20:07	20:32
17:26	18:25	19:13	19:53	21:01	21:23
18:40	19:44	20:45	21:30	22:39	23:04
19:41	20:40	21:45	23:01		-
20:43	21:47	22:48	-	-	-
21:57	22:59	-	-	-	-

Source: https://www.hakodate.travel/en/news/the-latest-timetable-of-hokkaido-shinkansen-bullet-train/

a How long does it take to ride the first train from Tokyo to Shin-Hakodate to the nearest half-hour?

b Gio wants to catch a train at Sendai and get to Tokyo by 15:00. What is the time of the latest train he should catch?

c How long does it take the 09:36 train from Tokyo to travel to Shin-Hakodate?

d Haruka arrives at Shin-Aomori station at 10:45. How long will she have to wait for the next train to Tokyo?

4 Siti flies from Jakarta to Tokyo. Her flight leaves at 21:55 and arrives at 07:25 local time.
The local time in Tokyo is 2 hours ahead of the local time in Jakarta.
Work out the flight time, in hours and minutes. [2]

[**Total: 2**]

5 Qian takes a walk of 37 minutes once a week from his house to the park.
Find the total time Qian spends walking after 12 weeks.
Give your answer in hours and minutes. [2]

[**Total: 2**]

REFLECTION

Look back at the exam skills questions. What do you think the marks were awarded for?

Are there marks that you don't think you would have achieved? What could you add to improve your answers?

13.3 Limits of accuracy – upper and lower bounds

UNDERSTAND THESE TERMS

- Upper bound
- Lower bound

1 Find the upper and lower bounds of these quantities.

   a 16 to the nearest whole number.

   b 3.7 to 1 decimal place.

   c 600 to the nearest one hundred.

   d 11.26 to 2 decimal places.

   e 0.357 to 3 significant figures.

2 The height, h m, of a building is 15.6 m, correct to 1 decimal place.
Copy and complete this statement about the value of h.
.... $\leqslant h <$ .... [2]

[Total: 2]

3 The length of a piece of rope is 5.7 m to the nearest 10 cm. The actual
length of the rope is L cm. Find the range of possible values for L. [2]

[Total: 2]

> **≪ RECALL AND CONNECT 2 ≪**
>
> Round these numbers.
>
> **a** 278 to the nearest 10.   **d** 2.019 to 3 significant figures.
> **b** 57.4 to the nearest whole number.   **e** 60.07 to 3 significant figures.
> **c** 9.27 to 1 decimal place.   **f** 0.0978 to 2 significant figures.

13.4 Conversion graphs and
13.5 Exchanging currencies

1 Use the conversion graph to convert these temperatures.

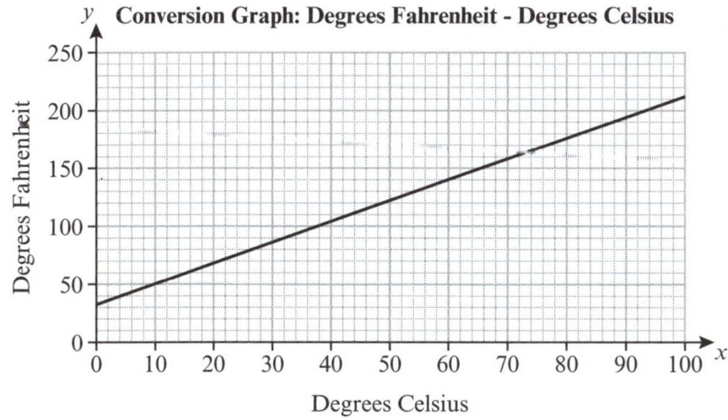

   a 30 °C = ______ °F   **b** 150 °F = ______ °C

   c 10 °C = ______ °F   **d** 200 °F = ______ °C

2 Use the ratio boxes to convert the currency.

a

Korean Won	Indonesian Rupiah
1	11.7
10 000	

b

Korean Won	Indonesian Rupiah
1	11.7
	200 000

c

Korean Won	Indonesian Rupiah
1	11.7
	1

3 On one day, 1 United Arab Emirates dirham = 0.27 US dollars.
Convert 500 dirham to US dollars.

4 Akiko wants to exchange Japanese yen for Danish krone.
She needs 1000 krone.
The exchange rate is 1 yen = 0.073 krone.
Work out how much yen she needs to exchange.
Give your answer to the nearest yen. [1]

[Total: 1]

5 An Australian tourist exchanges $5000 to Turkish lira at an
exchange rate of $1 = 25.54 lira.
She spends 102 700 lira during her trip.
How many dollars does she get back if the exchange
rate is $1 = 24.75 lira?
Give your answer to the nearest dollar. [3]

[Total: 3]

≪ RECALL AND CONNECT 3 ≪

Oranges cost $2.23 per kilogram.

a Write down the equation for the total cost, C, in terms of the number of
kilograms of oranges, k.

b Find the cost for 5 kilograms of oranges.

SELF-ASSESSMENT CHECKLIST

Let's revisit the Knowledge and Exam skills focus for this chapter.
Decide how confident you are with each statement.

	Now I can	Show it	Needs more work	Almost there	Confident to move on
1	convert between units in the metric system	When converting from 5 cm^2 to m^2, Sam has written 0.05 m^2. What mistake has he made?			
2	solve problems involving time calculations and timetables	Look up a local bus or train timetable. Pick two stops on the route. Can you calculate the duration between them?			
3	use a calculator to work out time calculations	If you were converting 1.2 hours to minutes, what buttons would you press on the calculator?			
4	find lower and upper bounds of numbers that are written to a given level of accuracy	Find the lower and upper bounds of 1.3 correct to 1 decimal place.			
5	use conversion graphs to change units from one measuring system to another	Draw a conversion graph to convert between miles and kilometres. How many kilometres are equivalent to 5 miles?			
6	use exchange rates to convert currencies	1 Mexican peso = 0.23 British pounds. Convert 25 000 pesos to pounds. Convert 500 pounds to pesos.			
7	understand the command word 'give' and answer 'give' questions	Write down two things that the command word 'give' could mean.			
8	understand how the number of marks can help when writing an answer.	Look back at the exam skills questions and write down what you think the marks would be given for.			

14 Further solving of equations and inequalities

In this chapter you will answer questions on:

- writing pairs of simultaneous equations to model situations

- solving pairs of simultaneous equations graphically and algebraically

- using number lines to represent and interpret inequalities.

EXAM SKILLS FOCUS

In this chapter you will:

- show that you understand the command words 'write down' and can answer 'write down' questions.

- reflect on your progress.

When you read an examination question, look carefully at the command words used. It is important to understand what each command word means and what it is asking you to do. In this chapter, look out for the questions containing the command words 'write down'.

Write down	give an answer without significant working.

When an examination question uses the command words 'write down', it is asking for a brief, direct answer that you can find without much or any working. In algebraic questions, this can include writing an expression, an equation or the value of a variable.

This chapter extends some skills that you have seen earlier in the course, for example, solving equations. It can be good to reflect on your progress and check how well you remember topics and skills that you have already revised. If you find yourself struggling with some types of questions, it can be helpful to go back and revise earlier related content.

14.1 Simultaneous linear equations

UNDERSTAND THESE TERMS

- Simultaneous
- Linear inequality

1   What word or words would complete the following statement?
The solution to simultaneous linear equations when looking at their graphs is found at the point of ___________________ between the two lines.

2   Use the graph to find the solution to these simultaneous equations.
$$3x - y = 2$$
$$x + y = 2$$

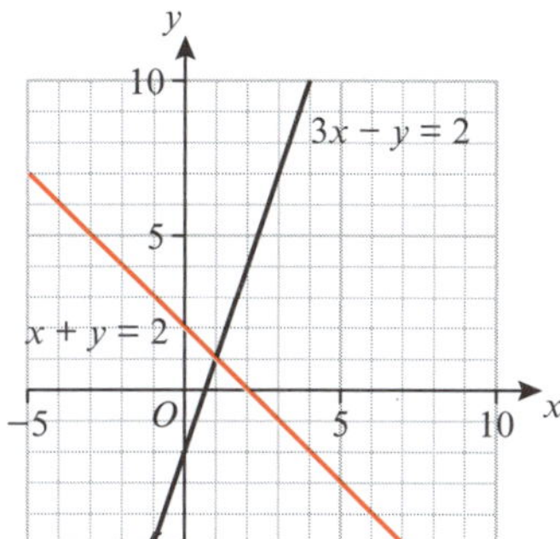

3   Shizuka wants to find the solution to the following simultaneous equations graphically.

$$2x + 3y = 6$$
$$\frac{1}{2}y = -x + 2$$

She draws this graph of the line $2x + 3y = 6$.

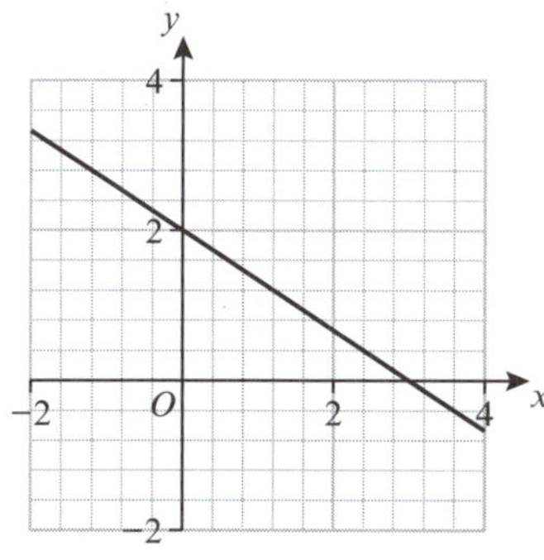

a   Draw the other line $\frac{1}{2}y = -x + 2$ and find the solution.

b   Draw the graph of $2x + 3y = 10$.
Explain why there are no solutions to these simultaneous equations.

$$\frac{1}{2}y = -x + 2 \quad \text{and} \quad 2x + 3y = 10$$

4   Determine if each pair of equations has one solution, infinite solutions or no solution.

Explain your reasoning. You may find it helpful to draw each pair of lines on a graph.

a $3x + 4y = 5$
  $6x + 8y = 10$

b $-x + y = 1$
  $-2x + 2y = 1$

c $y = 2x - 1$
  $y = 3x + 2$

5 Solve each pair of equations by substitution. Check your solution.

  a $3x - 4y = 7$
$$y = \frac{1}{2}x - 1$$

  b $3x - 4y = 2$
$$2x = 7 - 3y$$

6 Solve each pair of equations by elimination. Check your solution.

  a $4x + 3y = 20$
$$4x - y = 12$$

  b $2x + 3y = 4$
$$x - y = -3$$

7 Solve each pair of simultaneous equations. Check your solution.

  a $3x + \frac{2}{3}y = 4$
$$\frac{1}{2}x - y = 4$$

  b $2y = 5x - 4$
$$2x + \frac{1}{3}y = 5$$

8 It costs $\$h$ per hour plus $\$d$ per kilometre to rent a car.

  a Rai rents a car for 4 hours and travels 20 km. He pays \$60.
Write down an equation to show this information. [1]

  b Santosh rents a car for 6 hours and travels 50 km. He pays \$100.
Write down an equation to show this information. [1]

  c Solve the simultaneous equations to find the price per hour and the
price per km of renting the car. You must show all your working. [4]

[Total: 6]

9 Soledad buys six notebooks and three bookmarks for \$18.90.
She then buys five notebooks and four bookmarks from the same
store for \$17.40.
All the notebooks and all the bookmarks cost the same amount.

  a Write down a pair of simultaneous equations. [2]

  b Solve the equations to find the cost of a notebook and the
cost of a bookmark.
You must show all your working. [4]

[Total: 6]

≪ RECALL AND CONNECT 1 ≪

  a Rearrange the equation $3x + 2y = 1$ so that y is the subject.

  b Draw the graph of the line $2x - y = 3$.

> **REFLECTION**
>
> How can you recognise problems involving simultaneous equations if you are
> not told to use this method to solve them? How do you decide which method
> (elimination or substitution) to use when solving simultaneous equations?
> Reflect on the earlier topics you have revised. Do you have preferred methods
> for solving different types of problems? Why do you prefer those methods?

14.2 Linear inequalities

1   Show these inequalities on a number line.

  a $2 < k \leqslant 7$ **b** $-3.5 \leqslant q < 1.4$ **c** $-6.25 \leqslant w \leqslant -2.75$

  d $0 < r$ **e** $t \leqslant -1$ **f** $-1.2 \leqslant p \leqslant 2.3$

2   Write down all the integers that satisfy each inequality.

  a $-2 \leqslant n < 2$ **b** $2 < p < 5$ **c** $3 < s < 4$

  d $-5 \leqslant d < -3$ **e** $\dfrac{3}{2} < g < \pi$ **f** $-1 \leqslant h < \sqrt{10}$

3   The number line represents the possible values of m.

  a   Write the inequality shown on the number line.

  b   If m is an integer, write all its possible values.

4   Raditya measured the distance d metres that his toy car travelled as 278.4 m,
correct to the nearest 0.1 m.

  a   Write down an inequality that represents the value of d.   [2]

  b   Draw a number line to represent the inequality.   [2]

  [Total: 4]

5   The number line shows the number of units, p, of a product that a factory can
produce per day. Write down an inequality to describe the value of p.   [2]

  [Total: 2]

> **« RECALL AND CONNECT 2 «**
>
> Compare each pair of numbers by using the correct symbol (<, = or >).
>
> **a** $-3.7 \boxed{} -1.2$ **b** $\pi \boxed{} \sqrt{5}$ **c** $2^{-1} \boxed{} 0.5$

SELF-ASSESSMENT CHECKLIST

Let's revisit the Knowledge and Exam skills focus for this chapter.
Decide how confident you are with each statement.

	Now I can	Show it	Needs more work	Almost there	Confident to move on
1	write a pair of simultaneous equations to model a situation	The cost of 3 bags and 5 pens is $42. The cost of 2 bags and 3 pens is $26. Write down a pair of simultaneous equations.			
2	solve a pair of simultaneous equations graphically	Solve these simultaneous equations graphically. $x + 2y = 10$ $-2x + 3y = 1$			
3	solve a pair of simultaneous equations algebraically	Solve these simultaneous equations algebraically. $-3x + y = 10$ $2x + 3y = 8$			
4	use number lines to represent and interpret inequalities	Draw an inequality on a number line. Swap with a partner. Write down the inequality that your partner has drawn.			
5	understand the command words 'write down' and answer 'write down' questions	When asked to 'write down' a pair of simultaneous equations, what should you do and what should you not do?			
6	reflect on my progress.	Write a list of topics you feel confident on, and a list of topics you want extra practice on.			

15 Scale drawings, bearings and trigonometry

When you read an examination question, look carefully at the command word used. It is important to understand what each command word means and what it is asking you to do. In this chapter, look out for the questions containing the command words 'show (that)' and 'work out'.

Show (that)	provide structured evidence that leads to a given result.
Work out	calculate from given facts, figures or information with or without the use of a calculator.

When an examination question uses the command words 'show that', you need to use the information you are given and demonstrate why a stated result is true. You should write down the evidence and reasons that you are using. These might be facts, formulas or working.

If the question uses the command words 'work out', you should use information given in the question to find the answer. You should still write down all your working and the method that you have used to find the answer.

Try to stay calm when taking exams. When faced with an unfamiliar exam question, try to focus on what you know rather than what you don't know. This may help you answer some of the question, and possibly help you work out what steps you need to take next. And remember to take slow, deep breaths to help you stay calm.

15.1 Scale drawings and 15.2 Bearings

UNDERSTAND THESE TERMS

- Scale
- Bearing

1 A map of a country has a scale of 1 : 1000 000.
Which of the following is true?

   a 1 cm on the map represents an actual distance of 1000 km.

   b 1 cm on the map represents an actual distance of 1 km.

   c 1 cm on the map represents an actual distance of 10 km.

   d 1 cm on the map represents an actual distance of 1000 m.

2 The distance on a map is 5 cm. The actual distance is 200 km.

   a What is the scale?

   b Calculate the distance on the map for an actual distance of 90 km.

   c Calculate the actual distance for a distance on the map of 7.5 cm.

3 Write the three-figure bearing for each compass direction.

   a North-West   **b** South   **c** West   **d** South-West

4

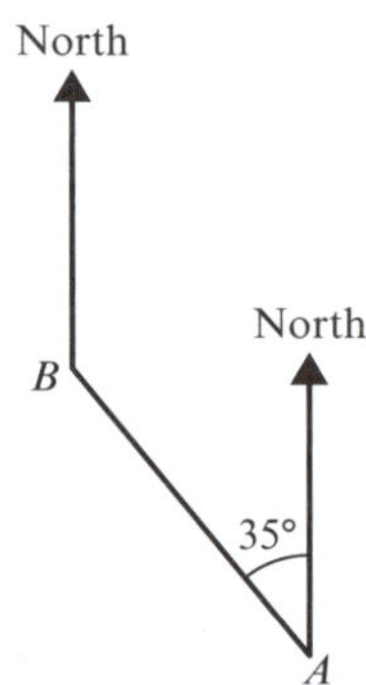

   a What is the bearing of B from A?

   b What is the bearing of A from B?

5 The bearing of town Y from town X is 105°. What is the bearing of town X from town Y?

6 Andy rides his bike from a starting point of a bike trail on a bearing of 050°.
Then he stops at a park.
What is the bearing of the park from his original position?

7 The scale drawing shows two cities, M and N. The scale is 1 centimetre represents 20 kilometres.

   M •————————————• N

   a Work out the actual distance in kilometres.   [1]

   b Another city, P, is 85 km away from M.

      i Work out the length of MP on the scale drawing in centimetres.   [1]

      ii Show that there is more than one possible position for P.   [1]

[Total: 3]

8   A building has a height of 24 metres. A scale drawing of the building
has a height of 16 cm.
Work out the scale used. Give your answer in the form $1:n$. [2]

[Total: 2]

9   The scale drawing shows the position of city H on a map.
The scale is 1 centimetre represents 10 kilometres.

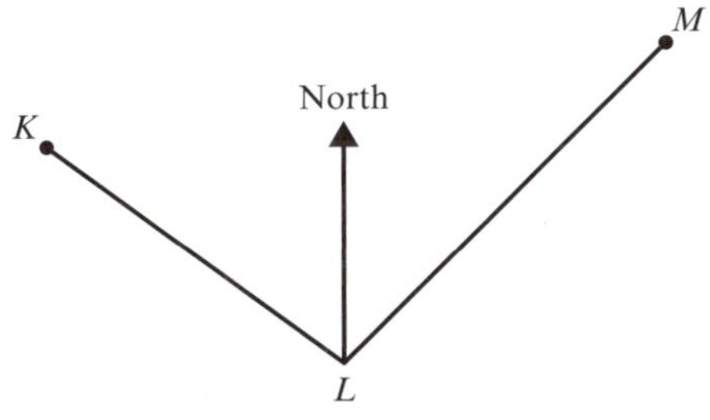

a   Town K is 40 km from city H on a bearing of 125°.
Copy the diagram and mark the position of K on the map. [2]

b   Work out the bearing of city H from town K. [2]

c   Another city L is on a bearing of 215° from city H.
Work out the bearing of city H from city L. [2]

d   The city L is 3 cm from city H on the map.
Mark the position of L on the map. [1]

e   Work out the actual distance between city L and city K. [2]

[Total: 9]

10 K is on a bearing of 292° from L. Angle KLM is 93°.
Show that the bearing of M from L is 025°. [2]

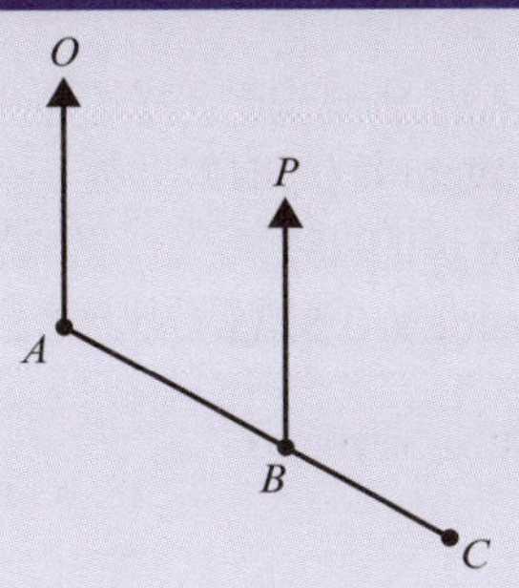

[Total: 2]

《 RECALL AND CONNECT 1 《

Look at the diagram. Lines OA and BP are parallel.

What word describes angle OAB and angle PBC?

Write an algebraic statement to describe how
angle OAB and angle PBC are related.

REFLECTION

Were there any questions you were not sure how to answer? How did you approach these questions?

What did you write down even if you were not able to answer the whole question?

What will you do next time you find a question that you are not sure how to answer?

15.3 Understanding the tangent, cosine and sine ratios and 15.4 Solving problems using trigonometry

UNDERSTAND THESE TERMS

- Opposite
- Adjacent
- Tangent ratio
- Sine ratio
- Cosine ratio
- Inverse function

1   Identify the hypotenuse, opposite side and adjacent side that correspond to angle A of the triangle.

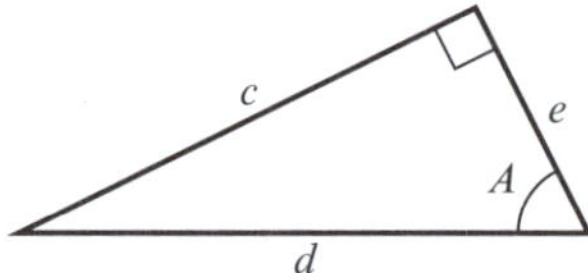

2   The diagram shows a right-angled triangle.

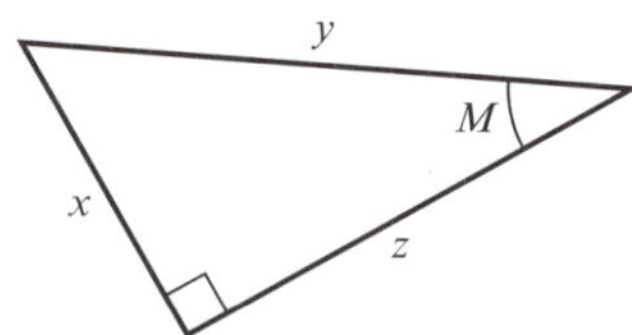

Express the following trigonometric ratios in terms of x, y and z.

a $\tan M$ b $\sin M$ c $\cos M$

3   Find these values. Give your answers to 3 significant figures.

a $\tan 27°$ b $\sin 48°$ c $\cos 86°$

4   Find

a   an acute angle whose tangent is 0.7812

b   an acute angle whose sine is 0.9781

c   an acute angle whose cosine is 0.5735.

5   Find the length of f. Give your answer to 1 decimal place.

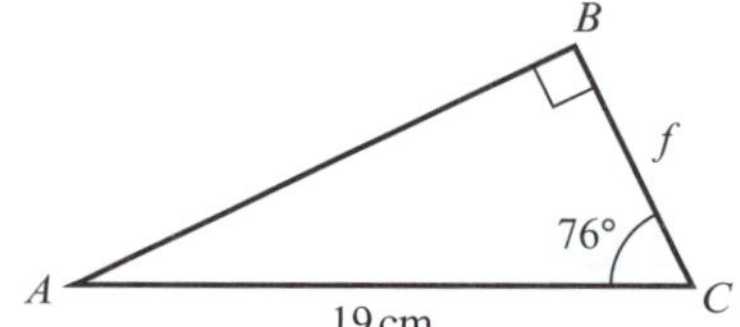

6   Find the angle a. Give your answer to 1 decimal place.

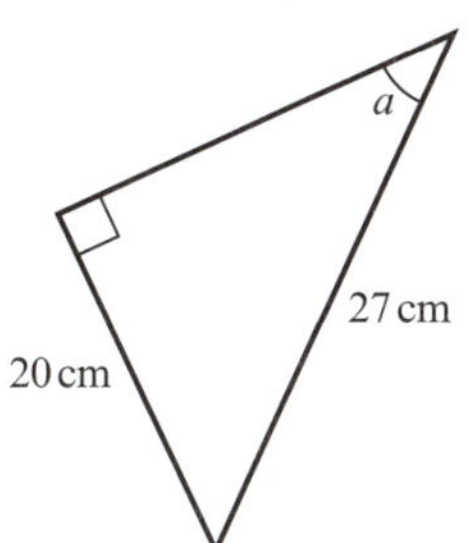

7   The diagram shows a right-angled triangle.
Show that the value of x correct to 3 significant figures is 16.4.   [3]

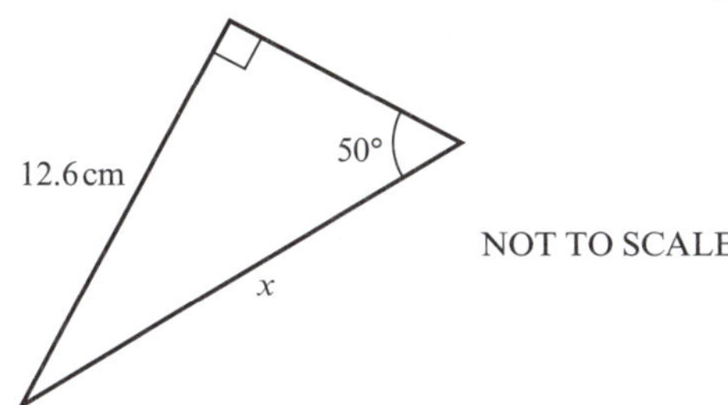

[Total: 3]

8   Amir wants to find the angle a made by a straight line with the x-axis
by drawing a vertical line to form a triangle as shown in the diagram.
Determine angle a, correct to 2 decimal places.   [3]

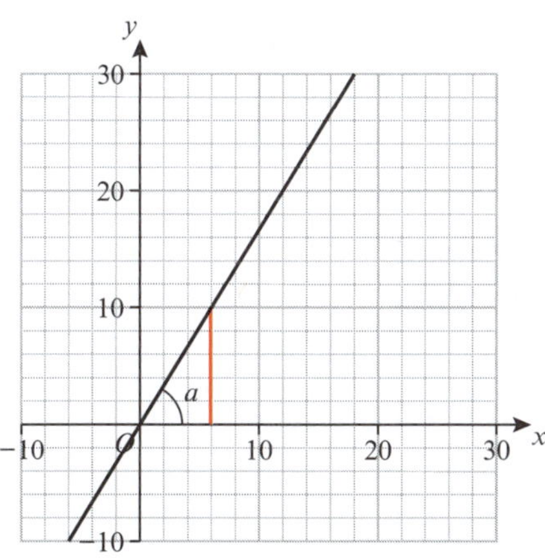

[Total: 3]

9   In a right-angled triangle ABC, the value of $\cos A = \dfrac{7}{25}$.
Show that the value of $\sin A = \dfrac{24}{25}$.   [3]

[Total: 3]

10   Marcella is building a wheelchair ramp. The ramp must be at
an angle of 4.5° to the ground. The ramp will be 15 cm high.
Work out the length of the base of the ramp.
Give your answer to the nearest centimetre.   [3]

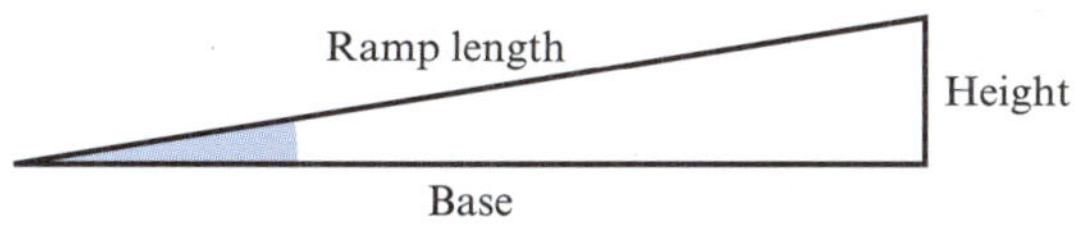

[Total: 3]

11 A flagpole is built on level ground.
The flagpole is 7.5 m high.
One end of a rope is fixed to the top of the flagpole, the other end is fixed
to the ground.
The rope makes an angle of 36° with the top of the flagpole.
Calculate the distance from the bottom of the flagpole to the point where
the rope is fixed to the ground. [2]

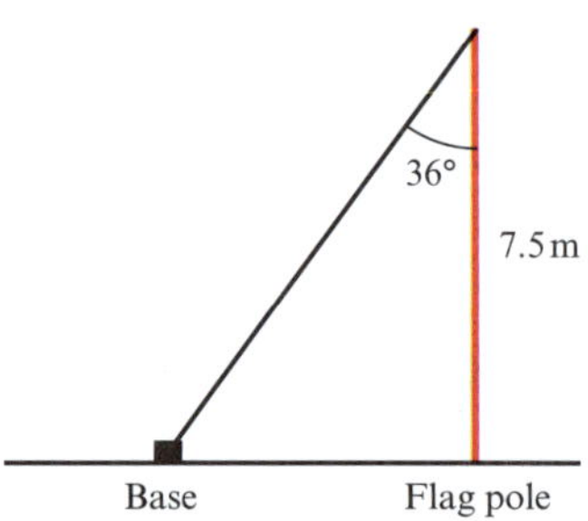

[Total: 2]

12 The diagram shows a bridge with pillars from which cables support
the bridge deck.
Two cables, *TA* and *TB*, are tied from the top of a tower.
Calculate the length of the cable *TB*. [4]

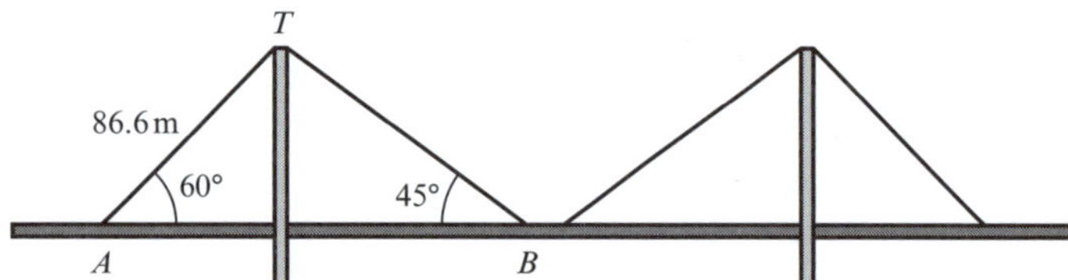

[Total: 4]

≪ RECALL AND CONNECT 2 ≪

ABC is a right-angled triangle. Find the length of *b* to 3 decimal places.

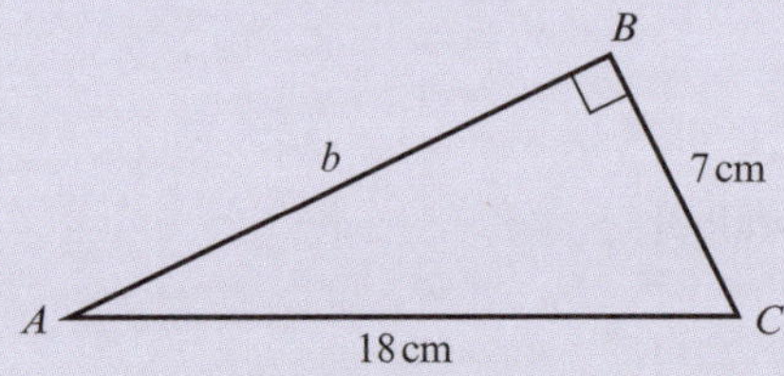

REFLECTION

How do you remember the trigonometric ratios? Would a mnemonic device be
useful to help you remember them?

If you can't remember which formula to use in an exam, try writing down all the
information that you know; it may help you to remember what calculations you
need to do.

SELF-ASSESSMENT CHECKLIST

Let's revisit the Knowledge and Exam skills focus for this chapter.
Decide how confident you are with each statement.

	Now I can	Show it	Needs more work	Almost there	Confident to move on
1	interpret scale drawings	Find a floor plan for a house online. Find the actual sizes of the house based on the scale drawing in the floor plan.			
2	calculate bearings	The bearing of B from A is 127°. Find the bearing of A from B.			
3	calculate sine, cosine and tangent ratios for right-angled triangles	Look at Section 15.3 Question 1. Write the ratios of sine, cosine and tangent of the angle A in terms of c, d and e.			
4	use sine, cosine and tangent ratios to calculate the angles in right-angled triangles	A right-angled triangle ABC has hypotenuse $AC = 15\,cm$ and side $AB = 7\,cm$. Calculate the angle C.			
5	use sine, cosine and tangent ratios to calculate the lengths in right-angled triangles	A right-angled triangle PQR has hypotenuse PR of length 17 cm and angle P is 25°. Calculate the length PQ.			
6	understand the command words 'work out' and answer a 'work out' question	Look through the chapter for the questions that use 'work out'. Write down what you can use from each question to find the answers.			
7	understand the command words 'show (that)' and answer a 'show (that)' question	Look through the chapter for the questions that use 'show (that)'. Write down any rules or evidence you should include in your answer.			
8	manage test anxiety when working on questions.	Write three things you can do to stay calm in an exam.			

16 Scatter diagrams and correlation

When you read an examination question, look carefully at the command word used. It is important to understand what each command word means and what it is asking you to do. In this chapter, look out for the questions containing the command words 'describe' and 'plot'.

Describe	state the points of a topic / give characteristics and main features.
Plot	mark point(s) on a graph.

If you see an exam question that uses the command word 'describe', you will need to write down any important features. Try to use key words when writing your answer. If a question uses the word 'plot', this means that you need to mark points accurately. Be careful when marking the points and make sure that you check the scale to ensure you draw the points in the correct places.

In this chapter, you may be asked to describe features of a scatter diagram or relationships between two data variables. To make sure you write a good answer, you should try to include key words, give reasons by describing what happens to one variable as the other changes, and try to relate your answer to the context of the question.

Whenever you are asked to draw a graph or diagram, it is important to make sure that you include all the main features and labels in your answer. If you need to draw a scatter diagram as part of your answer, make sure that you put the correct variable on each axis, mark the points accurately and include the axis labels. If you need to draw a line of best fit, make sure that you use a ruler and ensure it passes as close to as many points as possible.

16.1 Introduction to bivariate data

1   What are the type and strength of correlation shown by each of these scatter diagrams?

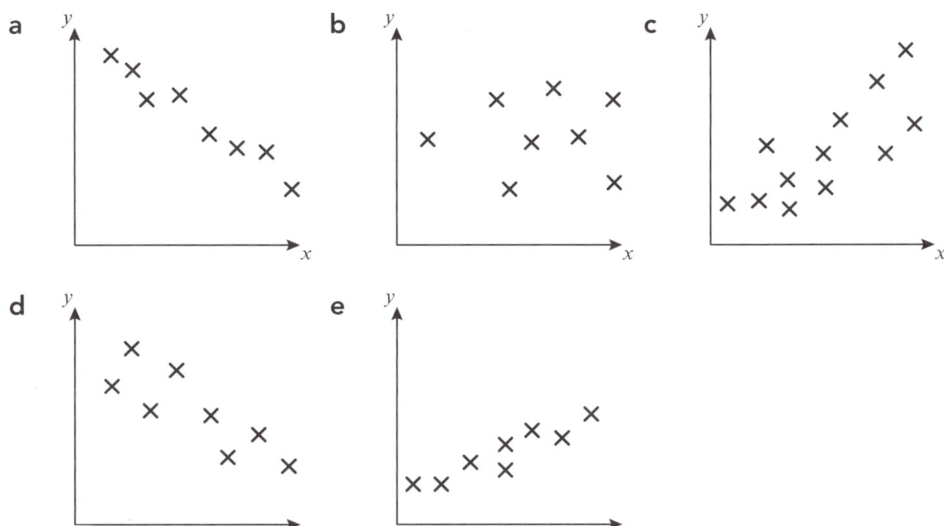

UNDERSTAND THESE TERMS

- Bivariate data
- Correlation
- Scatter diagram
- Negative correlation
- Positive correlation
- Zero correlation
- Dependent variable
- Line of best fit
- Extrapolation

2   The tables show the number of hours spent studying and the exam scores for a group of students.

Hours studied per week	Exam score (%)
1	65
2	55
3	74
4	57
4	60
4	70
5	90
6	65
8	57

Hours studied per week	Exam score (%)
8	69
8	70
9	73
10	78
12	85
14	87
14	88
16	90
18	87

a   Draw a scatter diagram with hours studied per week on the horizontal axis and exam score on the vertical axis.

b   State what type of correlation the diagram shows.

c   Draw a line of best fit.

d Use your line of best fit to estimate the exam score of a student who studied 7 hours per week.

e Use your line of best fit to estimate the number of hours studied per week for a student who received an exam score of 80%.

3 Twelve members of a gym record how many months they have been attending the gym and the amount of mass they are able to lift.

Months attending gym	1	2	3	4	5	6	7	8	9	10	11	12
Total mass able to lift (kg)	1.5	2	4.5	4	7	6.5	9.5	12	9	12	17	14

Use the table of data to decide if each of these statements is true or false.

a The amount of mass able to lift (in kg) is positively correlated with the number of months of regularly attending the gym.

b You cannot estimate the total weight able to lift for 6.5 months because there is no information in the data.

c Based on the trend, someone who attends the gym for 5 years will be able to lift around 72 kg.

4 Ilona records the height, in centimetres, and the arm span, in centimetres, of students in her class. Some of her results are shown in the scatter diagram.

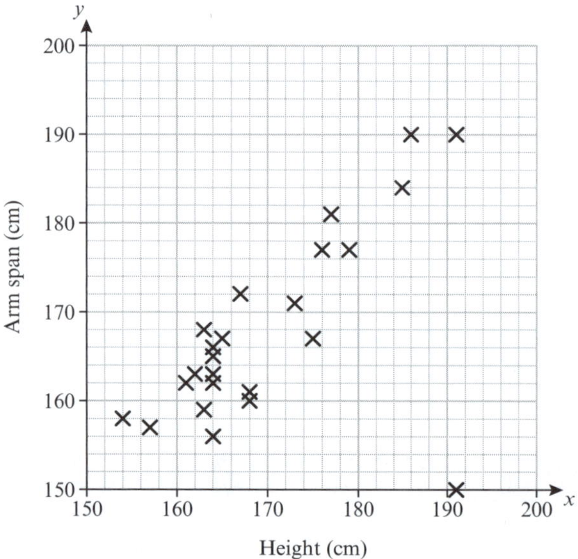

a The table shows two more results.

Height (cm)	166	173
Arm span (cm)	167	172

Plot these points on a copy of the scatter diagram.   [1]

b One student has a height of 186 cm.
Write down the length of that student's arm span.   [1]

c Another student has an arm span of 156 cm.
Write down that student's height.   [1]

d   Aisha says, 'This graph shows that the taller you are, the longer
your arm span will be.'
Do you agree with Aisha's statement?
Give a reason for your answer, referring to the graph.   [1]

e   Describe the correlation between height and arm span.   [1]

f   Draw a line of best fit on the scatter diagram.   [1]

g   Use your line of best fit to estimate the arm span of a student with
height 170 cm.   [1]

[Total: 7]

5   Andra collects data on the masses of cars, in kilograms, and their
fuel efficiency, in kilometres per gallon.

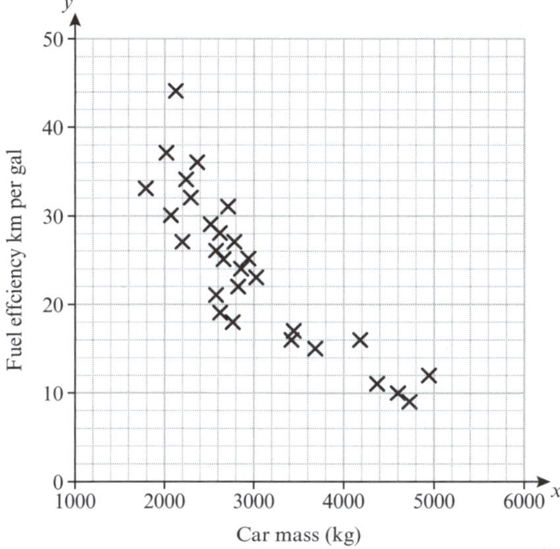

a   Describe the type of correlation between car mass and fuel efficiency.   [2]

b   Draw a line of best fit on a copy of the scatter diagram.   [1]

c   Use your line of best fit to find an estimate for the fuel efficiency of a
car of mass 4000 kg.   [1]

d   Use your line of best fit to find an estimate for the mass of a car with
fuel efficiency of 20 km per gal.   [1]

[Total: 5]

≪ RECALL AND CONNECT 1 ≪

The equation of a line of best fit for a scatter diagram is found to be $y = -3x + 5$.
What are the gradient and y-intercept of this line?

REFLECTION

How well did you answer the questions where you had to draw a scatter
diagram? Was there anything you missed out in your answers?

How well do you think you answered the 'describe' questions?
What information did you include? Was there any information that you
missed out? See if you can go back and improve your answers.

SELF-ASSESSMENT CHECKLIST

Let's revisit the Knowledge and Exam skills focus for this chapter.
Decide how confident you are with each statement.

	Now I can	Show it	Needs more work	Almost there	Confident to move on
1	draw scatter diagrams for bivariate data	Use the data from Section 16.1 Question 3 to draw a scatter diagram.			
2	identify whether or not there is a positive or negative correlation between two variables	Draw a diagram to illustrate what positive, negative and no correlation look like on a scatter diagram.			
3	decide whether a correlation is strong or weak	Collect data of students in your class on their shoe sizes and their height. Create a scatter diagram and describe the strength of the correlation.			
4	draw a line of best fit	Draw a scatter diagram with at least ten points and swap with a partner. Draw a line of best fit on your partner's diagram.			
5	decide how reliable predictions are	Look at the data in Section 16.1 Question 5. How reliable would it be to use the line of best fit to estimate the fuel efficiency for a vehicle of mass 6500 kg?			
6	understand the command word 'describe' and answer a 'describe' question	What should you include in your answer when a scatter diagram question asks you to describe the relationship between two variables?			
7	understand the command word 'plot' and answer a 'plot' question	How accurate do you need to be when plotting points on a graph?			
8	provide a good answer to an exam question.	Create a checklist of the main features of a scatter diagram and a line of best fit.			

Exam practice 4

This section contains past paper questions from previous Cambridge exams, which draw together your knowledge on a range of topics that you have covered up to this point. These questions give you the opportunity to test your knowledge and understanding.

The following question has an example student response and commentary provided. Work through the question first, then compare your answer to the sample response and commentary. Are your answers different to the sample responses?

1 **a** Sophie gets on a bus at 10 47 and she gets off the bus 36 minutes later.
Work out the time she gets off the bus. [1]

  b A television costs \$840 in the USA.
The same television costs 3549 ringgits in Malaysia.
The exchange rate is \$1 = 4.2 ringgits.
In which country is the television cheaper and by how many dollars? [2]

Cambridge IGCSE Mathematics (0580) Paper 32 Q1b, f, November 2024 **[Total: 3]**

Example student response	Commentary
a 10 11	This student has subtracted 36 minutes from 10 47 instead of adding 36 minutes. ***This answer scores 0 out of 1 mark.***
b \$840 × 4.2 = 3528 3549 − 3528 = 21 ringgits	The student has worked out the cost of the television in the USA in ringgits and has found the difference in the two prices. They have not stated which country the television is cheaper in, and they have not given the difference in price in dollars. ***This answer scores 0 out of 2 marks.***

The following question has an example student response and commentary provided. Work through the question first, then compare your answer to the sample response and commentary. Are your answers different to the sample responses?

2 **a** Write 5.26 pm using the 24-hour clock. [1]

  b A journey starts at 21 15 one day and ends at 04 33 the next day.
Calculate the time taken, in hours and minutes. [1]

  c Change 10 260 seconds into hours. [2]

Cambridge IGCSE Mathematics (0580) Paper 12 Q7, March 2022 **[Total: 4]**

Example student response	Commentary
a 17 26	This is the correct answer. **This answer scores 1 out of 1 mark.**
b 7 h 48 min	The student has worked out the number of whole hours correctly, but then they have added 15 to 33 instead of subtracting. **This answer scores 0 out of 1 mark.**
c 10 620 ÷ 60 = 171 hours	The student has correctly divided the number of seconds by 60, but has not realised that this would only give the number of minutes, not the number of hours. This would score 1 mark. To score the second mark they would need to convert the number of minutes into hours. **This answer scores 1 out of 2 marks.**

Here is a similar question that you should attempt. Use the information from the previous response and commentary to guide you as you answer.

3   A plane leaves Sydney at 21 48 local time to fly to Johannesburg.
    The flight takes 14 hours 15 minutes.
    The local time in Sydney is 8 hours ahead of the local time in Johannesburg.
    Find the local time in Johannesburg when the plane arrives.   [3]

Cambridge IGCSE Mathematics (0580) Paper 32 Q3b(i), June 2023   **[Total: 3]**

The following question has an example student response and commentary provided. Work through the question first, then compare your answer to the sample response and commentary. Are your answers different to the sample responses?

4   Victoria buys 5 cups of tea and 4 cakes for $15.69.
    Isabella buys 3 cups of tea and 7 cakes for $17.97.

    Write down a pair of simultaneous equations and solve them to find the
    cost of one cup of tea and the cost of one cake.
    You must show all your working.   [6]

Cambridge IGCSE Mathematics (0580) Paper 32 Q6d, November 2023   **[Total: 6]**

Example student response	Commentary
$5t + 4c = 15.69$ $3t + 7c = 17.97$	This student has written a correct pair of simultaneous equations. **This would score 2 marks.**
$15t + 12c = 15.69$ $15t + 35c = 89.85$	They have then attempted to make the coefficients equal, but they have made a mistake and have forgotten to multiply the right-hand side of one of the equations. **This would score 0 marks.**
$23c = 74.16$ $c = 3.22$	The student has used the correct method to eliminate a variable, but the value for c is incorrect due to their earlier mistake. **Since the method is correct, they would score 1 mark.**
$5t + 4(3.22) = 15.69$ $5t = 2.81$ $t = 0.56$ cake: \$3.22, tea: \$0.56	The student then has followed a correct method to find the value of t. Because of their previous mistake, their final answers are incorrect. **This answer scores 3 out of 6 marks.**

Here is a similar question that you should attempt. Use the information from the previous response and commentary to guide you as you answer.

5 In this part, all angles are in degrees.

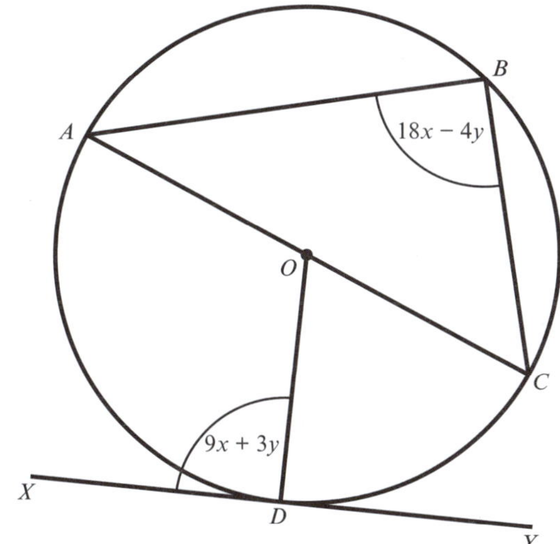

A, B, C and D lie on a circle, centre O, diameter AC.
XY is a tangent to the circle at D.

a Use the information in the diagram to complete these two simultaneous equations.

$9x + 3y =$ ....
$18x − 4y =$ .... [2]

b Solve your simultaneous equations.
You must show all your working. [3]

Cambridge IGCSE Mathematics (0580) Paper 32 Q4c, March 2022 [Total: 5]

The following question has an example student response and commentary provided. Work through the question first, then compare your answer to the sample response and commentary. Are your answers different to the sample responses?

6   The scale drawing shows the positions of three towns R, S and T, on a map.
RS and ST are straight roads between the towns.
The scale is 1 centimetre represents 8 kilometres. [Use Figure 5 on the Past Paper Practice Questions Resource Sheet.]

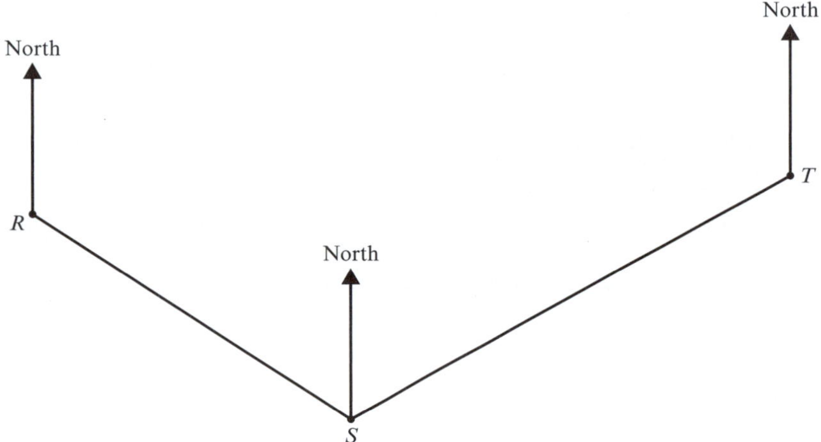

Scale: 1 cm to 8 km

a   Work out the actual distance between R and S. [2]

b   Another town, V, is on a bearing of 163° from R and on a bearing of 215° from T. Mark the position of V on the map. [2]

c   A man cycles at a constant speed of 24 km/h along the straight road from S to T.
After 1 hour and 50 minutes he stops at a café, C.
Mark the position of C on the map.
You must show your working. [3]

d   A hotel, H, is on a bearing of 321° from R.
Work out the bearing of R from H. [2]

e   Write the scale 1 cm to 8 km in the form 1 : n. [1]

Cambridge IGCSE Mathematics (0580) Paper 32 Q7, March 2023   **[Total: 10]**

Example student response	Commentary
a 6	The student has measured the distance between R and S on the diagram correctly, but they have not used the scale to find the actual distance. ***This answer scores 1 out of 2 marks.***
b 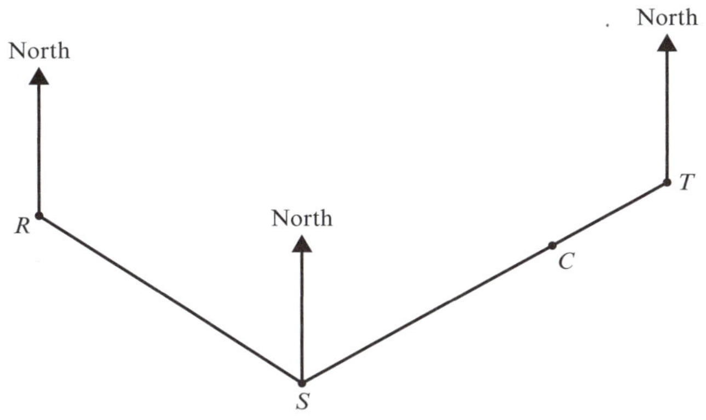 North North North R S C T	This student has drawn the bearing of V from R incorrectly. ***This answer scores 0 out of 2 marks.***
c time: 1 hour 50 minutes = 1.8333… h distance = 24 km/h × 1.8333… h = 44 km scaled distance: $\frac{44}{8}$ = 5.5 cm 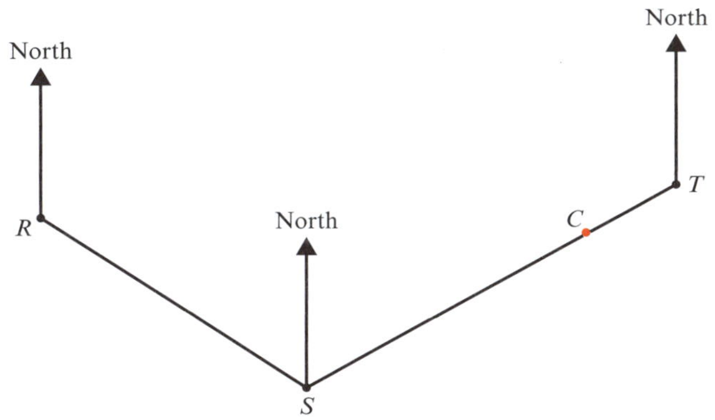 North North North R S C T	The student has converted the time into hours correctly, used it to find the distance with the speed-distance-time formula, then converted the actual distance to cm. ***This answer scores 3 out of 3 marks.***
d 360 − 321 = 39	The student has used the rules for angles around a point to find the other angle at R, but this is not the bearing of R from the hotel. They may have realised this if they had used a sketch. ***This answer scores 0 out of 2 marks.***
e 1 : 8000	The student has converted 8 km to metres, not to centimetres. ***This answer scores 0 out of 1 mark.***

The following question has an example student response and commentary provided. Work through the question first, then compare your answer to the sample response and commentary. Are your answers different to the sample responses?

7 Fidel gives different amounts of water to some plants.
The scatter diagram shows the height (cm) and the amount of water (ml) for each of 15 plants.

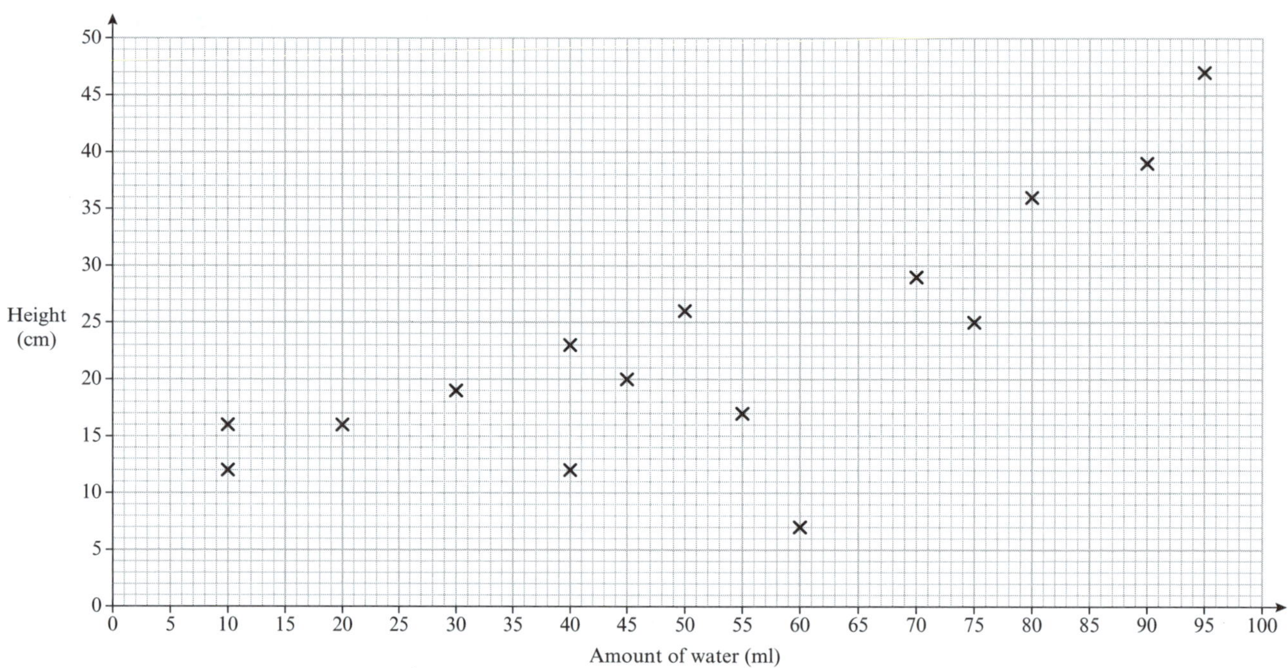

a Plot these two results on the scatter diagram. [Use Figure 6 on the Past Paper Practice Questions Resource Sheet.]   [1]

Amount of water (ml)	60	85
Height (cm)	27	41

b What type of correlation is shown in the scatter diagram?   [1]

c One of the plants had a lower height than expected for the amount of water given.
On the scatter diagram, put a ring around the point for this plant.   [1]

d **i**   On the scatter diagram, draw a line of best fit.   [1]

   ii   Another plant is given 65 ml of water.
   Use your line of best fit to estimate the height of this plant.   [1]

Cambridge IGCSE Mathematics (0580) Paper 32 Q4a–d, June 2023   **[Total: 5]**

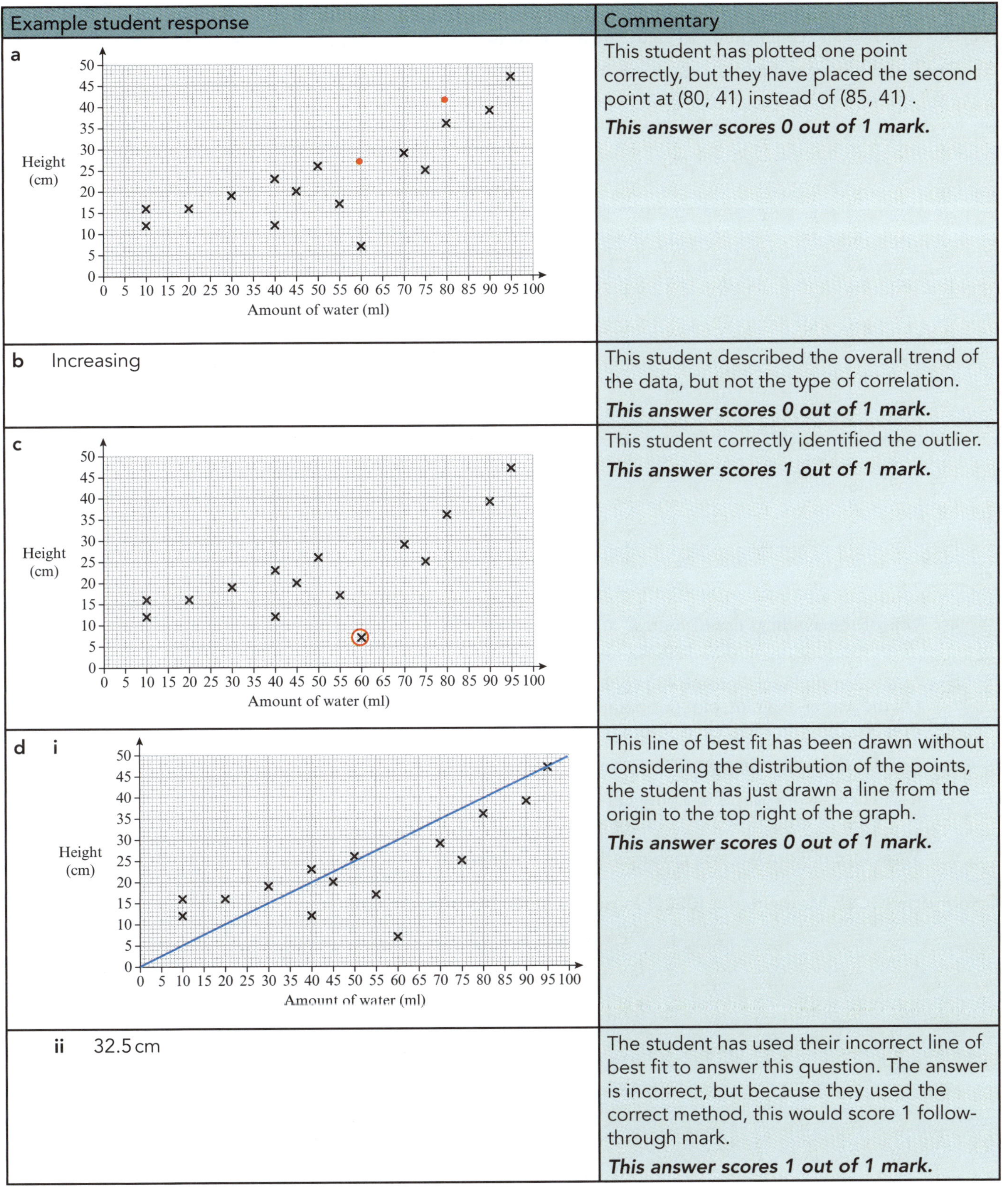

Example student response	Commentary
a	This student has plotted one point correctly, but they have placed the second point at (80, 41) instead of (85, 41) . **This answer scores 0 out of 1 mark.**
b Increasing	This student described the overall trend of the data, but not the type of correlation. **This answer scores 0 out of 1 mark.**
c	This student correctly identified the outlier. **This answer scores 1 out of 1 mark.**
d i	This line of best fit has been drawn without considering the distribution of the points, the student has just drawn a line from the origin to the top right of the graph. **This answer scores 0 out of 1 mark.**
ii 32.5 cm	The student has used their incorrect line of best fit to answer this question. The answer is incorrect, but because they used the correct method, this would score 1 follow-through mark. **This answer scores 1 out of 1 mark.**

Here is a similar question that you should attempt. Use the information from the previous response and commentary to guide you as you answer.

8 The scatter diagram shows the number of rooms and the number of people in each of eight buildings.

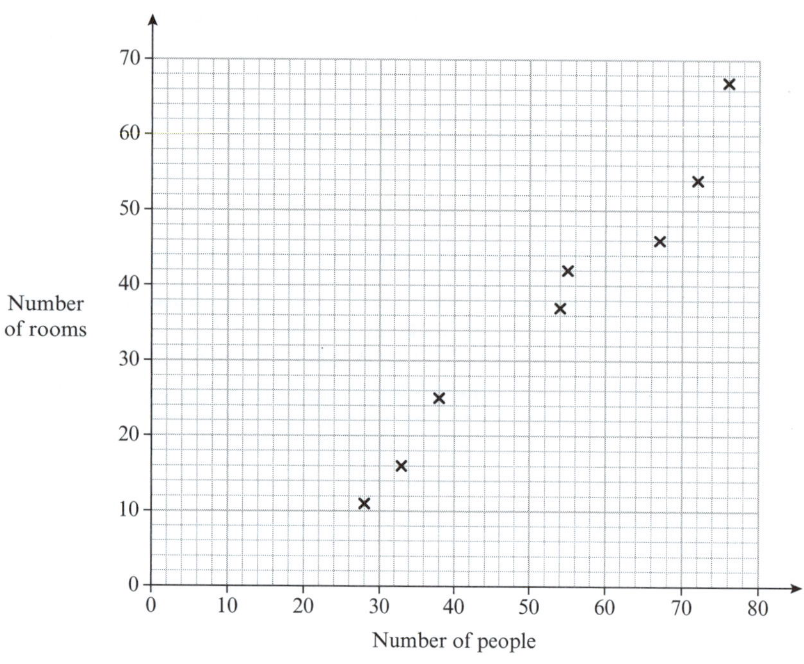

a One of the buildings has 67 rooms.
Write down the number of people in this building. [1]

b In another building there are 42 people and 33 rooms.
On the scatter diagram, plot this point. [Use Figure 7 on the Past Paper Practice Questions Resource Sheet.] [1]

c **i** On the scatter diagram, draw a line of best fit. [1]

ii There are 45 people in a different building.
Find an estimate for the number of rooms in this building. [1]

d What type of correlation is shown in the scatter diagram? [1]

Cambridge IGCSE Mathematics (0580) Paper 12 Q13, November 2024 [Total: 5]

17 Managing money

When you read an examination question, look carefully at the command word used. It is important to understand what each command word means and what it is asking you to do. In this chapter, look out for the questions containing the command words 'calculate' and 'determine'.

| Calculate | work out from given facts, figures or information. |
| Determine | establish with certainty. |

When an examination question uses the command word 'determine', it is asking that you to give an answer with certainty. This means that you should give reasons for your answer or show the method that you are using, even if you have used a calculator. If the question uses the command word 'calculate', you should use information and values that have been provided in the question to find the answer.

Build confidence working without a calculator by practising common non-calculator percentage methods. For example, when working with percentages, you could use written methods such as finding 10% and 1%, and use the results to calculate other values. As you work through this chapter, try answering the questions without a calculator and find methods that work for you.

17.1 Earning money

1 Find the total amount each person earned.

   a Hamish worked 15 hours at a rate of $6 per hour.

   b Anjali worked 12 hours at a rate of $8.50 per hour.

   c Keira worked for 25 hours at a rate of $7.75 per hour.

   d Zuri worked for 35 hours at a rate of $10.50 per hour.

2 Different employees of a company are paid the same amount each hour. Find each person's hourly rate of pay.

   a Toby earned $91 for 7 hours of work.

   b Dejen earned $375 for 15 hours of work.

   c Mei earned $825 for 22 hours of work.

   d Reina earned $243.75 for 25 hours of work.

3 The table shows the amounts paid to four employees before tax. The table also shows the tax paid and other deductions (which could include pension contributions).

Find the amount that each employee keeps after paying for tax and any other deductions they have.

	Employee	Amount earned before tax ($)	Tax paid ($)	Other deductions ($)
a	R Abbas	743.50	133.83	57.59
b	S Choi	1479.25	266.27	126.41
c	A Dai	837.75	150.80	87.95
d	M Rami	1032.50	185.85	189.73

4 Find each amount of tax.

   a 20% tax on $1500   **b** 15% tax on $12 000

   c 28% tax on $24 000   **d** 33% tax on $57 500

5 Turab works as a sales representative for a company that sells motorbikes.

He is paid $450 a week plus a commission of 2.5% of his sales.

   a He makes $90 000 in sales one week. Calculate the amount he earns that week.   [2]

   b Over the next four weeks he makes $350 000 in sales. Calculate the amount Turab earns.   [2]

[Total: 4]

6   Use the table to answer the questions.

Taxable income	Income tax payable
$0–8375	10% of the amount over $0
$8375–34 000	$837.50 plus 15% of the amount over $8375
$34 000–82 400	$4681.25 plus 25% of the amount over $34 000
$82 400–171 850	$16 781.25 plus 28% of the amount over $82 400
$171 850–373 650	$41 827.25 plus 33% of the amount over $171 850
$373 650+	$108 421.25 plus 35% of the amount over $373 650

Determine the income tax payable for a person earning

a $50 000 [2]

b $300 000 [2]

[Total: 4]

7   Rahul's standard hourly rate of pay is $10.50.
Rahul is paid 1.5 times his standard rate for every hour he works
on a Saturday and a Sunday.

Last week Rahul worked 33 hours in total from Monday to Friday.
On Saturday, Rahul worked from 15:00 to 21:00. On Sunday,
Rahul did not work.
Calculate Rahul's earnings. [3]

[Total: 3]

« RECALL AND CONNECT 1 «

The list shows Sairah's weekly earnings in dollars, $, for the last 8 weeks.

785.50, 687.50, 375, 537.25, 775, 650.50, 825, 735.75

Calculate Sairah's mean weekly wage.

REFLECTION

Have you ever had to carry out money calculations in your own life?
What methods did you use? Are they the same methods as you used in
these questions?

Are there any techniques you wish you had known before for doing calculations
outside of school?

UNDERSTAND THESE TERMS

- Simple interest
- Compound interest
- Principal
- Interest rate

17.2 Borrowing and investing money

1   Write the formula for simple interest. Define the variables that you used.

2   Write the formula for compound interest. Define the variables that you used.

3 For each investment, calculate
  i the simple interest
  ii the final value.

  a $200 invested at a rate of 5% for 6 years

  b $3000 invested at a rate of 3% for 5 years

  c $1200 invested at a rate of 3.5% for 4 years

  d $5000 invested at a rate of 1.5% for 7 years

4 These investments have compound interest applied.
For each investment, find
  i the value of each investment after the given time
  ii the interest earned.

  a $200 invested at a rate of 5% for 6 years

  b $3000 invested at a rate of 3% for 5 years

  c $1200 invested at a rate of 3.5% for 4 years

  d $5000 invested at a rate of 1.5% for 7 years

5 David is buying a laptop. The laptop costs $4600.
He pays for the laptop in instalments.
He pays a 25% deposit.
He pays interest of 8% on the remaining amount divided into 12 equal
monthly instalments.
Work out how much David pays each month. [3]

[Total: 3]

6 Han opens a bank account and deposits $20 000.
The account pays 3.5% simple interest each year.
How much is in the account after 12 years? [3]

[Total: 3]

7 Leena takes out a business loan of $70 000 with a compound interest rate of
6% over 5 years.
Calculate the total amount Leena repays after 5 years. [3]

[Total: 3]

8 Karina puts $8000 into a savings account.
The savings account pays compound interest.
The interest rate is 3.2%.

  a How much is in Karina's account after 5 years? [2]

  b Logan also puts his $8000 into savings account.
  Logan's account pays simple interest.
  After 5 years he has $9000.
  What was the interest rate of his account? [3]

[Total: 5]

17.3 Buying and selling

UNDERSTAND THESE TERMS

- Profit
- Loss
- Cost price
- Selling price
- Discount

1 **a** Write a formula for finding percentage profit.

b Write a formula for finding percentage loss.

2 Increase

a $150 by 4%   **b** $250 by 6%

c $1200 by 2.5%   **d** $3200 by 1.5%

3 Decrease

a $150 by 6%   **b** $250 by 5%

c $2400 by 12%   **d** $4200 by 7.5%

4 What was the percentage change in each case?

a Original price $25, final price $30

b Original price $25, final price $20

c Original price $55, final price $62.75

d Original price $90, final price $63

5 Marco bought a car for $18 000. He sold it 2 years later for $13 500.
What was the percentage loss?   [2]

[Total: 2]

6 Faith bought a chair for $10 at a market. She spent $15 more to
renovate the chair. After renovating it, Faith sold the chair for $85.
Calculate her percentage profit.   [3]

[Total: 3]

7 A café gives students a discount of 15% off the price of drinks.
The café does not give a discount on food.
Bhavia uses her student discount to buy a coffee worth $3.50
and a pastry worth $1.75 from the café.
How much does Bhavia pay in total using her discount?   [3]

[Total: 3]

8 Gianni sells pizza by the slice. The total cost to make each pizza is $2.70.
Each slice is one sixth of a whole pizza. He sells each slice for $2.50.
What is Gianni's percentage profit?   [3]

[Total: 3]

« RECALL AND CONNECT 3 «

Convert the fractions to percentages.

a $\dfrac{3}{5}$ b $\dfrac{3}{8}$ c $\dfrac{27}{20}$ d $2\dfrac{17}{40}$

REFLECTION

Have you tried answering the questions without a calculator? What methods have you used?

Are there some methods you prefer to others?

Have you found non-calculator methods for other topics?

SELF-ASSESSMENT CHECKLIST

Let's revisit the Knowledge and Exam skills focus for this chapter.
Decide how confident you are with each statement.

	Now I can	Show it	Needs more work	Almost there	Confident to move on
1	solve problems involving earnings	Tom earns $300 per week plus 2% on all the sales he makes. How much does Tom earn in a week where he sells $550 worth of products?			
2	calculate earnings after tax	Look up the income tax rate for a country of your choosing. Calculate each amount earned after tax is paid. a $50 000 b $35 000 c $84 000			
3	calculate simple interest	Calculate the value of a $4000 investment after 3 years at a rate of 2.5% per year simple interest.			
4	use the simple interest formula to calculate the principal amount, rate of interest and time period of a debt or investment	Use the simple interest formula to write a formula to calculate a the interest rate b the time period.			

CONTINUED

	Now I can	Show it	Needs more work	Almost there	Confident to move on
5	solve problems related to finance payments and amounts	Sam buys a laptop costing $2500. She pays a $300 deposit. She pays the remainder in monthly instalments. She pays interest of 8% on the remaining amount divided into 12 equal monthly instalments. Find the value of each instalment.			
6	calculate compound interest over a given time period	Zayd borrows $15 000 at a compound interest rate of 4.5% per year for 5 years. How much does Zayd repay?			
7	calculate the percentage profit or loss using given rates and prices	Find the percentage profit for an item bought for $58 and sold for $84.			
8	calculate the selling price or mark-up	Richard buys a phone for $899 and later sells it for a 30% loss. What was the selling price?			
9	understand the command words 'calculate' and 'determine'	Write down the differences between the command words 'calculate' and 'determine'.			
10	answer money questions without a calculator.	Pick four different numbers and, without using a calculator, work out **a** 70% **b** 15% **c** 48% of your numbers.			

18 Curved graphs

In this chapter you will answer questions on:

- constructing tables of values to draw quadratic graphs (parabolas)
- sketching quadratic graphs
- constructing tables of values to draw reciprocal graphs (hyperbolas)
- using graphs to solve quadratic equations.

In this chapter you will:

- show that you understand the command words 'plot' and 'sketch' and can answer 'plot' and 'sketch' questions
- show that you can write a good answer and know what a good answer looks like.

When you read an examination question, look carefully at the command word used. It is important to understand what each command word means and what it is asking you to do. In this chapter, look out for questions containing the command word 'describe'.

Plot	mark point(s) on a graph.
Sketch	make a simple freehand drawing showing the key features.

When an examination question uses the command word 'plot', you need to mark points clearly on a graph and sometimes join those points with a suitable line or curve. For a 'plot' question, it is important to draw the graph as accurately as possible. You need to ensure that each point is plotted to an accuracy of within half of the smallest grid square.

When you are answering a question that requires you to draw a graph, it is important to make sure you include all key features. You should ensure that the axes are labelled, the points are plotted accurately and, if the graph is a curve, make sure you join the points using a smooth curve. It is a good idea to check that your graph is the correct shape once you have finished.

When an examination question uses the command word 'sketch', it is asking for a simple, freehand drawing that shows the key features. For graphs, the key features are the shape, the places where the line or curve crosses the axes and any turning points. This is different from the 'plot' command word, because 'plot' requires accurate drawings of all points, not just the shape and key points.

18.1 Review of quadratic graphs (the parabola)

<table>
<tr><td>UNDERSTAND THIS TERM</td></tr>
<tr><td>•   Parabola</td></tr>
</table>

1 Copy and complete the following tables of values and plot the graphs on the same set of axes. Use values of -8 to 12 on the y-axis.

a

x	-3	-2	-1	0	1	2	3
$y = x^2 + 2$							

b

x	-3	-2	-1	0	1	2	3
$y = x^2 - 1$							

c

x	-3	-2	-1	0	1	2	3
$y = -x^2 + 6$							

d

x	-3	-2	-1	0	1	2	3
$y = -x^2 + 4$							

2 Match each parabola on the graph to its equation.

a $y = 5 - x^2$

b $y = 3 - x^2$

c $y = 5 + x^2$

d $y = x^2 + 3$

e $y = x^2 - 3$

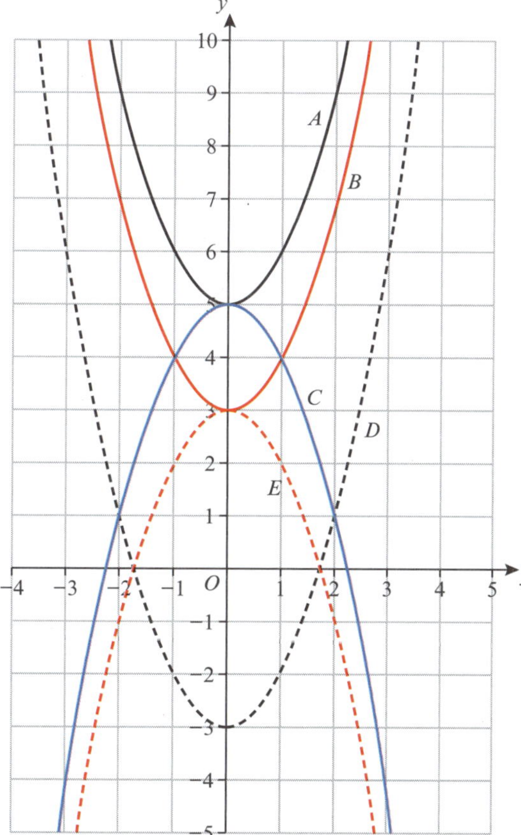

3 Here is the graph of $y = x^2$.

On a copy of the graph, sketch the graphs of

a $y = 2x^2 + 1$

b $y = -4x^2$

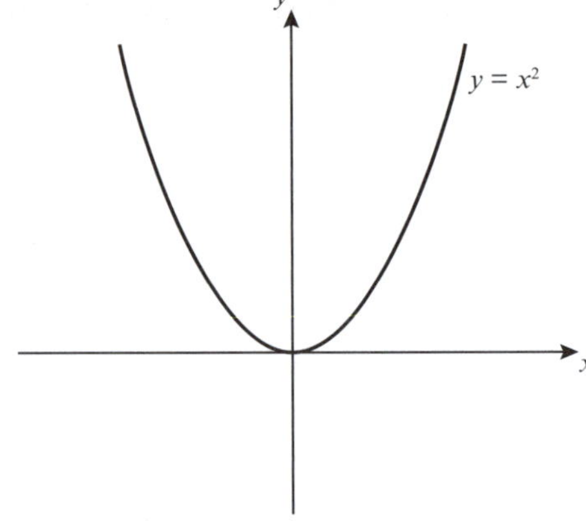

4 **a** Copy and complete this table of values for $y = x^2 - 2x - 5$.

x	−3	−2	−1	0	1	2	3
$y = x^2 - 2x - 5$				−5			−2

[3]

b Use the table of values to plot the graph of $y = x^2 - 2x - 5$, on a copy of the coordinate axes. [4]

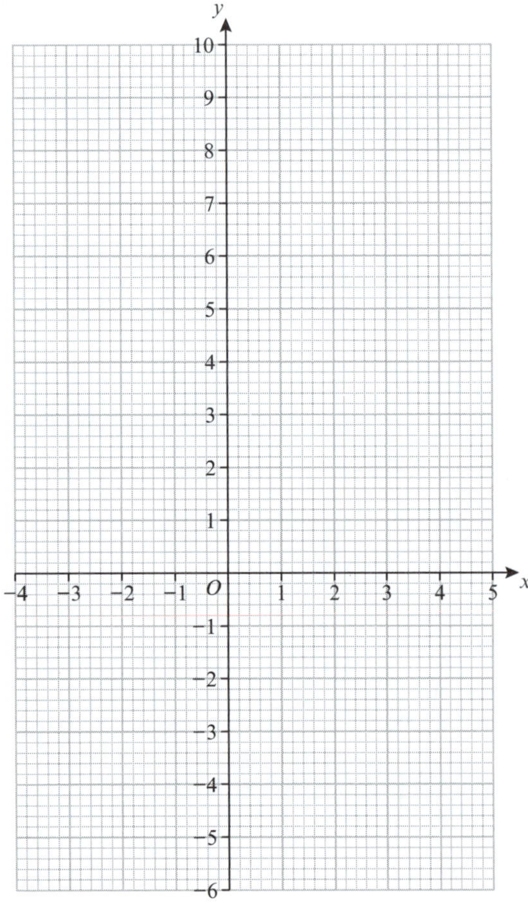

[Total: 7]

5 a Copy and complete this table of values for $y = -x^2 + 4x + 1$.

x	−2	−1	0	1	2	3	4	5	6
$y = -x^2 + 4x + 1$		−4				4	1		

[3]

b Use the table of values to plot the graph of $y = -x^2 + 4x + 1$, on a copy of the coordinate axes.   [4]

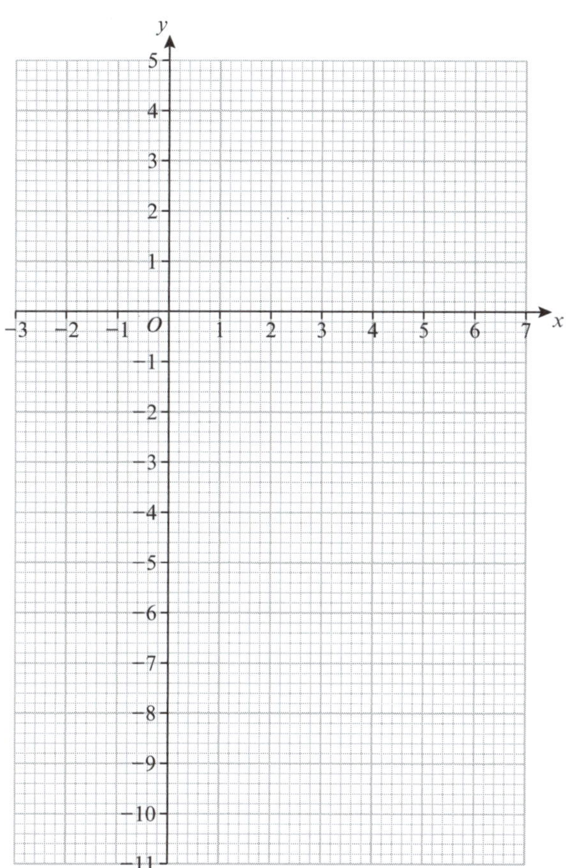

[Total: 7]

≪ RECALL AND CONNECT 1 ≪

a Expand and simplify $(2x + 5)(x - 4)$.

b Expand and simplify $(x + 2)^2$.

c Hence find an expression for $(2x + 5)(x - 4) - (x + 2)^2$.

REFLECTION

Were you able to complete the table for Question 4 without a calculator? Do you know how to use the functions on your calculator to find tables of values?

Are you confident with using the different functions of your calculator? Find out what functions your calculator has and which may help you in the exam.

18.2 Drawing reciprocal graphs (the hyperbola)

1 Copy and complete the following tables of values and plot the graphs on the same set of axes. Use values of −10 to 10 on the y-axis.

a

x	−5	−2	−1	−0.5		0.5	1	2	5
$y = \dfrac{2}{x}$									

b

x	−5	−2	−1	−0.5		0.5	1	2	5
$y = -\dfrac{2}{x}$									

c

x	−5	−2	−1	−0.5		0.5	1	2	5
$y = -\dfrac{4}{x}$									

d

x	−5	−2	−1	−0.5		0.5	1	2	5
$y = \dfrac{4}{x}$									

2 a Copy and complete the table for $y = -\dfrac{7}{x}$, giving values of y correct to 1 decimal place.

x	−8	−5	−2	−1		1	2	5	8
$y = -\dfrac{7}{x}$									

[3]

b Use the table of values to plot the graph of $y = = -\dfrac{7}{x}$, on a copy of the coordinate axes.

[4]

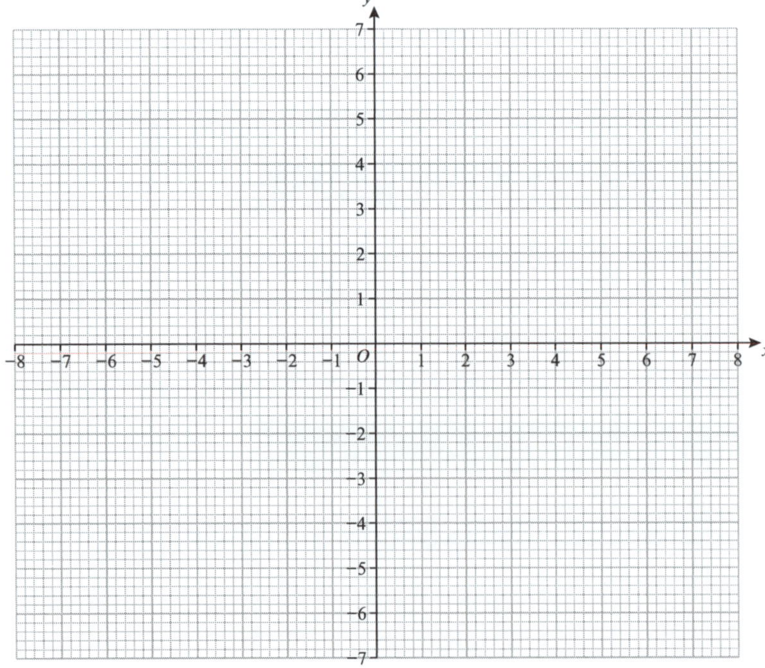

[Total: 7]

18.3 Using graphs to solve quadratic equations

1   The diagram shows the graphs of $y = -x^2 - 2x + 3$, $y = \frac{1}{2}x + 2$ and $y = -x + 1$.

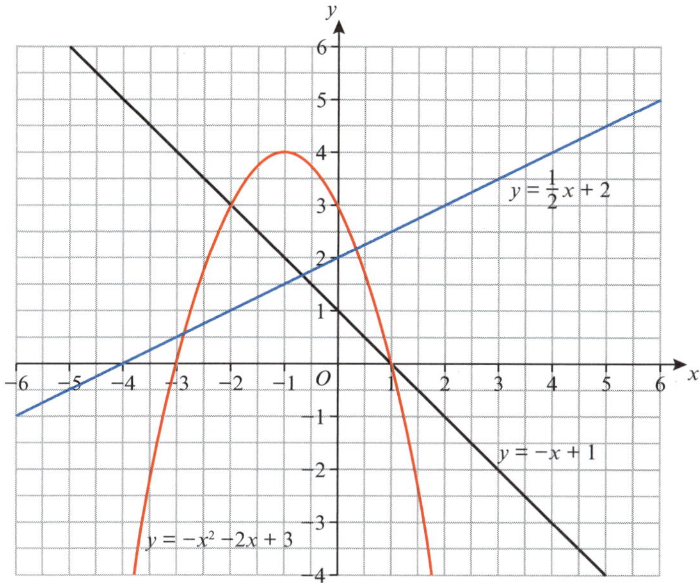

Use the diagram to write down the coordinates where

a $y = -x^2 - 2x + 3$ intersects $y = -x + 1$

b $y = -x^2 - 2x + 3$ intersects $y = \frac{1}{2}x + 2$

c $y = -x^2 - 2x + 3$ intersects the x-axis.

2   For each part, use two of the graphs $y = x^2 + 3x$, $y = -2$ and $y = 5$
to solve the equation.

a $x^2 + 3x = 0$

b $x^2 + 3x = -2$

c $x^2 + 3x = 5$

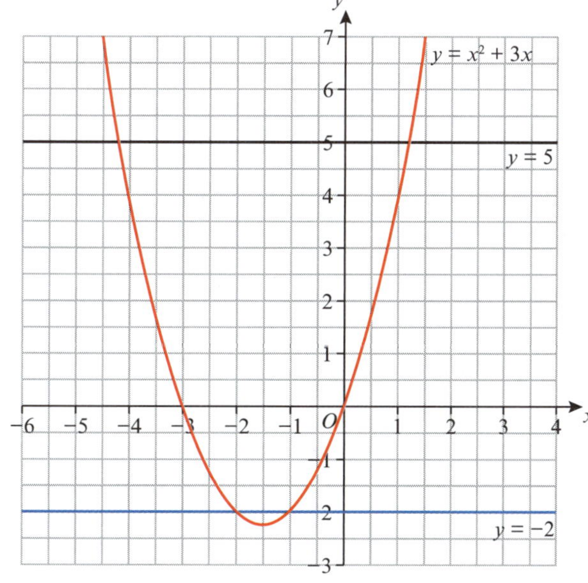

3 The diagram shows the graph of $y = x^2 - 5x + 2$.

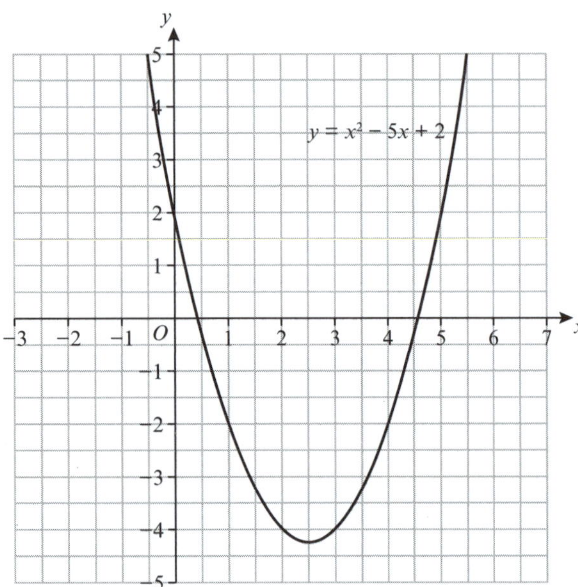

Use the graph to find the solutions of each equation to 1 decimal place.

a $x^2 - 5x + 2 = 0$ [2]

b $x^2 - 5x + 2 = 4$ [2]

c $x^2 - 5x + 2 = -3$ [2]

[Total: 6]

4 **a** Copy and complete the table of values for the equation $y = -x^2 + x + 4$. [2]

x	−3	−2	−1	0	1	2	3	4
y	−8			4				−8

b   Use the table of values to draw the graph of $y = -x^2 + 4x + 1$.
Use the grid provided.   [3]

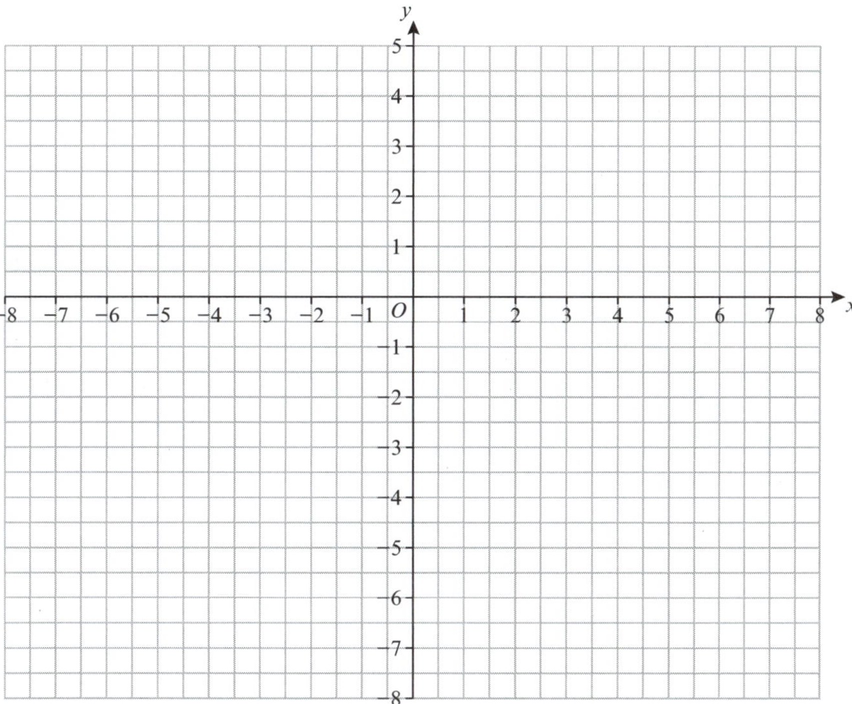

c   Write down the solutions to these equations.
   i $-x^2 + x + 4 = 0$ [2]
   ii $-x^2 + x + 4 = 2$ [2]
   iii $-x^2 + x + 4 = 1.5$ [2]

[Total: 11]

≪ RECALL AND CONNECT 2 ≪

Plot the graph of for $y = -\dfrac{1}{2}x + 3$ on the grid provided.

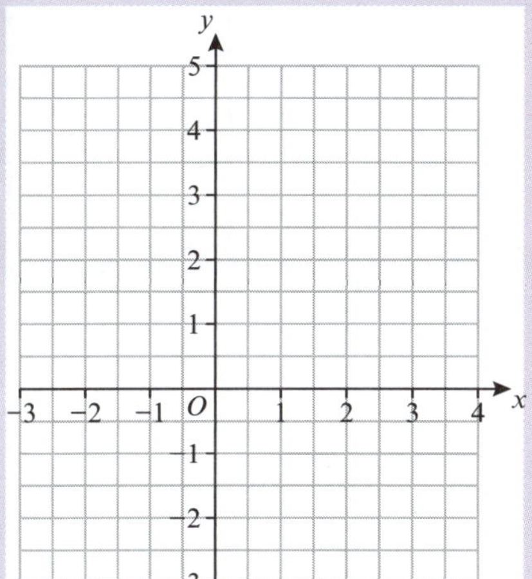

REFLECTION

How can you tell when to join the points on a graph or chart? How do you decide if the points should be joined with a smooth curve or a straight line?

Are you confident when joining the points on a curve freehand?

How could you practise this skill?

SELF-ASSESSMENT CHECKLIST

Let's revisit the Knowledge and Exam skills focus for this chapter.
Decide how confident you are with each statement.

	Now I can	Show it	Needs more work	Almost there	Confident to move on
1	construct a table of values to draw quadratic graphs (parabolas)	Write a quadratic function and swap with a partner. Draw the graph of your partner's quadratic function.			
2	sketch quadratic equations in the form $y = ax^2 + c$	Sketch the graphs of $y = x^2$, $y = -5x^2 - 1$, $y = 3x^2 + 2$.			
3	construct a table of values to draw graphs called hyperbolas	Construct a table of values for $y = \dfrac{3}{x}$ for $-4 \leqslant x \leqslant -1$, and $1 \leqslant x \leqslant 4$, and plot the graph.			
4	use graphs to find the approximate solutions to quadratic equations	List the steps to solve a quadratic equation using a graph.			
5	understand the command word 'plot'	At what level of accuracy should you plot your points to be awarded marks?			
6	understand the command word 'sketch'	Sketch the graphs in Section 18.3 Question 2.			
7	understand what a good answer looks like.	Write a list of rules for plotting a curved graph to ensure all marks are gained in an exam question.			

19 Symmetry

When you read an examination question, look carefully at the command word used. It is important to understand what each command word means and what it is asking you to do. In this chapter, look out for the questions containing the command words 'explain' and 'state'.

Explain	set out purposes or reasons/make the relationships between things clear/say why and/or how and support with relevant evidence.
State	express in clear terms.

When an examination question uses the command word 'explain', it is asking for a detailed response. You should include your reasoning in your answer and support your reasoning with any relevant evidence. If the question uses the command word 'state' then it is asking for a brief direct answer without explanation or detailed working. Be concise and only include the information the question asks for.

When revising for your exams, it can be helpful to look at the mark schemes for lots of different questions. The mark schemes describe how the marks are awarded. For example, a mark scheme for an 'explain' question will show the reasons that you would need to give in your answer. You can use this to help you understand whether you are including enough detail to gain all the marks.

19.1 Symmetry in two dimensions

<table>
<tr><td>

</td><td style="vertical-align:top;">

</td></tr>
</table>

1 Copy the shapes and draw on all the lines of symmetry.

a 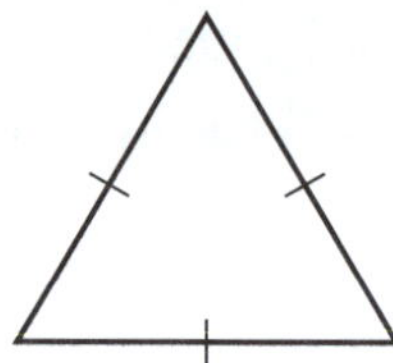   b 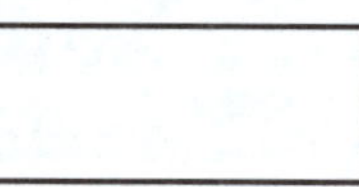

c    d 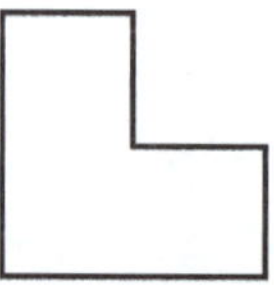

2 Write down the order of rotational symmetry for each shape in Question 1.

3 State the order of rotational symmetry for each shape.

a 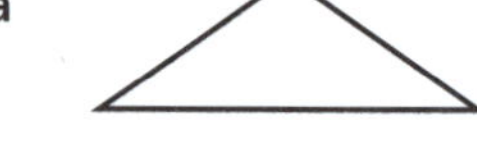

[1]

b 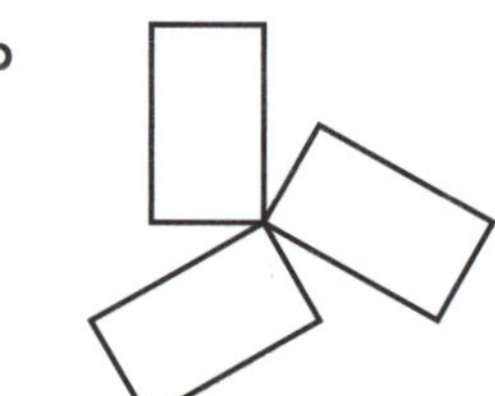

[1]

c 

[1]

d 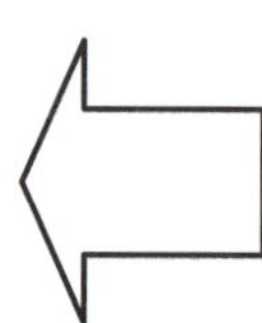

[1]

[Total: 4]

4 A quadrilateral has
- four equal sides
- rotational symmetry of order 4
- four lines of symmetry.

Explain why the quadrilateral cannot be a rhombus. [1]

[Total: 1]

5   Copy the diagram and shade the minimum number of squares so that it has

   a   exactly two lines of symmetry   [2]

   b   rotational symmetry of order 2.   [2]

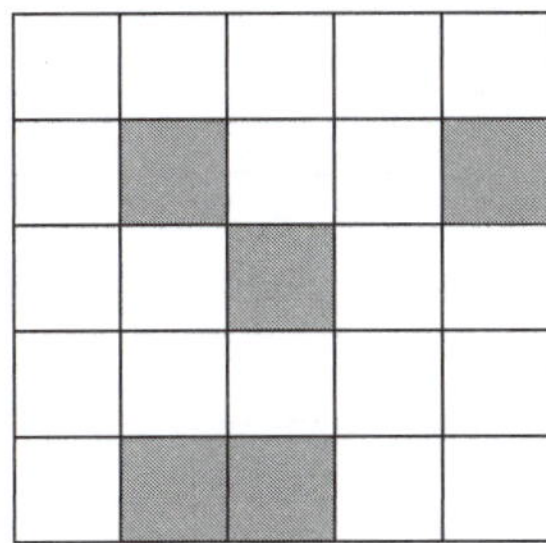

[Total: 4]

≪ RECALL AND CONNECT 1 ≪

Here is the graph of $y = x^2 - 5x$. Write down the equation of the line of symmetry of the graph.

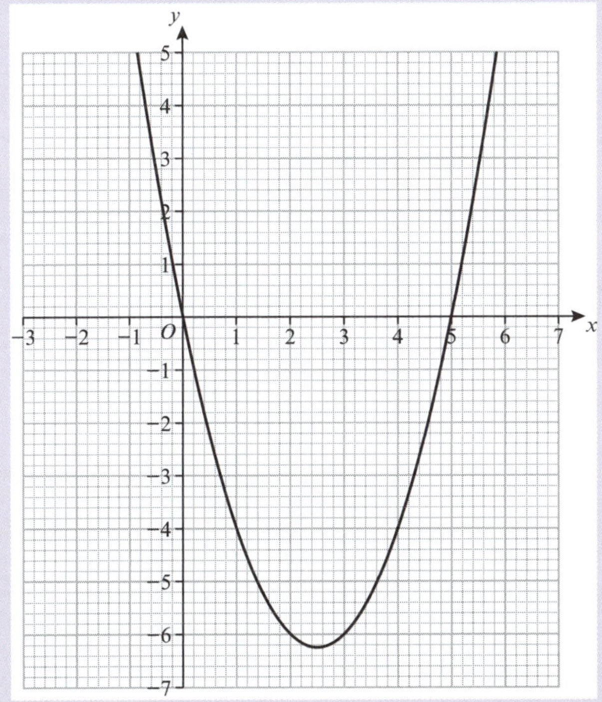

REFLECTION

Symmetry can be seen in lots of places, including in shapes and graphs.

Can you think of other topics that involve symmetry, or where using symmetry can help you solve problems?

19.2 Angle relationships in circles

1 Find the missing angles marked with letters.

a

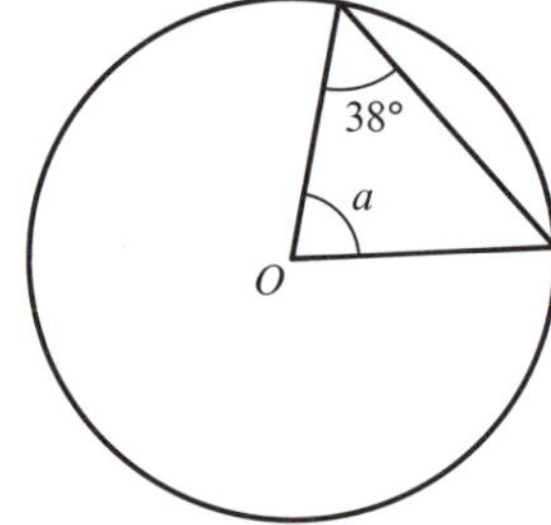

b

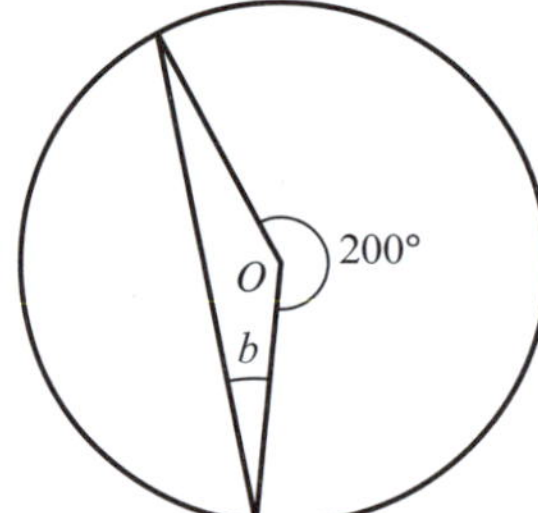

c

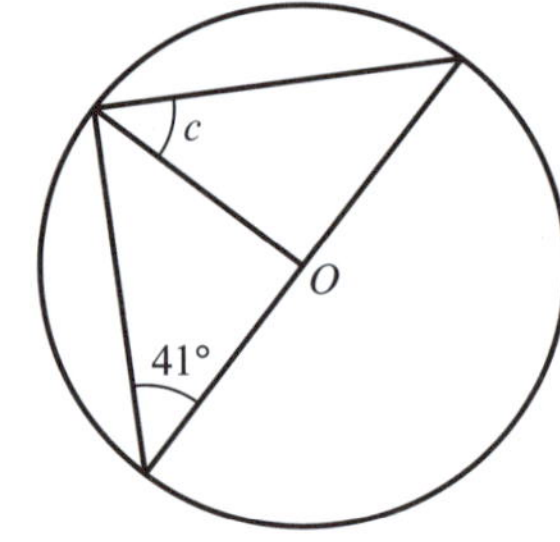

2 Find the missing angles marked with letters.

a

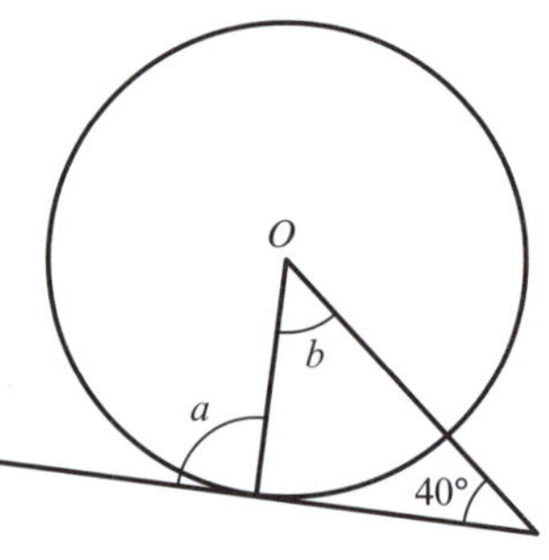

b

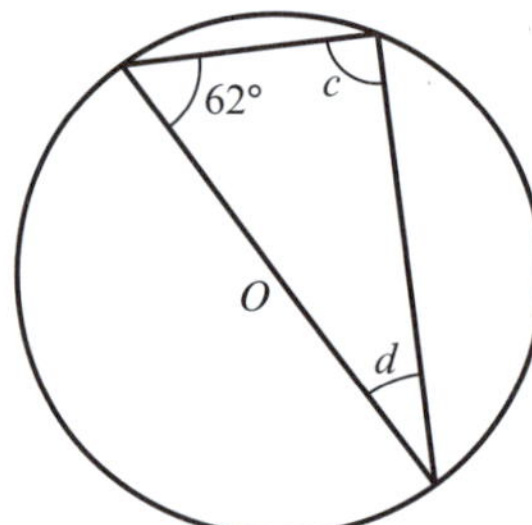

c

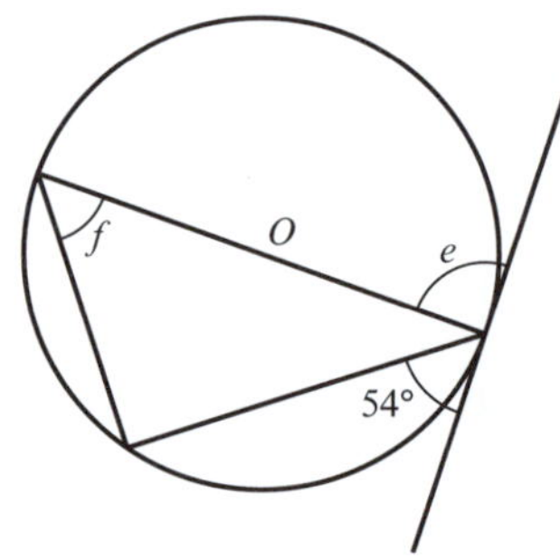

3   The diagram shows a circle centre O and the triangle ABC
where $\angle OAB = 45°$.

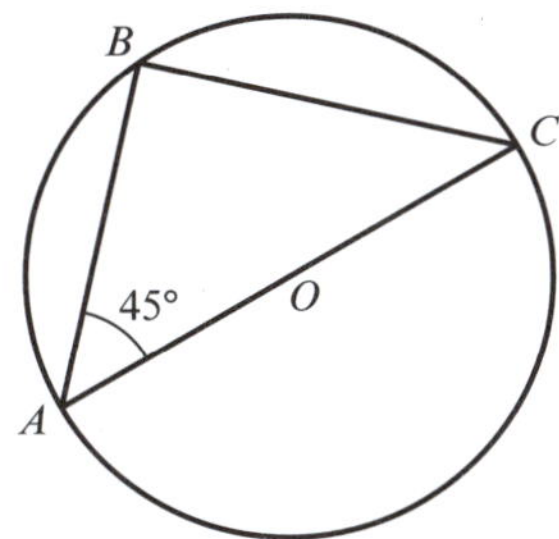

Explain why triangle ABC is isosceles. [2]

[**Total: 2**]

4   The diagram shows a circle centre O.
A and C are points on the circumference of the circle.
The tangent to the circle at A and the tangent to the circle at C intersect at B.

$\angle OCA = 25°$.

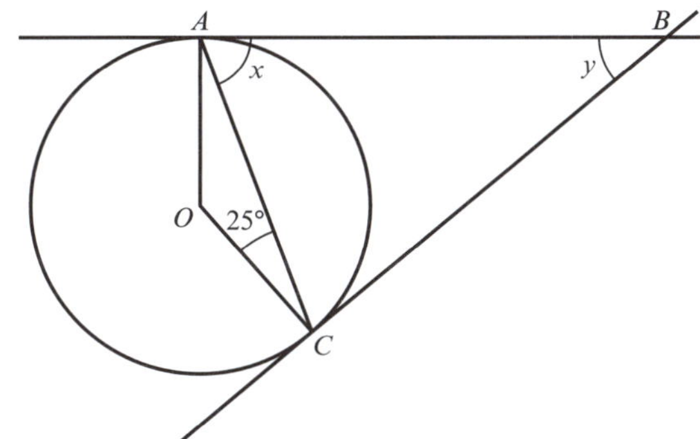

a   Calculate the size of angle x. [2]

b   Calculate the size of angle y. [2]

c   Explain why triangle ABC is isosceles. [2]

[**Total: 6**]

≪ RECALL AND CONNECT 2 ≪

The diagram shows a triangle ABC,
where AC is the diameter of a semicircle.

a   State the size of angle ABC.

b   Find the length AC.

c   Calculate the area of the semicircle.

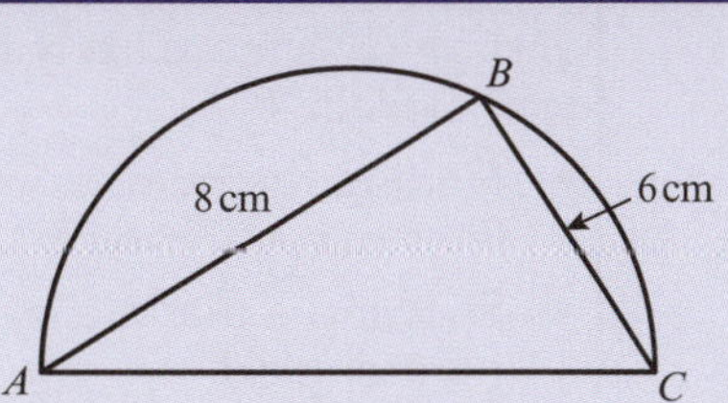

REFLECTION

When you need to give reasons in your answer, as you would for an 'explain' question, what can you do to ensure your reasons are clear and include all the necessary information?

Think about how you can apply this when giving reasons for answers about angle questions.

SELF-ASSESSMENT CHECKLIST

Let's revisit the Knowledge and Exam skills focus for this chapter.
Decide how confident you are with each statement.

	Now I can	Show it	Needs more work	Almost there	Confident to move on
1	identify line symmetry of two-dimensional shapes	Draw a shape which has 5 lines of symmetry.			
2	find the order of rotational symmetry of two-dimensional shapes	Draw a regular polygon with rotational symmetry order 8.			
3	apply symmetry properties of circles to solve problems	The diagram shows a circle with centre O. Calculate the size of x.			
4	understand the command words 'explain' and 'state'	Which of these question types is more likely to use the command word 'state' and which is more likely to use 'explain'? • Finding the number of lines of symmetry. • Showing a triangle is right-angled.			
5	understand mark schemes.	Look at Section 19.2 Questions 1 and 2. How many marks do you think each part might be worth? What would each mark be awarded for?			

20 Ratio, rate and proportion

When you read an examination question, look carefully at the command word used. It is important to understand what each command word means and what it is asking you to do. In this chapter, look out for the questions containing the command words 'calculate' and 'work out'.

| Calculate | calculate from given facts, figures or information. |
| Work out | work out from given facts, figures or information with or without the use of a calculator. |

You will take two mathematics examination papers. Paper 1 is a non-calculator paper. Paper 3 is a calculator paper. 'Work out' and 'calculate' questions can appear on either paper. For Paper 3 you can use a calculator, but for Paper 1 you will not have a calculator. Use the non-calculator questions in this chapter to show that you can understand and answer questions without a calculator.

Some of the questions in this chapter make connections with other topics in mathematics. This can help you recall and revise the other topics and strengthen your understanding by seeing how different topics link together. The 'Recall and connect' questions also help you to make these connections.

20.1 Working with ratio

UNDERSTAND THIS TERM

- Ratio

1   Mia has 4 red counters and 5 blue counters. Write down the ratio of

   a   red counters to blue counters

   b   blue counters to red counters.

2   Write each ratio in its simplest form.

   a $4:10$ **b** $9:3$ **c** $350:500$ **d** $0.5:0.75$

3    Write down the ratio of

   a   1 millimetre to 1 metre   **b**   1 kilogram to 1 gram

   c   1 hour to 1 minute   **d**   1 centimetre to 1 metre.

4   Write each ratio in its simplest form.

   a   2 metres : 20 millimetres   **b**   45 minutes : 6 hours

   c   8 cm : 64 mm   **d**   2.5 litres : 600 millilitres

5   Saskia mixes orange paint, using red and yellow paint in the ratio red : yellow $= 2:5$

   She uses 60 ml of red paint.
   How much yellow paint does she use?

6   Divide

   a   \$300 in the ratio $2:3$ **b**   60 kg in the ratio $7:5$

   c   2 litres in the ratio $1:2:5$ **d**   120 cm in the ratio $3:7:6$

7   The angles in a triangle are in the ratio $2:3:4$.
Calculate the size of the largest angle.   [2]

                                                          [Total: 2]

8   Manjit sells some books.
He sells 51 fiction books, 27 history books and 33 art books.
Find the ratio of the number of fiction books : history books : art books in its simplest form.   [2]

                                                           [Total: 2]

9   There are 288 people in a cinema.
The ratio of adults : children $= 5:3$.
Work out the number of children in the cinema.   [2]

                                                           [Total: 2]

10   Sunita makes some biscuits.
Each biscuit is either almond, chocolate or vanilla, in the ratio
almond : chocolate : vanilla $= 4 : 5 : 3$.
24 biscuits are vanilla.
Show that Sunita makes 96 biscuits.   [2]

[Total: 2]

11   A train has first-class and standard seats in the ratio
first-class : standard $= 2 : 7$
There are 100 more standard seats than first-class seats.
Work out the number of first-class seats.   [2]

[Total: 2]

≪ RECALL AND CONNECT 1 ≪

What angle fact did you use to answer Question 7?

Write down an expression that you could use to help you solve this problem.

REFLECTION

Do you remember what you learned about writing expressions in Chapter 2 and
solving equations in Chapter 5?

One way to check is to answer the 'Recall and connect' questions. These
questions do not test everything you need to know from previous chapters.
How will you check that you remember skills from earlier chapters?

20.2 Ratio and scale

1   Express the following ratios in the form $1 : n$.

    a $5 : 20$ **b** $4 : 10$ **c** $2\,\text{cm} : 30\,\text{mm}$ **d** $4\,\text{cm} : 1\,\text{km}$

2   Express the following ratios in the form $n : 1$.

    a $16 : 8$ **b** $15 : 3$ **c** $20 : 12$ **d** $36 : 8$

    e $2\,\text{cm} : 4\,\text{mm}$ **f** $100\,\text{g} : 1\,\text{kg}$ **g**   3 hours : 30 seconds

3   A scale model is made at a scale of $1 : 20$.
Find the real distance in centimetres of the following lengths on the model.

    a $3\,\text{cm}$ **b** $4\,\text{mm}$ **c** $7\,\text{cm}$ **d** $2.5\,\text{cm}$

4   The scale of a map is $1 : 25\,000$.
Find the distances on the map for these real distances.

    a   Village A to Village B is $7\,\text{km}$.

    b   Village B to village C is $5\,\text{km}$.

5 Fionn makes a scale model of a house.
On the model, the height of the house is 40 cm.
The actual height of the house is 8 metres.
Find the scale of the model in the form $1:n$. [2]

[Total: 2]

6 The scale of a map is $1:50\,000$.
On the map, the distance between two stations is 13 cm.
Calculate the actual distance between the two stations.
Give your answer in kilometres. [2]

[Total: 2]

≪ RECALL AND CONNECT 2 ≪

Can you recall the conversion facts for metric units of length, for example metres to centimetres or kilometres to metres?

How could memorising these conversion facts help you to answer scale questions?

20.3 Rates and 20.4 Kinematic graphs

UNDERSTAND THESE TERMS

- Rate
- Speed

1 5 ml of water drips from a tap every 10 seconds.
Write the rate of water dripped

    a in millilitres per minute

    b in millilitres per hour

    c in litres per hour.

2 20 000 people live in a town of area 8 km².
What is the number of people per km²?

3 A train travels 280 km in 3.5 hours.
What is the average speed of the train?

4 Alix walks at an average speed of 4.2 km/h for $3\frac{1}{4}$ hours.
Find the distance that Alix walks.

5 Rani drives at an average speed of 60 km/h.
How long it would take her to drive 180 km?

6   Miko cycles from *A* to *B*.
The travel graph shows this journey.

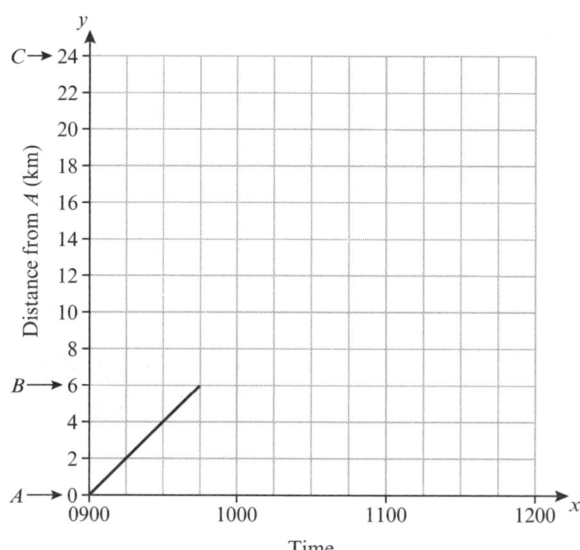

a   Write down the time that Miko leaves *A*.   [1]

b   Work out how long, in minutes, it takes Miko to cycle from *A* to *B*.   [1]

c   Miko stays at *B* for 15 minutes.
Then he cycles to *C* at a constant speed of 12 km/h.
Copy and complete the travel graph.   [2]

d   Work out the average speed for the whole journey from *A* to *C* in km/h.   [2]

[Total: 6]

7   The travel graph shows Tatsue's journey to work.

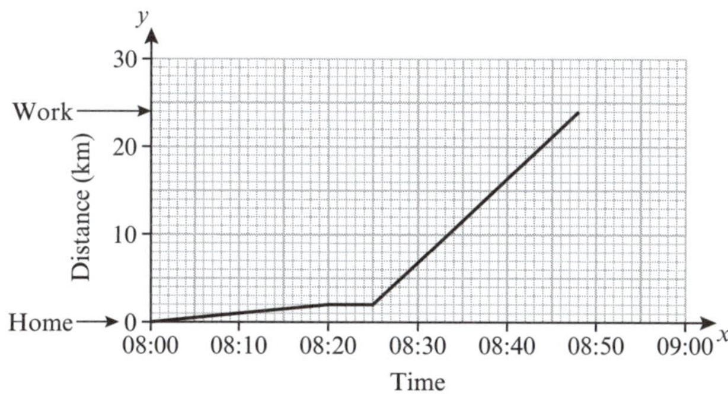

a   Explain what is happening between 08:20 and 08:25.   [1]

b   Between which times is Tatsue's speed the fastest?
Give a reason for your answer.   [2]

c   Calculate Tatsue's average speed for the whole journey.
Give your answer in kilometres per hour.   [3]

[Total: 6]

8   A bus travels at an average speed of 30 km/h.
Calculate how long, in hours and minutes, this bus
takes to travel 42 km.   [3]

[Total: 3]

9 Convert 5.4 km/h into m/s. [2]

[**Total: 2**]

REFLECTION

In the previous section you used conversion facts for metric units of length. Which other units do you need to convert to change speeds to different units? What about changing millilitres per second to litres per hour?

What methods will you use to revise and remember these conversion facts?

20.5 Proportion

UNDERSTAND THESE TERMS

- Direct proportion
- Inverse proportion

1 Five pens cost $6.25.
What would 12 pens cost?

2 To make 8 pancakes you need 200 g of flour.
How much flour do you need for each quantity of pancakes?

    a 12 pancakes   **b** 60 pancakes

3 A car travels 10 km in 14 minutes.
How long will the car take to travel 35 km at the same speed?

4 It takes 3 people 4 days to paint a house.
Working at the same rate, how many days would it take

    a 2 people   **b** 6 people?

5 A bus travelling at 20 km/h takes 42 minutes to travel from the bus station to the hospital.
How long will this journey take if the bus travels at 30 km/h?

6 The graph shows the directly proportional relationship between lengths in miles and lengths in kilometres.

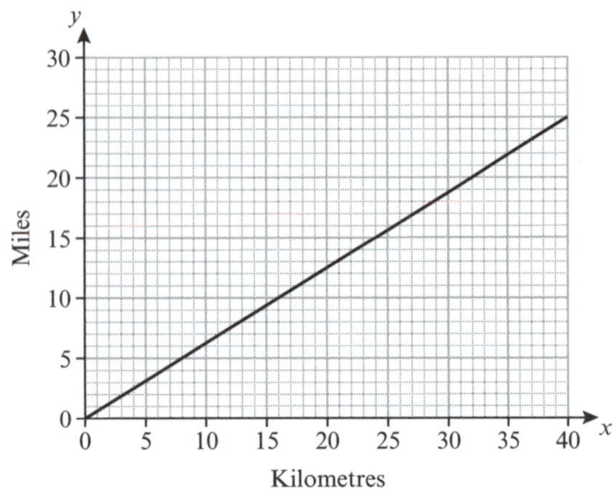

    a Use the graph to estimate how many miles are equal to 15 km.

    b Convert 75 miles to kilometres.

7 $1 = 85.4 rupees
Convert 5124 rupees into dollars.   [2]

[Total: 2]

8   1 yard = 0.9144 metres
Convert 5 yards into centimetres.
Give your answer to the nearest centimetre.   [3]

[Total: 3]

9   Work out which box of rice is the best value.
You must show your working.

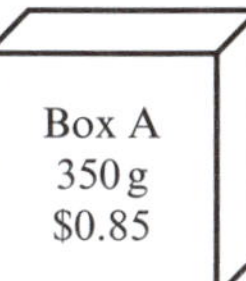

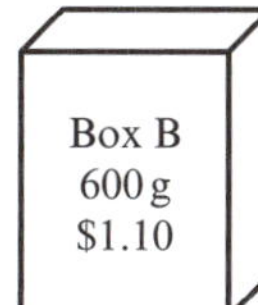

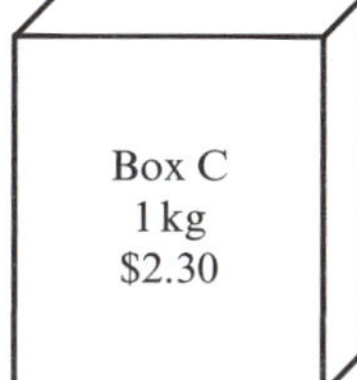

[3]

[Total: 3]

SELF-ASSESSMENT CHECKLIST

Let's revisit the Knowledge and Exam skills focus for this chapter.
Decide how confident you are with each statement.

	Now I can	Show it	Needs more work	Almost there	Confident to move on
1	simplify a ratio	Write the ratio 24 : 30 : 48 in its simplest form.			
2	use equivalent ratios	A shop sells boxes of cereal in the ratio large boxes : small boxes = 3 : 5. The shop sells 30 more small boxes than large boxes. How many boxes do they sell in total?			
3	divide in a given ratio	Divide $72 in the ratio 4 : 5.			
4	write a ratio in the form $1 : n$	Write the ratio 5 cm : 1 m in the form $1 : n$.			
5	use a scale	Find a real map. Use the scale of the map to work out the distance between two towns on the map.			

CONTINUED

	Now I can	Show it	Needs more work	Almost there	Confident to move on
6	calculate speed	A car travels 140 km in 4 hours. Calculate the average speed of the car.			
7	convert units of speed	Convert 5 m/s into km/h.			
8	interpret distance–time graphs	Draw a distance–time graph to represent a journey. Swap with a partner and try to describe the journey from the graph.			
9	solve direct proportion problems	12 pencils cost $4.80. What do 7 pencils cost?			
10	solve inverse proportion problems	It takes 3 people 6 hours to clean all the rooms in a hotel. How long would it take 4 people to clean all the rooms?			
11	understand the command words 'calculate' and 'work out'	What is the same about answering a 'work out' question and a 'calculate' question? When can you use a calculator when answering these questions?			
12	find answers to 'non-calculator' questions	Divide £40 in the ratio 3 : 5.			
13	make connections with other topics in mathematics.	Write down all the topics you used in this chapter.			

Exam practice 5

This section contains past paper questions from previous Cambridge exams, which draw together your knowledge on a range of topics that you have covered up to this point. These questions give you the opportunity to test your knowledge and understanding.

The following question has an example student response and commentary provided. Work through the question first, then compare your answer to the sample response and commentary. Are your answers different to the sample responses?

1 **a** A waiter works 29 hours a week in the café.
He is paid $9.50 per hour.
He is paid for 52 weeks of the year.
Work out his total pay for the year. [2]

   b The chef is paid 32% more than the waiter per hour.
Work out how much the chef is paid per hour. [2]

Cambridge IGCSE Mathematics (0580) Paper 32 Q1b, March 2023 **[Total: 4]**

Example student response	Commentary
a $29 \times 9.50 = \$275.50$	The student has worked out the weekly wage correctly. However, they have not used the weekly wage to calculate the total pay for the whole year. ***This answer scores 1 out of 2 marks.***
b $9.50 \times 0.32 = \$3.04$	The student has used the correct method to find 32% of the waiter's wage. This is the amount of increase, not the chef's wage. ***This answer scores 1 out of 2 marks.***

Here is a similar question that you should attempt. Use the information from the previous response and commentary to guide you as you answer.

2 Asha works in a café.

Her wage is calculated using the formula: wage = hourly rate × number of hours + bonus

Her hourly rate is $11.52.

One week Asha works 25 hours and receives a bonus of $5.40.

Work out her wage for this week. [2]

Cambridge IGCSE Mathematics (0580) Paper 12 Q2, November 2023 **[Total: 2]**

The following question has an example student response and commentary provided.
Work through the question first, then compare your answer to the sample response and
commentary. Are your answers different to the sample responses?

3   Alexa, Ben and Chloe own a restaurant.
They invest \$12 000 at a rate of $n\%$ per year simple interest.
At the end of 3 years the value of the investment is \$12 900.
Find the value of n. [3]

Cambridge IGCSE Mathematics (0580) Paper 32 Q4c, June 2020 [Total: 3]

Example student response	Commentary
$\dfrac{12900 \times 100}{3 \times 12000} = 35.83\%$	The student has used a rearrangement of the simple interest formula. However, they have not found the interest by subtracting the principal sum. ***This answer scores 0 out of 3 marks.***

Here is a similar question that you should attempt. Use the information from the
previous response and commentary to guide you as you answer.

4   The owners of some land buy new equipment for a playground.
They borrow \$8500 for 4 years at a rate of 6.5% per year compound interest.
Calculate the amount they repay at the end of the 4 years.
Give your answer correct to the nearest dollar. [3]

Adapted from Cambridge IGCSE Mathematics (0580) Paper 32 Q7c, June 2024 [Total: 3]

The following question has an example student response and commentary provided.
Work through the question first, then compare your answer to the sample response and
commentary. Are your answers different to the sample responses?

5   a   Complete the table of values for $y = x^2 - 3x - 6$. [3]

x	−3	−2	−1	0	1	2	3	4	5	6
y	12		−2					−2		12

   b   On the grid, draw the graph of $y = x^2 - 3x - 6$
for $-3 \leqslant x \leqslant 6$. [4]
[Use Figure 8 on the Past Paper Practice Questions
Resource Sheet.]

   c   Write down the equation of the line of symmetry
of the graph. [1]

   d   Use your graph to solve the equation $x^2 - 3x - 6 = 0$. [2]

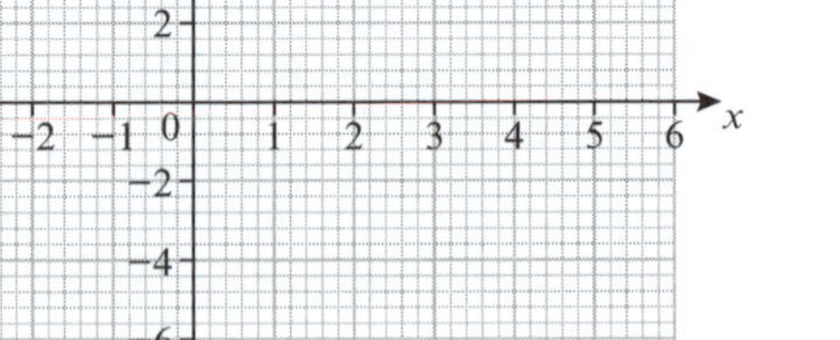

Cambridge IGCSE Mathematics (0580) Paper 32 Q9, June 2020 [Total: 10]

Example student response	Commentary
a −4, −6, −8, −8, −6, 4	The student has made a mistake when calculating the first value by not using brackets when entering −2 in their calculator, and has got an incorrect value of $y = -4$ for $x = -2$. However, the rest of the values are correct. ***This answer scores 2 out of 3 marks.***
b	The student has plotted all their points from their table correctly and they have drawn a smooth curve through their points. However, as one of the values in their table was incorrect, the graph is not completely correct. ***This answer scores 3 out of 4 marks.***
c 1.5	The student has written only the x-value and has not written the equation of the line. ***This answer scores 0 out of 1 mark.***
d −2.4, 4.4	The student has used their incorrect graph to read the values. However, their values are correct according to their graph. ***This answer scores 2 out of 2 marks.***

Here is a similar question that you should attempt. Use the information from the previous response and commentary to guide you as you answer.

6   **i**   Complete the table of values for $y = \dfrac{-6}{x}$.   [3]

x	−6	−4	−3	−2	−1.5	−1		1	1.5	2	3	5	6
y	1		2	3		6		−6		−3	−2		−1

ii On the grid, draw the graph of $y = \dfrac{-6}{x}$ for $-6 \leqslant x \leqslant -1$ and $1 \leqslant x \leqslant 6$.
[Use Figure 9 on the Past Paper Practice Questions Resource Sheet.] [4]

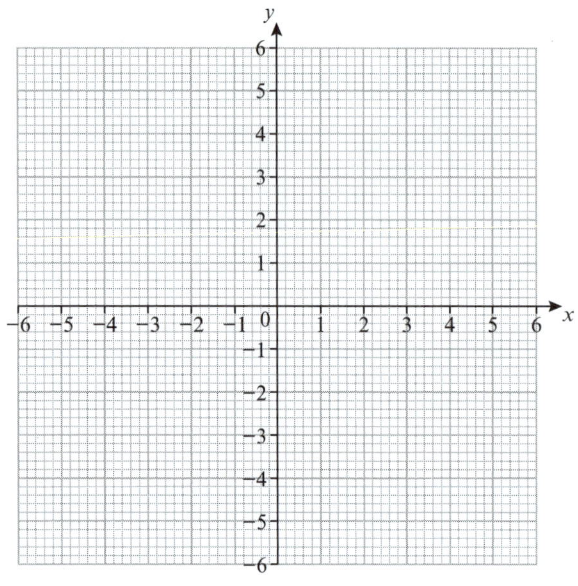

iii Write down the order of rotational symmetry of the graph. [1]
iv Write down the equation of each line of symmetry of the graph. [2]
v On the grid, draw the line $y = 2.5$. [1]
vi Use your graph to solve the equation $\dfrac{-6}{x} = 2.5$. [1]

Cambridge IGCSE Mathematics (0580) Paper 32 Q2a, June 2022 [Total: 12]

The following question has an example student response and commentary provided. Work through the question first, then compare your answer to the sample response and commentary. Are your answers different to the sample responses?

7

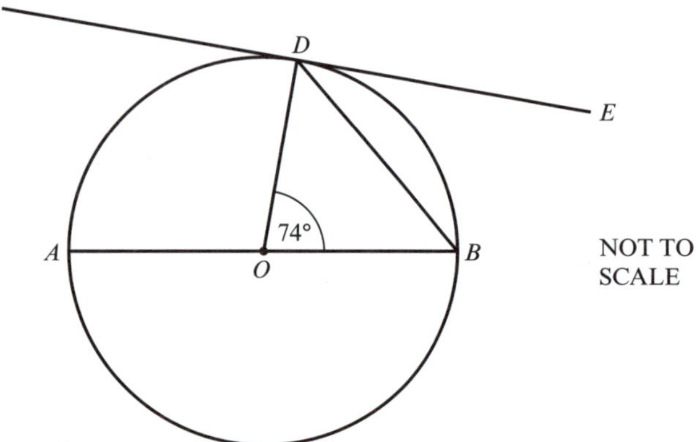

The diagram shows a circle, centre O, with diameter AOB.
The line CDE touches the circle at D and angle $DOB = 74°$.

i Write down the mathematical name of the line CDE. [1]
ii Work out angle ODB. [2]
iii Work out angle BDE.
Give a geometrical reason for your answer. [2]

Cambridge IGCSE Mathematics (0580) Paper 32 Q5c, June 2024 [Total: 5]

Example student response	Commentary
i Chord	The student has used the wrong name for the line *CDE*. **This answer scores 0 out of 1 mark.**
ii 74°	The student has recognised that the triangle is isosceles, however they have not used the angle facts for isosceles triangles correctly. **This answer scores 0 out of 2 marks.**
iii 90 − 74 = 16° A tangent is perpendicular to the radius.	The student has used the correct geometric reason and a correct method, but used their incorrect answer from part (ii). Therefore follow-through marks are awarded. **This answer scores 2 out of 2 marks.**

Here is a similar question that you should attempt. Use the information from the previous response and commentary to guide you as you answer.

8

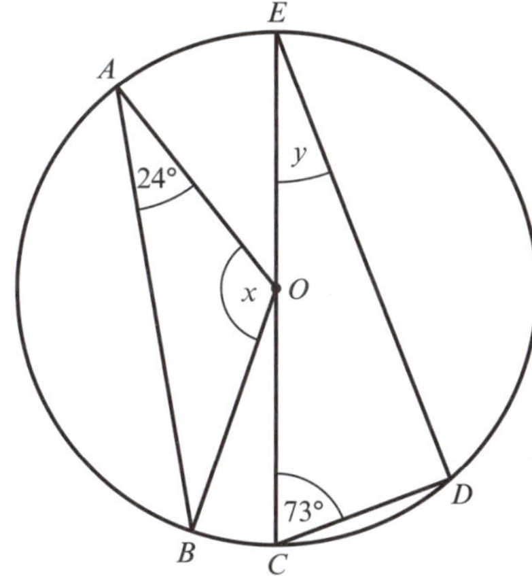

The diagram shows a circle, centre O, with diameter CE.
A, B, C, D and E lie on the circumference of the circle.

i Find the value of x.
Give a reason for your answer. [3]

ii Find the value of y.
Give a reason for your answer. [2]

iii Draw a tangent to the circle at A.
[Use Figure 10 on the Past Paper Practice Questions Resource Sheet.] [1]

Cambridge IGCSE Mathematics (0580) Paper 32 Q3c, March 2020 [Total: 6]

21 More equations, formulae and functions

When you read an examination question, look carefully at the command word used. It is important to understand what each command word means and what it is asking you to do. In this chapter, look out for the questions containing the command words 'write down' and 'work out'.

Write down	give an answer without significant working.
Work out	calculate from given facts, figures or information with or without the use of a calculator.

When a question in the examination uses the command words 'write down', it is asking for a brief, direct answer that you can find without doing much or any working. To answer a 'write down an equation' question, you should include any letters and numbers that are given in the question. If the question uses the command words 'work out' you should use information given in the question to find the answer. Even if you use a calculator to answer the question, it is important that you show your method and working.

The number of marks for an examination question can help you understand how much work you need to do on the question. If you get the wrong solution and show no working, you will get zero marks, but if you show some correct working, you could get one mark even if your final solution is incorrect.

21.1 Setting up equations to solve problems

1 For each statement, write down an equation using x as the unknown number.
Solve your equation to find the value of x.

   a   When a number is multiplied by 7, the result is 56.

   b   When a number is divided by 6, the result is 8.

   c   Three more than a number is 5.

   d   Five less than a number is -4.

   e   When a number is subtracted from 15, the result is 6.

   f   When a number is trebled, the result is 27.

2 Write down and solve an equation to find the value of the unknown number.

   a   The sum of a number and three times the number is 20.

   b   Multiply a number by 4, then subtract 7, is equal to 9.

   c   When a number is divided by 3 and then 4 is added, the result is 11.

   d   Multiply a number by 3, then subtract 4, is equal to the number plus 12.

   e   When a positive number is squared and then 5 is added, the result is 21.

3 For each diagram, write down and solve an equation to find the value of the letter.

a
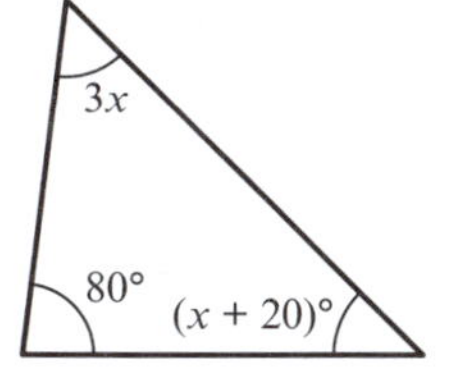

b
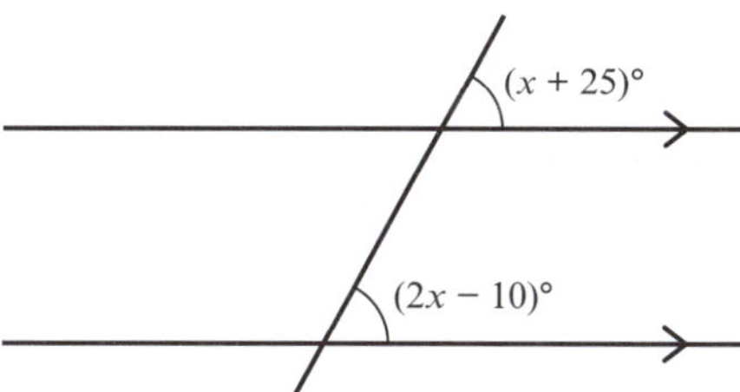

c
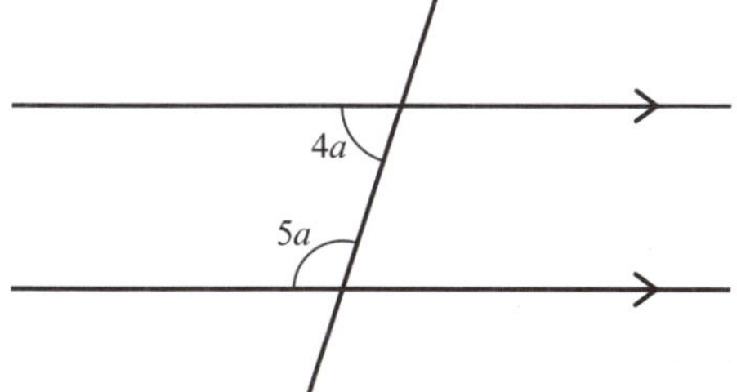

d
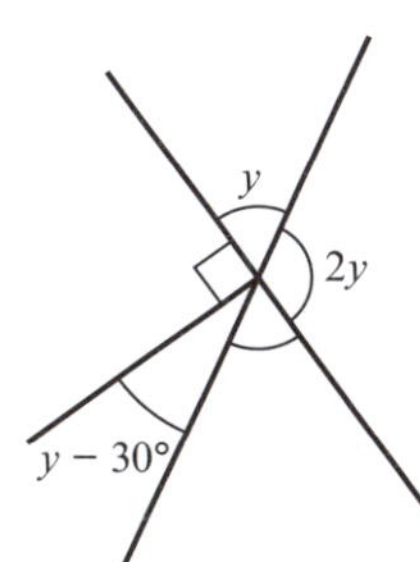

4  Tom is n years old.
Ben is 10 years older than Tom.
Sally is 3 years younger than Ben.
The sum of their ages is 53.
Use this information to write down an equation and solve it to find
the value of n.   [4]

[Total: 4]

5 The perimeter of this triangle is 36 cm.
Work out the value of x.   [3]

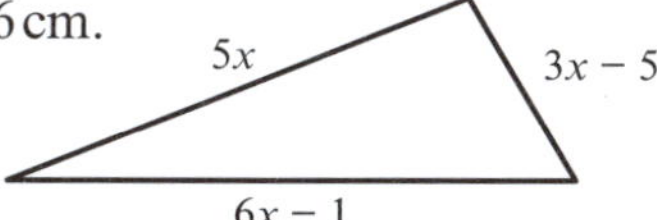

[Total: 3]

6  Lisa thinks of a number n, doubles it and subtracts 13.
The result is 37.
Write this as an equation in terms of n and solve the equation. [3]

[Total: 3]

7 The diagram shows an isosceles trapezium.

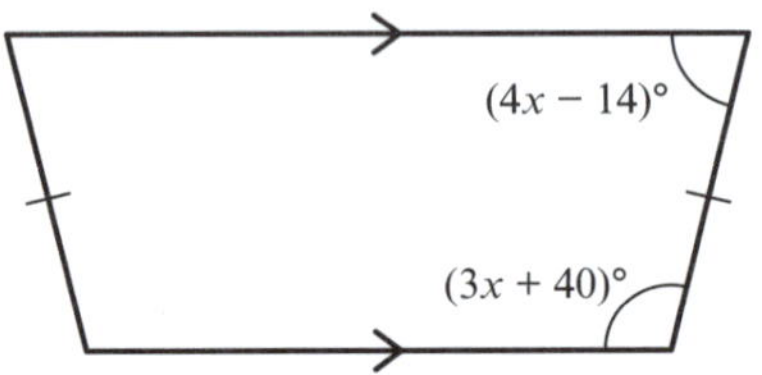

NOT TO SCALE

Work out the size of the largest interior angle of the trapezium. [4]

[Total: 4]

8 Malek has a box of counters and a bag of counters.
The box contains x counters.
There are four times as many counters in the bag than in the box.
Malek now takes six counters out of each container.
There are now seven times as many counters in the bag than in the box.
Use this information to write down an equation and solve it to find the
value of x. [3]

[Total: 3]

≪ RECALL AND CONNECT 1 ≪

Copy and complete these angle facts.
a   Angles on a straight line add to ......
b   Angles in a triangle add to ......
c   Angles in a quadrilateral add to ......
d   Angles around a point add to ......
e   Vertically opposite angles are ......
f   Co-interior angles add to ......
Make a list of the facts you still need to memorise.

REFLECTION

Question 8 asked you to write down an equation. To answer a 'write down'
question, you need to use the information given in the question. What
information from the question did you use to write your equation?

Which stages of the answer were the three marks given for?

21.2 Using and rearranging formulae

1  $Y = 5t + 4$
Find the value of Y when $t = 3$.

2  $F = ma$
Find the value of F when $m = 12$ and $a = 4$.

3 $P = \dfrac{F}{A}$
Find the value of P when $F = 20$ and $A = 1.6$.

4 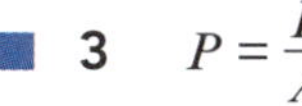 $v = u + at$
Find the value of v when $u = 2$, $a = 5$ and $t = 6$.

5  $y = mx + c$
Find the value of y when $m = 4$, $x = -3$ and $c = 9$.

6  $P = 2(l + w)$
Find the value of P when $l = 7$ and $w = 6$.

7 Make x the subject of each formula.

a $5x = n$	**b** $rx = n$	**c** $x + 3 = t$	**d** $x + p = t$
e $x - 5 = m$	**f** $x - b = c$	**g** $8 + x = t$	**h** $d + x = q$
i $\dfrac{x}{4} = k$	**j** $\dfrac{x}{d} = t$	**k** $\dfrac{6}{x} = f$	**l** $\dfrac{m}{x} = g$
m $N = 3x + 2$	**n** $T = 4x - 9$	**o** $w = \dfrac{x}{2} + 5$	**p** $v = \dfrac{x}{4} - t$

8 $S = \dfrac{D}{T}$
Find

   a the value of S when $D = 70$ and $T = 5$

   b the value of D when $S = 40$ and $T = 3$

   c the value of T when $S = 18$ and $D = 54$.

9 $y = mx + c$
Find

   a the value of y when $m = -2$, $x = 1$ and $c = 5$

   b the value of m when $y = 11$, $x = 3$ and $c = -4$

   c the value of c when $y = 14$, $m = -3$ and $x = -2$.

10 Make x the subject of the formula $y = kx^2$.   [2]

[Total: 2]

11 Franco calculates his wages in dollars, W, using the formula: $W = 20h + b$,
    where h is the number of hours he works and b is a bonus payment.

    a   Work out Franco's wages when he works 35 hours and gets a $45 bonus.   [2]

    b   One week Franco's wages are $700. His bonus is $80.
    Work out the number of hours Franco worked that week.   [2]

[Total: 4]

12 $P = 4r - 3$
    Make r the subject of this formula.   [2]

[Total: 2]

13 Make x the subject of this formula $y = \dfrac{x}{5} - c$.   [2]

[Total: 2]

⟪ RECALL AND CONNECT 2 ⟪

Look at Questions 6, 8 and 9. Have you seen or used these formulae before?
What do the letters in these formulae represent?

Do the same for any other formulae you recognise, for example you may have
used the formulae from Questions 2, 3 and 4 in science.

REFLECTION

What is the difference between a formula and an equation? When do you use
equation-solving techniques with formulae?

Can you think of different methods to find the value of a letter that is not
the subject?

Which method did you use in Questions 8, 9 and 11?

Which method do you prefer? Do you always prefer the same method? Why?

SELF-ASSESSMENT CHECKLIST

Let's revisit the Knowledge and Exam skills focus for this chapter.
Decide how confident you are with each statement.

	Now I can	Show it	Needs more work	Almost there	Confident to move on
1	set up an equation to solve a problem	Casey thinks of a number n, trebles it and adds 9. The result is 30. Write this as an equation in terms of n and solve the equation.			

CONTINUED

	Now I can	Show it	Needs more work	Almost there	Confident to move on
2	use a formula	$R = 3x + k$ Work out the value of R when $x = 5$ and $k = 2.7$.			
3	rearrange a formula	Find a formula you have used in another chapter. Rearrange this formula to make another letter the subject.			
4	understand the command words 'work out' and 'write down'	For 'work out' and 'write down' questions, you are given all the information you need in the question. What is different about how you answer them?			
5	use the marks available in an exam question to help write good answers to questions.	If a question is worth 2 or more marks, what should you include in your answer?			

22 Transformations and vectors

When you read an examination question, look carefully at the command word used. It is important to understand what each command word means and what it is asking you to do. In this chapter, look out for questions containing the command word 'describe'.

Describe	state the points of a topic / give characteristics and main features.

When a transformation question in the examination uses the command word 'describe', you need to write your answer and include the name of the transformation (reflection, rotation, translation or enlargement) and the main features of the transformation.

Here are some tips on how to give a good answer to a question asking you to describe the features of transformations.

- Reflection: include the equation of the mirror line.

- Rotation: write the centre of the rotation, the direction of the rotation (clockwise or anticlockwise) and the angle of the rotation.

- Translation: write the column vector.

- Enlargement: write the centre of the enlargement and the scale factor.

Some transformation questions ask you to 'draw' your answer. This means you need to draw the transformation of a shape on the grid, using a ruler and pencil. Draw shapes as accurately as possible.

22.1 Simple plane transformations

1   The grid shows quadrilateral A.

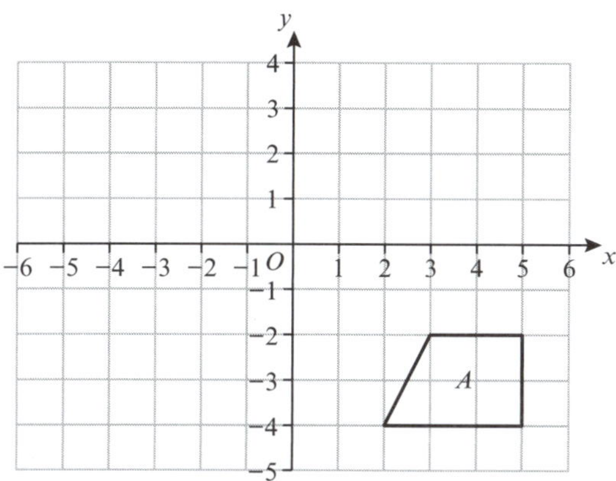

On a copy of the grid

a   reflect quadrilateral A in the line $x = 0$

b   translate quadrilateral A by the vector $\begin{pmatrix} -2 \\ 5 \end{pmatrix}$

c   rotate quadrilateral A 90° clockwise, centre $(4, -2)$.

2   The grid shows a triangle.

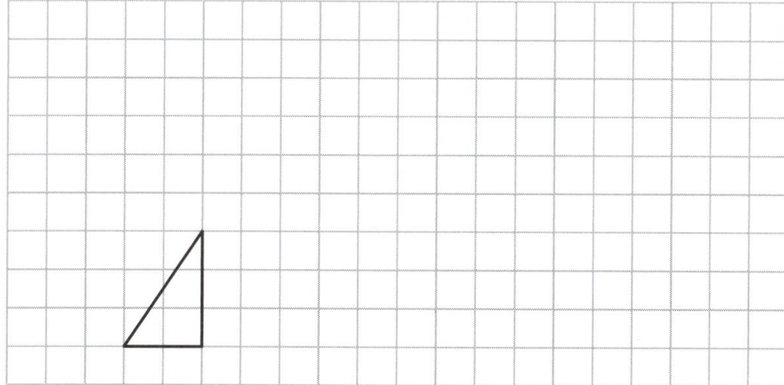

On a copy of the grid

a   draw an enlargement of the triangle with scale factor 2

b   draw an enlargement of the triangle with scale factor $\frac{1}{2}$

c   draw an enlargement of the triangle with scale factor $1\frac{1}{2}$.

3   Copy the grid and quadrilateral A from question 1.
On the grid, enlarge triangle A by scale factor 3, centre $(5, -4)$.

4   The grid shows triangles D, E, F, G, H, I, J and K.

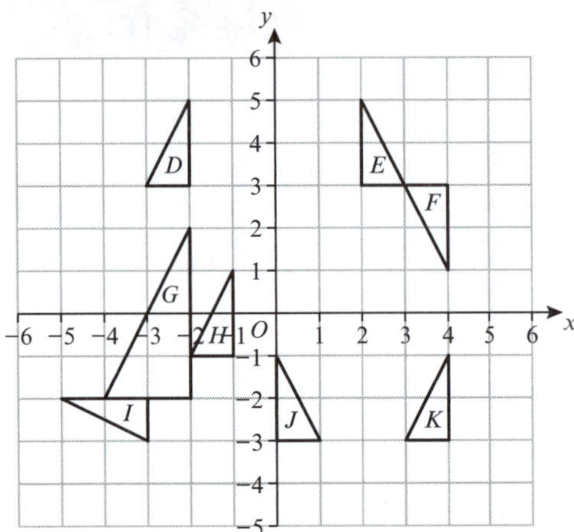

Describe fully the single transformation that maps

a   triangle D onto triangle E **b**   triangle E onto triangle F

c   triangle J onto triangle K **d**   triangle D onto triangle K

e   triangle D onto triangle I **f**   triangle H onto triangle G

g   triangle G onto triangle H.

5   The grid shows triangles L, M and N.

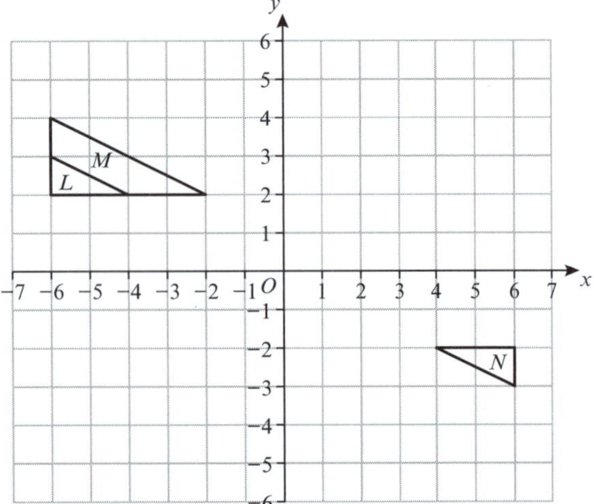

a   Describe fully the single transformation that maps triangle L onto
triangle M.   [3]

b   Describe fully the single transformation that maps triangle L onto
triangle N.   [3]

c   On a copy of the grid, draw the image of triangle L after a translation
by the vector $\begin{pmatrix} 3 \\ -5 \end{pmatrix}$.   [2]

d   On a copy of the grid, draw the image of triangle N after a reflection
in the line $y = -2$.   [2]

[Total: 10]

6   The grid shows quadrilaterals Q, R and S and the point P.

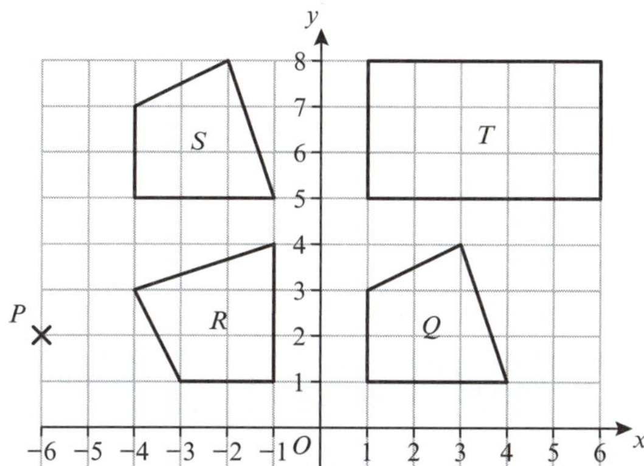

a   On a copy of the grid, mark the image of point P after a reflection in the line $x = 0$.   [1]

b   Describe fully the single transformation that maps quadrilateral Q onto quadrilateral R.   [3]

c   Describe fully the single transformation that maps quadrilateral S onto quadrilateral Q.   [2]

Quadrilateral Q has been enlarged with centre $(1, 0)$ to give quadrilateral T. The grid is large enough to show only one vertex and part of two sides of the quadrilateral T.

d   Write down the scale factor of the enlargement.   [1]

e   Find the coordinates of the other three vertices of quadrilateral T.   [3]

[Total: 10]

≪ RECALL AND CONNECT 1 ≪

Here are four triangles on a grid:

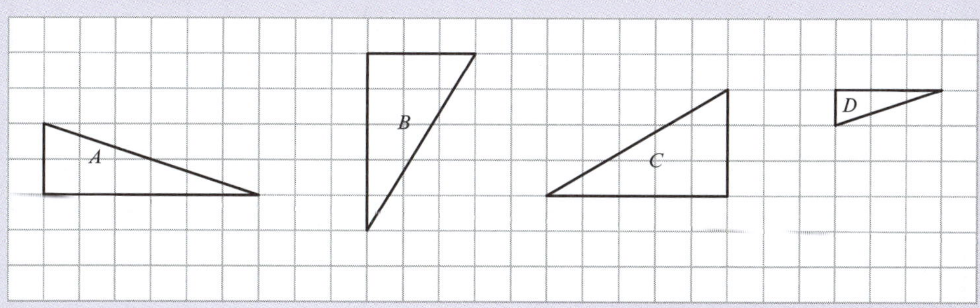

Which two triangles are congruent?

Which two triangles are similar?

Which transformations give congruent shapes? Which transformation gives similar shapes?

How can you use these facts to help you check your answers to 'Draw the image…' questions?

REFLECTION

How did you use coordinates, equations of straight lines and scale factors in these questions? Did you remember them, or did you have to look them up in earlier chapters?

How will you remember how to write a good answer for a 'Describe the transformation…' question? Make some notes that will help you to remember the information to include for each transformation.

SELF-ASSESSMENT CHECKLIST

Let's revisit the Knowledge and Exam skills focus for this chapter.
Decide how confident you are with each statement.

	Now I can	Show it	Needs more work	Almost there	Confident to move on
1	describe a reflection	Describe fully the single transformation that maps **a** triangle A onto triangle B **b** triangle B onto triangle A.			
2	describe a rotation	Describe fully the single transformation that maps **a** triangle C onto triangle D **b** triangle D onto triangle C.			
3	describe a translation	Draw a shape and its translation on a coordinate grid. Ask a partner to do the same. Swap diagrams and describe each other's translations.			

CONTINUED

	Now I can	Show it	Needs more work	Almost there	Confident to move on
4	describe an enlargement	Describe fully the single transformation that maps **a** triangle G onto triangle H **b** triangle H onto triangle G.			
5	draw a reflection	Draw the image of triangle J after a reflection in the line $x = -1$.			
6	draw a rotation	Draw a triangle on a coordinate grid. Swap your drawing with a partner. Rotate your partner's triangle by 90° anticlockwise, centre (0, 0).			
7	draw a translation	Translate your partner's triangle that you rotated in Question 6 by the vector $\begin{pmatrix} 1 \\ -3 \end{pmatrix}$.			

CONTINUED

	Now I can	Show it	Needs more work	Almost there	Confident to move on
8	draw an enlargement	Draw the image of triangle L after an enlargement by scale factor $\frac{1}{4}$, centre $(-4, -2)$. 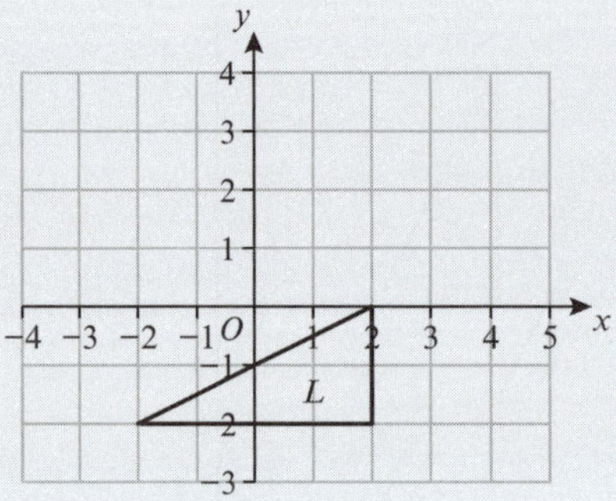			
9	understand the 'describe' command word and answer 'describe' questions	Answer the 'describe' questions in this chapter correctly, giving all the information needed.			
10	write a good answer to a transformation question.	Write down the three pieces of information you need to include when you describe an enlargement.			

23 Probability using tree diagrams and Venn diagrams

When you read an examination question, look carefully at the command word used. It is important to understand what each command word means and what it is asking you to do. In this chapter, look out for the questions containing the command words 'calculate' and 'work out'.

Calculate	work out from given facts, figures or information.
Work out	calculate from given facts, figures or information with or without the use of a calculator.

When an examination question uses one of the command words 'calculate' and 'work out', make sure that you look for the information in the question. Whether or not you use a calculator to answer the question, you should make sure to include your working or method in your answer.

Probability questions with tree diagrams and Venn diagrams often have several parts. Take time to read through the whole question carefully. If you cannot complete one part of a question, do not give up on the rest of the question. It is always worth attempting the remaining parts as you may be able to do these without having done a previous part. If you answer one part of a multi-part question incorrectly and then use this answer in your working for the next part, you can still get method marks in your working through the rest of the question. These are called 'follow through' marks.

When you have answered all the questions you can, go back to any questions you missed out or could not answer. You may find you can make a start on them or even answer them completely. It's always worth having another go.

23.1 Using tree diagrams to show outcomes and
23.2 Calculating probability from tree diagrams

1 Sushma spins this fair spinner twice.

    a Copy and complete this tree diagram.

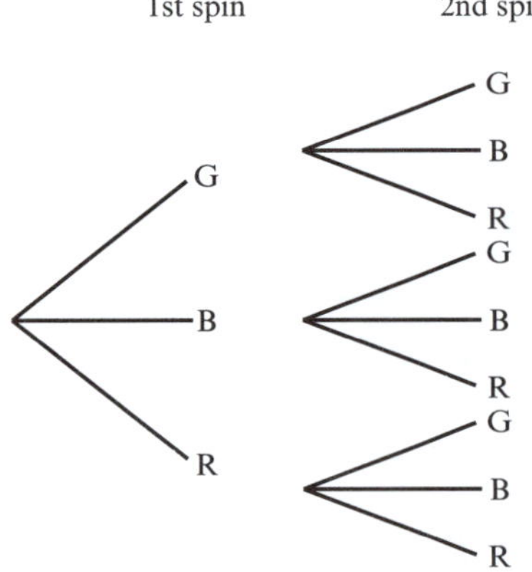

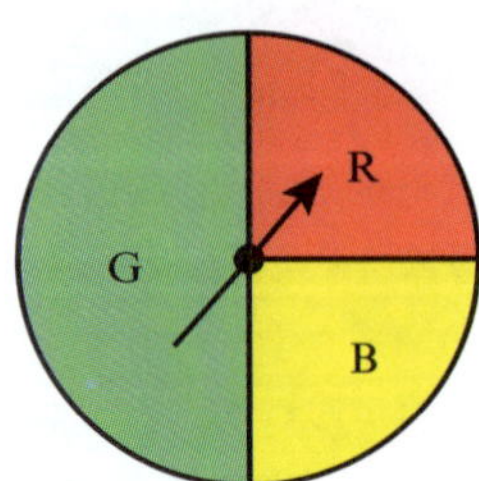

    b Find the probability that the spinner lands

      i on Blue both times

      ii once on Red and once on Green

      iii on the same colour twice

      iv on two different colours.

2 A game of snooker uses 22 balls.
15 of the balls are red.
Marvin puts the 22 snooker balls in a bag. He picks one ball at random,
notes its colour and then replaces it in the bag.
He then picks another ball at random.

    a Copy and complete the tree diagram.

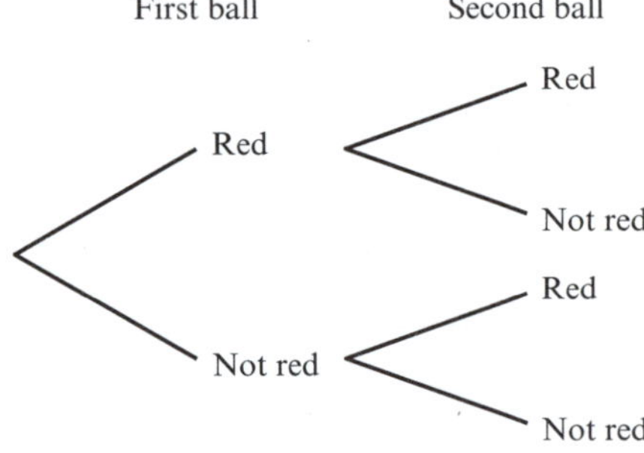

    b Find the probability that Marvin picks

      i two red balls

      ii no red balls

      iii at least one red ball.

3 Drake kicks a ball at a target twice.
The probability that Drake hits the target each time is 0.7.

    a Draw a tree diagram to show the outcomes.

    b Find the probability that Drake hits the target exactly once.

    c Find the probability that Drake hits the target at least once.

4 **a** A box contains these cards.

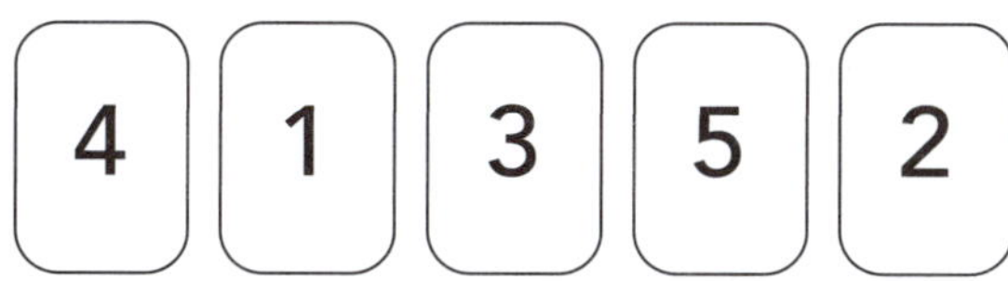

    One of the cards is picked at random.

    Find the probability that the number on the card is a factor of 21.   [1]

  b A bag contains four blue cards and five red cards.
Mila picks one card at random, notes its colour and then replaces
it in the bag.
She then picks another card at random.

    i Copy and complete the tree diagram.   [1]

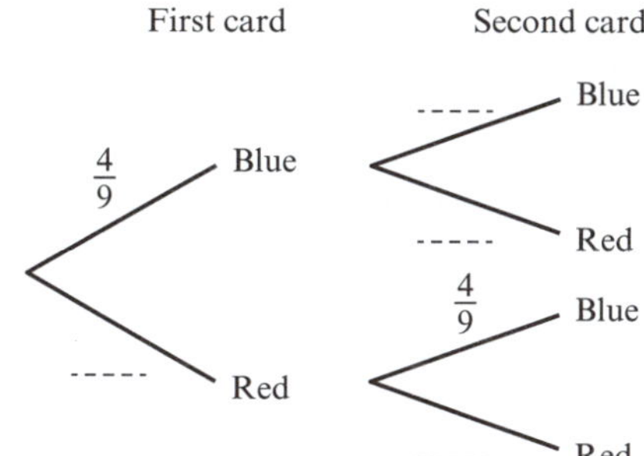

    ii Work out the probability that both cards Mila picks are red.   [2]

[Total: 4]

5 **a** Farad spins a fair spinner numbered 1 to 7.

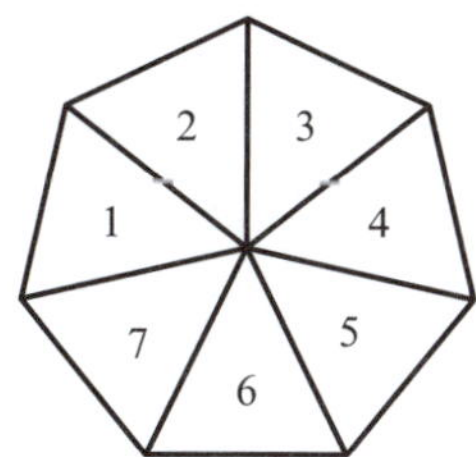

    Explain why the probability that the spinner lands on a square
number is $\frac{2}{7}$.   [2]

b Farad spins the spinner a second time.

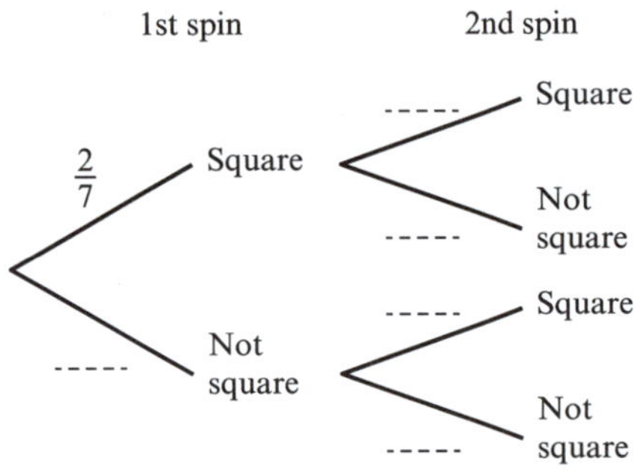

i Copy and complete the tree diagram. [2]

ii Calculate the probability that the spinner lands on a square number both times. [2]

[Total: 6]

≪ RECALL AND CONNECT 1 ≪

Work out

a $1 - \dfrac{3}{8}$ **b** $\dfrac{2}{5} + \dfrac{1}{5}$ **c** $\dfrac{2}{5} \times \dfrac{3}{5}$

d $1 - 0.7$ **e** $0.25 + 0.42$ **f** 0.3×0.2

How have you used these skills in the probability tree questions?

23.3 Calculating probability from Venn diagrams

1 The Venn diagram shows information about the number of customers at a café who chose beans (B) and cheese (C) toppings for a baked potato.

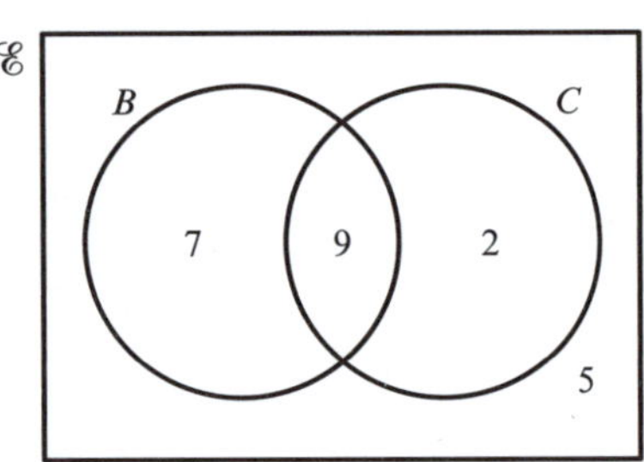

a Find the total number of customers at the café.

b Find

    i $n(B)$

    ii $n(C)$

    iii $n(B \cup C)$

    iv $n(B \cap C)$.

   c One of the customers is chosen at random.

      i Find the probability that this customer chose beans and cheese.

      ii Find the probability that this customer did not choose beans.

2 **a** $\mathscr{E}$ = {people at a sports centre}
T = {people who play tennis}
G = {people who play golf}

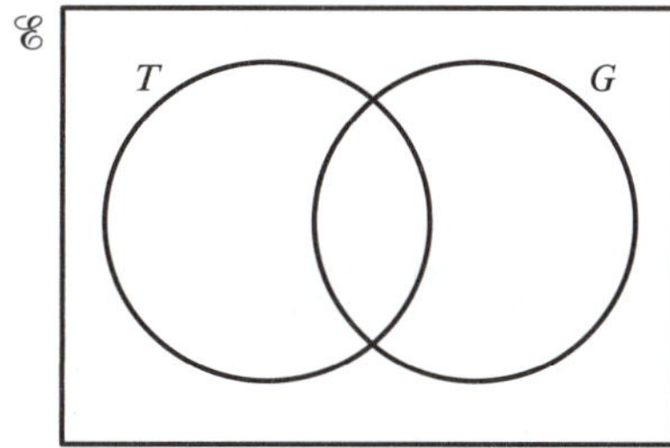

There are 100 people at the sports centre.
65 people play tennis.
20 people play both tennis and golf.
14 people do not play tennis and do
not play golf.
Copy and complete the Venn diagram.

 b A person at the sports centre is chosen at random. Find the probability that this person

   i plays tennis

   ii plays golf but not tennis

   iii plays golf and tennis

   iv does not play tennis.

3  $\mathscr{E}$ = {students in a class}
P = {students who like pop music}
C = {students who like classical music}
There are 27 students in the class.
11 students like classical music.

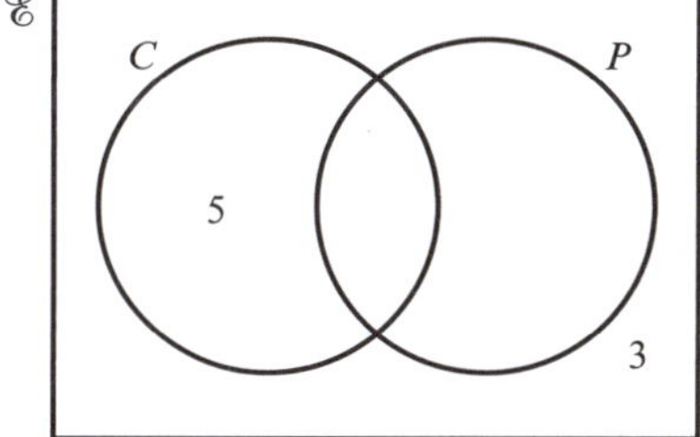

 a Copy and complete the Venn diagram. [2]

 b Work out $n(P \cup C)$. [1]

 c Work out the probability that a student chosen at random does not like classical music. [1]

[Total: 4]

4 The Venn diagram shows information about the number of students in a college who study Spanish (S) and Mandarin (M).

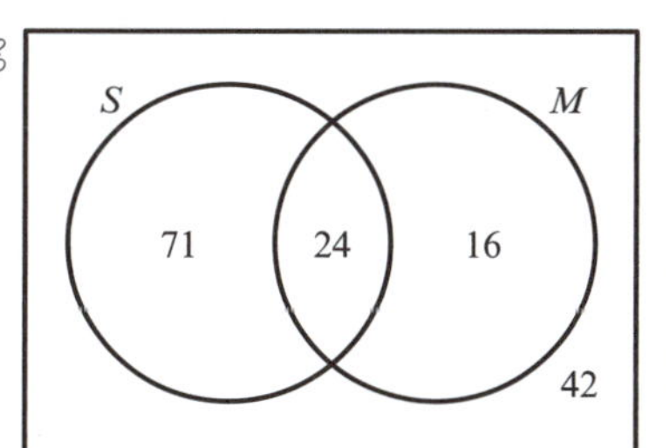

 a Work out the number of students in the college. [1]

 b Work out $n(S \cup M)$. [1]

 c Explain in words what the number 71 in the Venn diagram represents. [1]

 d One of the students is chosen at random. Find the probability that this student studies both Spanish and Mandarin. [1]

[Total: 4]

REFLECTION

One way to manage test anxiety is to make sure you have learned and practised all the skills you need.

One way to check is to answer questions like the ones in this section. How will you check that you remember skills from earlier chapters?

SELF-ASSESSMENT CHECKLIST

Let's revisit the Knowledge and Exam skills focus for this chapter.
Decide how confident you are with each statement.

	Now I can	Show it	Needs more work	Almost there	Confident to move on
1	calculate probabilities from a tree diagram	The tree diagram shows the probabilities of a fair spinner landing on odd and even numbers. Calculate the probability of the spinner landing **a** on two even numbers **b** once on odd and once on even **c** on odd on the first spin and even on the second spin.			

CONTINUED

	Now I can	Show it	Needs more work	Almost there	Confident to move on
2	complete a tree diagram to show outcomes	Zach has a fair spinner with the numbers as shown. He spins the spinner twice. 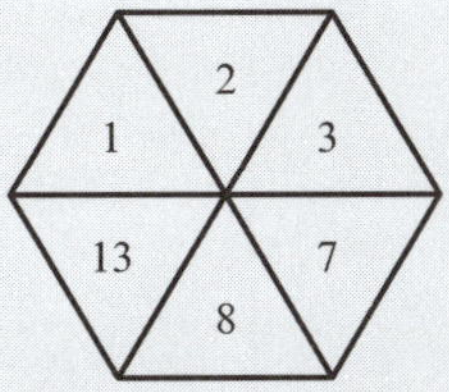 Copy and complete the tree diagram. 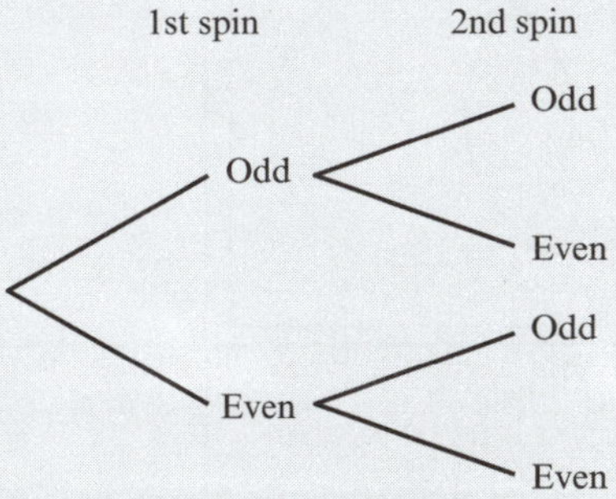			
3	work out probabilities from a Venn diagram	Carry out a survey in your class to find out how many people do two different sports, for example football and/or swimming. Draw a Venn diagram to show the results. Work out the probability that a student chosen at random does **a** both sports **b** one of the sports.			

CONTINUED

	Now I can	Show it	Needs more work	Almost there	Confident to move on
4	complete a Venn diagram	36 people go to a restaurant. 15 people order main course (M) and dessert (D). 8 people order main course only. 2 people do not order any food. Copy and complete the Venn diagram.			
5	understand the 'work out' command words and answer 'work out' questions	For the Venn diagram you drew above, explain how you would use the information in the diagram to work out the probability that a person chosen at random ordered dessert.			
6	understand the 'calculate' command word and answer 'calculate' questions	Write down some things to remember to help you answer a 'calculate probabilities from a tree diagram' question.			
7	develop strategies for coping with test anxiety.	Write yourself some tips on what you can do if you cannot answer a question in an examination.			

This section contains past paper questions from previous Cambridge exams, which draw together your knowledge on a range of topics that you have covered up to this point. These questions give you the opportunity to test your knowledge and understanding.

The following question has an example student response and commentary provided. Work through the question first, then compare your answer to the sample response and commentary. Are your answers different to the sample responses?

1   Write the ratio $5 \times 10^{-1} : 2 : 3 \times 10^1$ in its simplest form. [2]

Cambridge IGCSE Mathematics (0580) Paper 12 Q14, June 2022   **[Total: 2]**

Example student response	Commentary
$5 \times 10^{-1} : 2 : 3 \times 10^1$ $= 0.5 : 2 : 30$	The student has written the numbers in their simplest form, but not the ratio. A ratio in its simplest form does not include decimals or fractions. Because the simplification is incomplete, this would score 1 mark. ***This answer scores 1 out of 2 marks.***

The following question has an example student response and commentary provided. Work through the question first, then compare your answer to the sample response and commentary. Are your answers different to the sample responses?

2   1 mile = 1.609344 kilometres
   Change 6 miles into metres.
   Give your answer correct to the nearest metre. [3]

Cambridge IGCSE Mathematics (0580) Paper 32 Q7a, March 2022   **[Total: 3]**

Example student response	Commentary
6 miles = 6 × 1.609344 km = 9.656064 km 9.656064 km = 9.656064 × 100 = 966 m to the nearest metre	This student has correctly converted 6 miles into kilometres, but they have used the wrong conversion to convert kilometres into metres. ***This answer scores 1 out of 3 marks.***

The following question has an example student response and commentary provided.
Work through the question first, then compare your answer to the sample response and
commentary. Are your answers different to the sample responses?

3   The area of some land is in the ratio park : gardens : playground = 11 : 2 : 3.
    The park has an area of $4620\,m^2$.

    a   Work out the area of the gardens and the area of the playground.   [3]

    b   The park area of $4620\,m^2$ is made up of paths and grassland.
        18% of the park area is paths.

        i   Show that the grassland area is $3788.4\,m^2$.   [1]
        ii   Seed for the grassland is sold in bags.
             The seed in one bag covers an area of $280\,m^2$.
             The bags cost \$72 each for the first 5 bags and then \$58 each
             for any extra bags.
             Calculate the cost of the seed needed to cover the grassland.   [4]

Cambridge IGCSE Mathematics (0580) Paper 32 Q7a, b, June 2024   [Total: 8]

Example student response	Commentary
a 4620 11 + 2 + 3 = 16 4620 ÷ 16 = 288.75 Gardens = 2 × 288.75 = 577.5 Playground = 3 × 288.75 = 866.25	The student has shared 4620 in the given ratio, however $4620\,m^2$ is just the area of the park, not the total area of the land. To answer the question correctly, the student could have used equivalent ratios to calculate the areas of the gardens and the playground. Note that the student could answer the questions in part (b) correctly, even though their answer to part (a) is wrong. **This answer scores 0 out of 3 marks.**
b i 4620 18% of 4620 = 831.6	Notice that the question uses the command words 'show that' which means you need to provide enough evidence to explain the result. The student has correctly calculated 18% of 4620, however to get the mark they need to write a calculation to show that 4620 − 831.6 is equal to the area given in the question. **This answer scores 0 out of 1 marks.**
b ii 3788.4 ÷ 280 = 13.53 14 bags needed	The student would score 1 mark for calculating 3788.4 ÷ 280 and 1 mark for concluded that 14 bags would be needed.
14 × 72 = \$1008	This is not the correct answer. The student has worked out the cost if all bags cost \$72 but the question states that the first 5 bags are \$72 and any extra are \$58. The student should have used all the information in the question to calculate the correct price and gain the remaining 2 marks. **This answer scores 2 out of 4 marks.**

Here is a similar question that you should attempt. Use the information from the previous response and commentary to guide you as you answer.

4   **a**   Prakash buys 45 flowers from a shop.

> **<u>Special offer</u>**
> Buy 3 bunches of flowers
> for the price of 2 bunches.

   Each bunch has 5 flowers.
   The price of one bunch of flowers is \$2.68.
   Using the special offer, work out how much Prakash pays for the 45 flowers.   [3]

   b   15 of the flowers are red.
   18 of the flowers are orange.
   The rest of the flowers are yellow.
   Write down the ratio of the number of red flowers : orange flowers : yellow flowers.
   Give your answer in its simplest form.   [2]

   c   Prakash gives the 45 flowers to his family.
   He gives his grandmother x flowers.
   He gives his mother 8 more flowers than his grandmother.
   He gives his cousin 6 fewer flowers than his grandmother.
   He gives his sister twice as many flowers as he gives his cousin.

   i   Use this information to show that $5x - 10 = 45$.   [3]

   ii   Solve the equation $5x - 10 = 45$.   [2]

   iii Find the number of flowers that Prakash gives to his cousin.   [1]

Cambridge IGCSE Mathematics (0580) Paper 32 Q7, March 2021   **[Total: 11]**

The following question has an example student response and commentary provided.
Work through the question first, then compare your answer to the sample response and commentary. Are your answers different to the sample responses?

5   The grid shows three shapes, *A, B* and *C.*

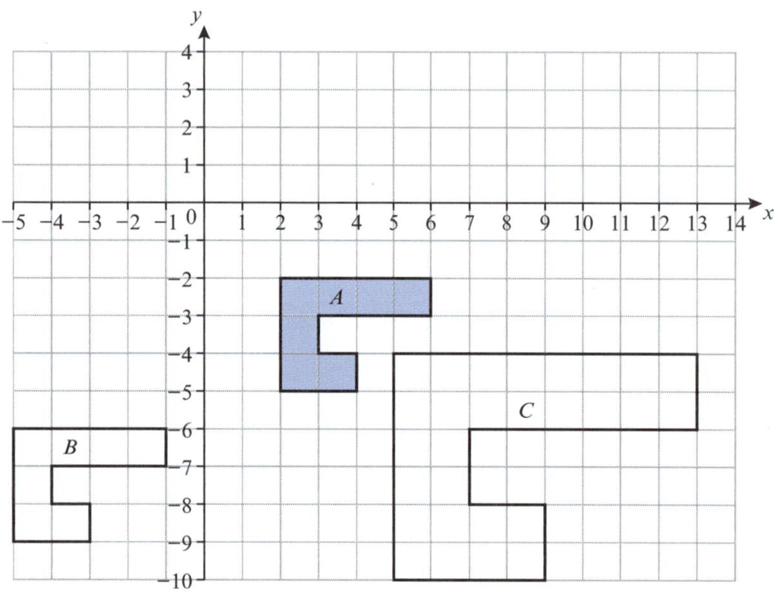

a   Describe fully the **single** transformation that maps

   i   shape *A* onto shape *B* [2]

   ii   shape *A* onto shape *C.* [3]

b   On the grid, draw the image of shape *A* after a rotation, 90° clockwise, centre (6, −3).
[Use Figure 11 on the Past Paper Practice Questions Resource Sheet.] [2]

Cambridge IGCSE Mathematics (0580) Paper 32 Q9, June 2022 **[Total: 7]**

Example student response	Commentary
a i translation	The student has written the correct transformation, however they have not included the column vector for the translation. ***This answer scores 1 out of 2 marks.***
ii scale factor 2, centre (−1, 0)	The student has written the correct scale factor and the correct centre. The student would score 1 mark each for these. To score the third mark, the student also needs to write the name of the transformation. ***This answer scores 2 out of 3 marks.***

b

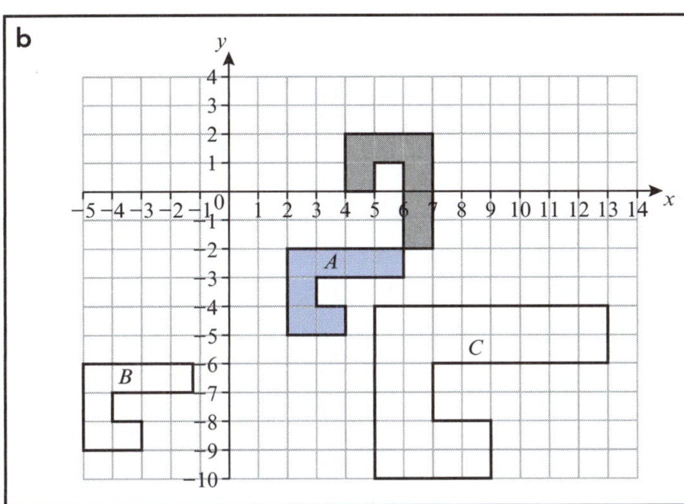

The student has correctly rotated the shape *A* by 90° which would score 1 mark, but they have rotated about the wrong centre, so they would not get the second mark.

This answer scores 1 out of 2 marks.

Here is a similar question that you should attempt. Use the information from the previous response and commentary to guide you as you answer.

6   The diagram shows four flags, *F*, *A*, *B* and *C* on a grid.

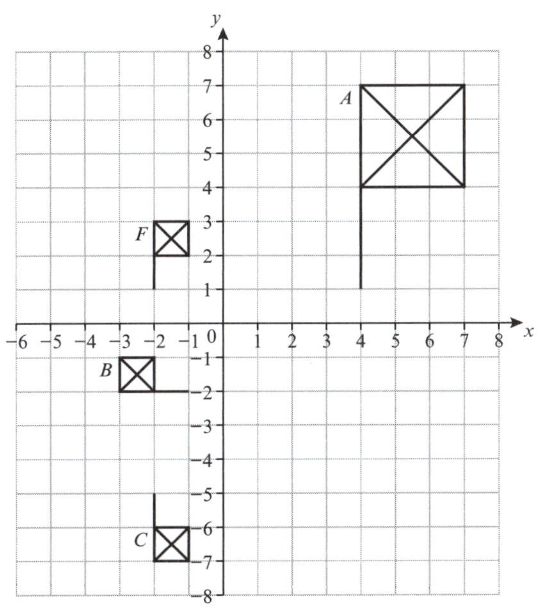

a   Describe fully the **single** transformation that maps

    i   flag *F* onto flag *A*   [3]

    ii   flag *F* onto flag *B*   [3]

    iii   flag *F* onto flag *C*.   [2]

b   On the grid, draw the image of flag *F* after a translation by the vector $\begin{pmatrix} 3 \\ -4 \end{pmatrix}$.   [2]
    [Use Figure 12 on the Past Paper Practice Questions Resource Sheet.]

Cambridge IGCSE Mathematics (0580) Paper 32 Q6, November 2022   **[Total: 10]**

The following question has an example student response and commentary provided.
Work through the question first, then compare your answer to the sample response and
commentary. Are your answers different to the sample responses?

7 **a** $\mathcal{E}$ = {people in a group}
B = {people who own a bicycle}
C = {people who own a car}
There are 120 people in the group.
21 people own a bicycle.
15 people own both a bicycle and a car.
35 people do not own a bicycle and do not own a car.

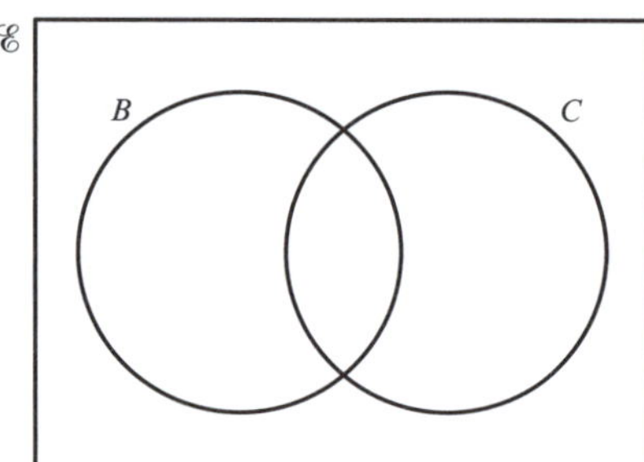

  i Complete the Venn diagram.
[Use Figure 13 on the Past Paper Questions resource sheet.] [2]

  ii A person from the group is chosen at random.
Find the probability that this person owns a car. [1]

b 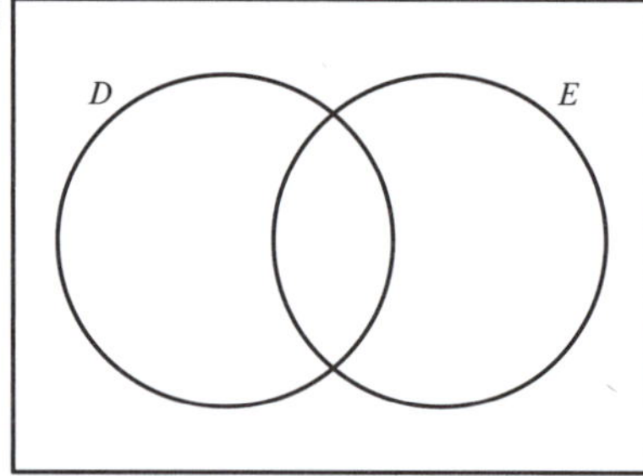

Shade the region $D \cup E$.
[Use Figure 14 on the Past Paper Practice Questions Resource Sheets.] [1]

Cambridge IGCSE Mathematics (0580) Paper 12 Q17, November 2022 [Total: 4]

Example student response	Commentary
a i $\mathcal{E}$ B · · · C 21 · 15 · 49 35	The student has correctly found and written 15 in the intersection and 35 outside sets B and C. This would score 1 mark. The other numbers in the Venn diagram are incorrect. 21 people own a bicycle so the total for set B should be 21. **This answer scores 1 out of 2 marks.**

ii 15 + 49 = 64 people own a car. 120 people in total. Probability person owns a car is $\dfrac{64}{120}$	This answer is not correct, because the numbers in the Venn diagram are not correct. However, this answer would score 1 follow-through mark because the method is correct and the student has used the values from the correct parts of their diagram. **This answer scores 1 out of 1 mark.**
b (Venn diagram with universal set $\mathscr{E}$, two overlapping shaded circles D and E)	This is the correct answer. **This answer scores 1 out of 1 mark.**

8 Now that you've gone through the commentary, try to write an improved answer to the parts of the question where you lost marks. This will help you check if you've understood why each mark has (or has not) been allocated. Use the commentary to guide you as you answer.